Born during the war-torn years of the nineteen forties in the North West of England to a working class family.

Nurtured within the then embryonic National Health Service and post-war education system whose attempts at creating a healthy, well-rounded, socialist child failed miserably. Schooled at a 'Boy's Technical School' (which thought itself akin to Harrow or some other rich self-serving establishment) it wasn't until after enrolment he was to discover only a large termination 'fee' would enable him to escape it's claustrophobic, torturous environs. (He still maintains the day he 'left' school was the best day of his life).

Following a spell of 'real' blood and gore in his native town he then embarked upon a life on the ocean waves only to be inexorably drawn back, in due course, to the comforting ways of his former life and a series of strange and sometimes dangerous enterprises the like of which were to eventually become his nemesis. At forty years of age a leap into the unknown on a quest to find the new 'beginning' took him from his native soil and on to new horizons.

Today he lives in another country. But he won't say which.

Fair Fortune

(Atlas D 'fou).

ISBN: 978-1-84944-046-2

British Library Cataloguing in Publication Data.
A catalogue record for this book is available from the British Library.

Published by UKUnpublished

UKUnpublished
.CO.UK

www.ukunpublished.co.uk
info@ukunpublished.co.uk

'BLACK Hors D'Oeuvres'

(Scripts on Black)

BY

Atlas D'four

War came to the world twice in the first half of the twentieth century. Fathers of the first generation and their sons as well as mothers and their daughters all fell foul of the madness of the times. Many perished wiping out many thousands of family lines in a space of less than 30 years. Hundreds of thousands of books have been written about both conflicts but few in the field of non-fiction have had the opportunity to be privy to the personal lives of the combatants during the action absorbed as they generally are in the wider scope of battle, strategy and tactics.

'Black Hors d'oeuvres' breaks the mould of general non-fiction and tells the story of two very separate 'operations' but both from the same theatre of war. A unit of volunteer soldiers told from their own personal experience. From the eagerness of youth full of ignorant bravado to the career soldier's overwhelming caution to the memories of the old and the experience that the true obscenity of war has brought them in the past and - the lonely quest of one extraordinary college student who suddenly finds himself thrust into a world of espionage and death. Both have the same objective in mind, to bloody the nose of the insolent Nazi war machine that has come to despoil their calm and beautiful land. For this was the Viking Kingdom of Norway in the year 1940 – and most certainly no place for foul harbingers of death.

Black Hors d'oeuvres.

Norway. A zone of gentle peace and ambient tranquillity. A land of ice and snow and a saga king, whose vaults, as legend would have it, were filled with the purest gold.

For the Nazi tyrant, a zone of destiny and German European domination. For the British First Sea Lord of the Admiralty, a zone of action and a personal restoration of fortunes. Both desire to 'snack' on the Black Hors d'oeuvres - - - .

Yet all that glitters in the Viking's Kingdom is not necessarily of the purest metal. As those who seek shall find -.

17ᵗʰ July 1976.   Chichester. West Sussex. England.

Black, wispy and distinctly oily. Such was the pungent smoke curling lazily in the mild breeze down the side of the crematoria chimney and along the verdigris-layered edges of the copper clad roof. John G. Ashington followed its course through misted eyes.

The 'G' stood for Gregers. Not Gregory. Norwegian. Or so his mother had told him. It wasn't hers. The pungent smoke that was. Her ashes already lay scattered amongst the petal strewn rose beds of the 'Garden of Remembrance'. The Graves Attendant had looked a little strange as John Ashington handed him the small leather pouch instead of the usual plastic urn to inter behind the yellow ochre memorial plaque. But given some of the events the man would have witnessed in his twenty years with his present employers John Ashington wasn't surprised when the man quickly recovered to proceed with the task to hand.

Watching the man putting the final touches to his handiwork John Ashington chose one of the wooden benches facing east. He preferred the sun to his back. He wanted to watch the lengthening shadows furl slowly towards her final resting-place. Yes. That was it. A finality. A closing down of things. The life experience. End of 'part one'. Part two was already evolving. The memories. So many pleasurable memories. And the anticipation of so many still to come. All a necessary part of the grieving process. One life was at an end but life must go on.

The pouch contained a photograph of the medal, the letter and a small sprinkling of her ashes. There were no final instructions. Nor had she wanted to discuss the matter. She knew she was dying. That was enough for her to contend with. He had respected her wishes which when it came down to the final analysis made things all the more difficult. How would she have wanted things done? In the event he just hoped he had done everything satisfactorily and had chosen wisely.

It was written on plain paper and dated the 22ⁿᵈ June 1943. The letter read;

My little Joyce. I am lonely. I am sad. Yesterday I think of you. Today and tomorrow. I am not far from you. I can not say. It is forbidden.
Are you well? I am well. The nights I do not forget. You also – Yes? The war is not good. We are not together. Soon we are. I hope. Yes – I promise. Soon.

I love you. I love you. I love you. Very much.   GREG'S.
xxxxxxxxxxxxxxxxxxxxxxxxxxxxxxxxxxxxxxxxxxxxxxx

The photocopy of the letter lay alongside a similar but well-worn photograph of the medal on the arm of the bench. The medal was in the shape of a 'knight's cross' and bore a coat of arms at its centre. A single gold sword adorned the red, white and blue ribbon. At a guess the inscription was in Norwegian. Which answered one of the dozens of questions revolving around John Ashington's head.

She had been a wonderful mother and he had loved her dearly. But at times had been angry with her. Like now. Why had she to die before such details regarding his 'father' could come to light? A soldier who died in the war. No proper name. No description of great import. Tall and good looking was how she had described him. But then wasn't that always the case when seen through the eyes of a lover? Even when small, squat and Mongoloid? A one night stand? She hadn't described it as such, but that could be a drawn conclusion devoid as it had been of further revelations. And now all this from the executors of her will!

He inherited everything. Naturally. There was no one else. Not that he was aware of? The will made no mention of the medal itself. It was as though she had decided he should use his own discretion, should he want to know more. The photograph of the medal was the key. The letter from 'Greg's' short for Gregers. That was no surprise. Norwegian. It was a start.

The Norwegian Charge Des Affaires had been more than helpful. The medal was indeed Norwegian. The Norwegian War Cross. A rare decoration. Quite valuable and issued in only very rare circumstance. Its British equivalent, the Victoria Cross. For valour. Few such medals had been conferred during the Second World War. Many, like his father's, posthumously.

21ˢᵗ August. 1976.   Buckinghamshire.   England.

The house imposed itself before a thick backdrop of tall fir trees and came at the end of a neat and well tended gravelled driveway. Nothing fussy. All in 'apple-pie' order. Cared for, was how one might describe it. Colonel Wilson was now Sir James Wilson. In his late sixties at a guess. Wrinkles, hair turning white but the skin held a healthier pallor. Slightly tanned. Someone who didn't winter at home? And there was a brightness to the eyes. Mischievous almost.

"I first met Gram in early 1942. He was keen. Good looking as I remember". The elderly man searched John Ashington's face.

"Younger even than you are now I warrant. You say he could be your father? There's a slight resemblance." The old man sighed. "It was a long time ago." John Ashington bit back the urge to ask another question. It would profit him more to let the old man take his time. More pointed questions could come later.

"We were receiving hundreds of Gram's countrymen in the early days. All through 1940 and '41', less so by '42'. He was a relative latecomer to the party. Through Sweden as I recall. Although I can't swear to it. It wasn't easy once the Germans had got their act together." Sir James paused to pour them both a drink. Home-made lemonade, slightly sparkling. John Ashington suspected a small hidden alcohol content, but said nothing. The old man replaced the jug on the table.

"How much do you already know about his work for the resistance?"

"Nothing Sir – That is, the embassy mentioned he was involved in some kind of covert operations and suggested you might be the best person of whom to make further enquiries." The old man smiled took a sip of his drink and cleared his throat.

"I suppose what I meant to say was – How much do you want to know?" Surprise must have registered on John Ashington's face for it brought a wide smile to the old man's lips.

"War is very often a dirty business. Most of what is given out in the public domain has generally been thoroughly sanitised. As children it is depicted in the comic books as the brave, courageous, determined Adonis, leaping into the heavens his machine pistol spitting fire. The enemy brutish, ugly, monocled Hun types, reeling back under the fearsome onslaught in abject terror as our hero storms victorious through the exploding battlefield. The adult version – slightly less theatrical, but still along the same lines. Nothing could be further from the truth. War – not to put too fine a point on it – is sheer bloody mayhem. It's dirty. It's cruel and it's sheer hell on earth and no less so for those like Gram who were directly on the sharp end of it all, who put their pride and love of country before everything else – including their lives." Sir James folded his arms across his chest. "So – young Gregers – I ask again. How much do you really want to know about this man?"

John Ashington narrowed his eyes hesitating only a fraction before answering.

"Everything Sir." he replied.

The patio was bathed in bright sunlight. One of those rare warm sultry afternoons of an English summer. Sir James took a long drink of his lemonade.

"As I said. Gram came to us in '42'. He and two others from Southern Norway. It was our job to assess them. We needed men who wanted to 'get back' at the Germans. Agents. Nationals like Gram who could easily avoid drawing attention to themselves. Men who could organise resistance. Keep the Germans busy. Tie down their manpower. That sort of thing. S.O.E. Special Operations Executive. Sounds frightfully important doesn't it? Not really. We called it 'the Firm'. By the time Gram arrived we had a number of training establishments dotted about the place. Sabotage training. Survival techniques. That sort of thing. He, as I recall, went through three or four of them before his final course at Stodham Park. That was our Propaganda School. He was sent back to Norway just before the Christmas – 1943. He had been trained in sabotage. His area was to be 'shipping'. You know the sort of thing, pop a little explosive charge inside the hull just below the water line. A delayed fuse. Off she sails and a little while later – Boom – No ship. Another cargo of iron ore misses its docking for the Krupps foundries. A few less guns for the Wehrmacht, a few less tanks for the SS. All very useful to the Allied war effort. The problem - ." The old man stopped, rubbed his chin hesitantly, then shrugged before continuing. "The problem was Gram tended to have very itchy feet. No patience. Needed action this day and all that. It was winter. Targets in the Oslo fjords were few and far between. So he teamed up with other operatives working in the city. These became known to the Gestapo as the 'Oslo Gang', a name they themselves found very much to their liking, so much so they adopted it for themselves and continue to use it for the rest of the 'occupation'.

That winter of '43 – 44' was one of the worst times for those of us in the 'Firm' who were working with the Norwegian units. Many of our 'boys' had been arrested by the Gestapo. It was obvious there was a traitor somewhere in the resistance. It was a jittery time all round. I remember it was about then he blew up the Labour Offices in Oslo. To destroy the Labour Conscription files. The Germans were rounding up all able-bodied men for work in Germany on their war effort so Gram and his friend Sonsteby, if I remember rightly, blew all their carefully indexed efforts to bits. They were terribly upset about it, the Germans I mean, months of work all up in smoke." Sir James chuckled to himself. John Ashington took the jug of lemonade and re-filled the proffered glass. The old man was getting into his stride. It was well to encourage him. Ashington replaced the jug on the table.

"How did he die -?"

The old man sank back into his garden chair and studied the frenzy of crystal bubbles battling their way to the surface through the opaque liquid in the long drinking glass.

"Bravely." he replied presently. "As most of them did." He paused for a moment lost in the memories.

"Gram loved the intrigue, the bizarre psychological aspects of it all. In another time, another space, he would have probably become a politician or a political pundit. He was fascinated by the use of propaganda as a weapon. Far more effective than guns he would say. It was his love of intrigue got him killed."

"Do you know the details?" John Ashington leaned forward.

"The Gestapo. They set a trap. Gram and another man made contact with a German national whom it appeared was willing to give them some important information. The German, as it eventually transpired, was an 'agent provocateur'. The pair of them unfortunately walked into a hail of bullets. Gram was killed instantly; the other man later took his own life to avoid torture by the Gestapo."

John Ashington tried to picture the event in his mind. It was of course impossible. Nevertheless, it served to put the reality to one important question that had lingered at the back of his mind for as long as he could remember. His 'father' really was dead. Which was why he had never come looking for them. Because he couldn't.

"Which is why he won this -?" He slipped the photograph of the medal across the table. Sir James hunched forward in his seat. He looked, not touching.

"The Norwegian War Cross?" he replied, more a half question than a statement. "No. Hardly. Medals of that status are few and far between. There were dozens of men just like Gram. Hundreds I suppose in the Milorg and Linge resistance groups. Possibly thousands if you include the Noric members. No – that award is another story. Not one we at the 'Firm' can take any credit for. It happened right at the beginning. 1940. The only reason we knew about it was the de-briefing all people like your father had to go through before they could be accepted into SOE. We had to be sure the Germans weren't slipping any of their own people into our nets. Those were dangerous times."

Sir James rose from his chair motioning for him to remain seated and turned towards the house. "Two minutes."

He returned in less than the stated time clutching a file of papers to his chest.

"This was his. It contains his own hand written report. There's a typed translation into English. It's a copy I'm afraid. The original is still with the 'Firm's' archives. It's no longer covered by the 'Official Secrets Act' but I would rather not part with it. There's no reason why you shouldn't read it - -. Tell you what. I have a few things I need to do. Why don't you make yourself comfortable, have some more of this excellent lemonade -. Sir James turned the handle of the jug towards him. "- Take your time. I'll come back later." Before John Ashington could object the old man turned away and disappeared beyond the confines of the rose strewn 'French' windows.

The file lay on the table its paper contents well fingered and worn along the edges. A white cotton ribbon, only now it was yellowed and discoloured with age, fastened the bundle together. John Ashington stared at it. Here was something written in his 'fathers' own hand. Written long before he had known his mother. The afternoon sun had crept cautiously around the edge of the tall tree line. It was cooler now. A breeze fondled the dainty bow of the ribbon. It jerked, to and fro, almost as if to say – come on then, what are you waiting for -? John Ashington looked up. The sky was as it had been for most of the afternoon, a mass of pale blue. Not the merest trace of a cloud. Where had the breeze come from? Wherever, it was gone now. He reached forward. "Well mother - ." he whispered. "Is this what you really wanted?"

No: 1372.   14th May 1942.

'My name is ----------------. I was born ----------------. This report is, to the best of my knowledge, a true record of events that began on the 9th April 1940 at ---------
---, Norway until my arrival at ------------, England on the -------------.

My friends and I were taking the ski-train to Gielo when news of the German Occupation of our country broke - - - - - - - - - - .

'In the Beginning'.

Fri. 5th April. 1940. 'Finse'. Southern Norway. 2200hrs.

It had snowed heavily most of the previous evening. At the tiny mountain hamlet of 'Finse' the snow now lay in drifts five feet deep at the tree line and banked up over the hotel windows so that one could have jumped off the roof to the ground without fear of injury. It was holiday time for most Norwegians. These small skiing villages to the west of Oslo attracted old and young alike. After a particularly harsh winter the coming of spring was heralding a much welcome relief. The air was warming. A time to relax from the rigours of the northern winds as the ice on the lakes and fjords began to thin out releasing its suffocating vice-like grip. Gram was due back home by Sunday night at the latest. His work was important for the money it earned but he tried not to let it interfere with his studies at the University. Economics and Politics. He wasn't sure about Economics. It all seemed very impractical. But Politics, now that was something else.

Kristina was the name of the girl behind the bar. She was reasonably good-looking, in a mid-European sort of way. But at nineteen years of age that wasn't the first thing on his mind. Nor was the constant prattle emanating from the wireless at the back of the bar. There was a war on. The Germans and the British again. He was sympathetic to the British point of view. That ridiculous goose-stepping German dictator had gone completely overboard with Poland. Someone needed to give him a bloody nose, if only to bring him to his senses.

Kristina was still busy. Gram took his drink and strolled over to the doors of the hotel veranda which had been cleared of the snow. From here he could see the little railway station and the forest of brightly painted skis staked into the drifts alongside the wooden platform. In the late evening sun the reflected brightness of the mountains shone down on the ski-tracked slopes which reached as far as the eye could see on and across the still frozen lake to the coast and the fjords beyond. It was beautiful. Calm. Peaceful. But then Gram had never known it to be otherwise. The European War was far away. Norway was a neutral country. She didn't take sides. All the pundits were forecasting an early end to the hostilities. It was seven months since the British had declared war on Germany. But very little had happened. An Armistice was the most likely outcome. The Germans and the Russians had both got what they wanted. There seemed precious little the British or the French could do about it, nothing that is that would make any real difference. Tomorrow it could all be over. Suddenly he remembered Kristina, or at least his groin did. He gave the distant pale blue diamond studded panorama one final look spun around expectantly and bounced back inside. At nineteen years of age one was 'ever hopeful'.

'The Lion' & 'The Wolf'.

January – March 1940.

Neutrality was never much of a burden for the Lion or the Wolf. Norway, Denmark or, as was shown later, the smaller nations of the Low Countries. None would be allowed to disrupt the war aims or policies of the belligerent nations. Winning was all that mattered and nothing would ultimately be allowed to stand in the way. For Britain's First Sea Lord Winston Churchill, the daily shipments of iron ore across Norway destined for German war production was a form of succour to Britain's enemies. Neutrality, in his eyes, should stand for higher goals. Zero aid in the matter of materials of war. Nothing more. Nothing less. "Smaller nations must not tie our hands when we are fighting for their rights and freedoms," said Churchill to his parliamentary colleagues in early December 1939 on the matter of the mining of Norway's seas and fjords in a bid to halt the iron ore traffic.

The outbreak of the Russian-Finnish War (known as the Winter War) on November 30th 1939, gave Churchill a possible excuse to force the issue. A Norwegian campaign using Allied troops (Operation Wilfred) would enter Norway under the guise of passing aid to the Finns. Preparations were put in hand for a landing in the north of Norway but these were thwarted by an armistice agreed between the Russian and Finnish governments on the 13th March 1940.

Meanwhile the 'Wolf' had his own agenda.

Aware of British intentions Adolf Hitler the German chancellor ordered his Generals, specifically General Jodl, to prepare for an invasion of Norway in mid – December. Code-named 'Oyster'.

In less than two weeks the proposed plans were produced for the German High Command Wehrmacht's (OKW) approval. On the 10th January 1940, these listed the Norwegian ports of Oslo, Kristiansand, Arendal, Stavanger, Bergen, Trondhiem and Narvik as the principal operational areas with further inland objectives to be served by paratroopers of the 7th Air Divisions. The man in charge would be Hitler's fifty-five year old General, Nikolaus Von Falkenhorst.

On the 1st of March 1940, (Hitler had delayed the invasion dates for reasons of a political nature) the German dictator signed the first of his directives for Norway's occupation and issued his final orders, now renamed 'Fall Westerbung/ Case Weser Exercise' and this only five days before the British

Norwegian Expedition forces were stood down due to the Russo-Finnish Pact.

At 02-10hrs on the 3ʳᵈ April 1940 the first of the German ships loaded to the gunwales with war materials for occupation left their Baltic Sea ports. The die was cast for neutral Norway and her smaller, totally defenceless cousin, Denmark.

Hitler and his General's had been careful not to broadcast their intentions too openly. The Nazi government had many enemies both within and without. It wasn't until the 6ᵗʰ of April that General Hans Oster of Vice Admiral Canaris's Abwehr (German Intelligence Services) was able to inform his Dutch contact in the Hague of the German plans *(Not for the one and only time – See Black Dove & Black Dawn, same author)*. This information was quickly in the hands of the British and French governments who speedily passed it on to the intelligence services of both Denmark and Norway. Alas it was all too late. On that same night Germany's Naval fleet sailed from their ports with less than twenty-four hours to go before the invasion was due to begin.

Only now was the mine laying operation and the ships carrying the troops for 'Operation Wilfred', demanded by Churchill months earlier, allowed to proceed.

In a speech to Britain's Conservative Party Association the then Prime Minister Mr Neville Chamberlain just three days earlier had taunted the German Chancellor with: "Herr Hitler has missed the boat." It was quite obvious that someone had done just that. It was also equally obvious it wasn't the 'Wolf'.

On the 8ᵗʰ of April as the silent shadows of the mountains slid effortlessly by over the peaceful waters of the Norwegian fjords, the forces of terror and enslavement crept relentlessly onwards. The subjugation of the neutral people and lands of Scandinavia was about to begin.

Tuesday 9th April 1940. 'Drobak'. Southern Norway. 06-00hrs.

What should have been a simple ceremonial march at the head of his troops into the friendly suburbs of Oslo, the Norwegian capital, had proven anything but. General Von Falkenhorst also required a complete change of clothing.

"Get that damn thing off the wall"; the General growled casting a disapproving eye at a portrait of Norway's King Haakon hanging over the office fireplace. His ADC Major Lindauer side-stepped the General's imposing bulk and quickly removed the offending article placing it under the desk. Unfortunately for the Major the picture was too large to fit the smaller knee-space.

"Just put it against the wall", breathed the General in exasperation, "- and not facing outwards."

The Mayor of Drobak's town hall office would have to serve as the General's temporary headquarters for the time being. It wasn't in the invasion plans but then neither was having his only heavy cruiser, the 'Blucher' blown out from under his feet.

"It seems our intelligence reports regarding our Norwegian 'friends' are about as accurate as our assurances we were to be offered no resistance Major. What was the name of that fort again?"

"Oskarborg General. We were informed its guns were obsolete museum pieces."

"Then it's just as well they weren't modern artillery pieces otherwise we might well have lost the whole fleet - - -," the General snapped.

Major Lindauer moved one of the office chairs before the dying red embers of the fireplace. He searched his brain for something he could report to promote a change in his commanding officers present ruffled demeanour.

"The latest reports from our advance units put them within ten kilometres of the city General. Once we have control of the radio station the people will quickly realise how hopeless their situation is and all resistance will cease."

General Falkenhorst pushed the proffered chair aside with the toe of his boot.

"And in the meantime my men die like flies Major and Germany loses what little it has left of its scarce naval resources. What the hell happened to the help we were supposed to receive from those Nas-sam people -?"

As if in reply to the General's question at that moment the door flew open. The visitor didn't so much as enter as present himself. He wore a grey mackintosh and pinstriped trousers. He was squat, flabby-faced and sported a shock of sandy coloured hair.

The General gave the man a distasteful stare.

"You. Do you speak German?" he snapped, before the visitor could announce himself.

The man blinked in surprise. "Well er. Yes. I do General."

"Good. In that case you will take a message for me. You are to find your Major Quisling. You are to tell him I insist he present himself here immediately. At once – do you hear? Within the hour. No excuses. Do you understand?"

"Well er. Yes Herr General but -."

General Falkenhorst's temper was never long and after paddling for some time through the black icy waters of a Norwegian fjord had not better improved.

"But! What do you mean - But?"

The man was by now visibly agitated.

"But Herr General – I am Major Quisling."

"YOU!" The General made no effort to conceal his obvious disbelief. Nor apparent disappointment.

"You are Major Quisling?"

"Yes Herr General. Major Vidkun Quisling at you service. I came as soon as I could. We were supposed, were we not, to join forces in Oslo? When I received news of the incident at Oskarborg I - - .""

"Incident! Incident! You call having my flag ship blasted to bits and my troops shot to pieces an incident? The Norwegians are not supposed to be resisting. You Quisling assured the Fuhrer there would be no call to arms. Would you kindly explain what went wrong – Herr Major -?"

Vidkun Abraham Lauritz Jonsson Quisling was the leader of the Nasjonal Samling, the Norwegian Nazi Party. A movement he himself conceived following his removal from political office in 1933 as Norway's Minister of Defence. Years of previous army service including a period as Military Attaché for the Norwegian Government in Moscow had left him vehemently anti-Communist and hence a prime mover of far right wing policies. Quisling had an accord of sorts with the German Chancellor Adolf Hitler. An agreement as to the conduct of Case Weser-Exercise. He was also not a man to be easily intimidated and as a politician knew full well how not to answer awkward questions. As now.

"The Fuhrer promised me that your forces would occupy only the ports. The rest of Norway and its subsequent administration was to be left to me. Your ships General not only carried troops but hundreds of German civilians destined to take over all the key administrative posts. This I know as a fact General from some of the survivors who made it ashore with yourself. Kindly explain to me General what went wrong with our previous arrangement?" General Falkenhorst blinked in surprise. He was unused to people speaking to him in such a manner, especially civilians.

"Wrong? What went wrong? I haven't the faintest idea what you are talking about. I am a soldier Major Quisling, not a politician. I know nothing of your 'civil' arrangements. How does your question explain why your fellow countrymen are shooting my men and putting up such resistance? Hundreds of my men have already been killed. This is treachery. The Fuhrer will hear of your disloyalty. You can be very sure of that."

Quisling stepped into the room and threw the door closed behind him.

"Disloyalty Herr General! There is no disloyalty on my part. You must blame the King of Norway for what has happened. The people fight on his wishes. His anti-German feelings are well known. If you want the fighting to stop, it is he who must be found and quickly – otherwise."

"Then what are you waiting for?" The General fixed his eyes on the man's face. "I suggest you treat the matter with the utmost urgency before any more of my men are slaughtered."

A satisfied smile crept up Quisling's features.

"Surely such a matter is of a military nature General. You possess the men and the materials and the means with which to carry out such an operation. Such things are not my responsibility."

The General looked the man up and down. He detested bureaucrats. Always hiding behind their pathetic rules and regulations. Never getting their hands dirty and always covering their arse's whenever the slightest whiff of danger presented itself. This one was typical and what's more an arsehole of a traitor to boot. What was true was such a mission could never be entrusted to such a sycophantic specimen as this. The General snorted his disgust.

"So. Where will this King go? Are you at least able to tell me that?"

"It is possible he and his retinue will go north to Hamar. From there they may try east to Sweden or alternately the West Coast – whichever proves to be the most practicable."

The General turned to his ADC. "Possible north, possible east, possible west – Wonderful. I despair -. Contact Wing Commander Goetz. Tell him my orders are to dispatch aircraft to the main road junctions north of the city. They are to disrupt and destroy any traffic they find there."

"Jawhol General." Lindaur strode for the door.

"As for you Herr Quisling. You will return to Oslo. Do you think you could muster enough forces to put a guard around the Central Bank? My orders are to transport all gold reserves immediately to Berlin for safekeeping. My ships are still waiting to pass Drobak. Your Norwegian countrymen there are refusing to surrender."

The smile on Quisling's face slowly began to fade to be replaced by one of acute pain.

"I er-. The er-. I'm afraid the er – gold reserves – have already gone from the city General."

"GONE! Already gone? Ninety thousand kilos of bullion? Gone? Gone where?" exploded the General.

Major Quisling averted his eyes from the Germans outraged stare and looked down at his feet, possibly hoping the highly polished timber might provide some fortuitous route of escape. "I er – That is, we don't exactly know General. That is, we are not quite sure. But wherever it is it cannot be too far away – as yet," he added hopefully.

A Saga King & His People.

When Norway ceded from Sweden in 1905 the young Prince Charles of Denmark was offered the Norwegian throne. He was crowned King Haakon V11 and was held in very high esteem by his Norwegian subjects. A Viking King he was furious the Germans should assault his adopted country and threaten its freedoms. Aware that his older brother King Christian of Denmark whose country was small, flat and with no standing army would have no choice other than to capitulate, he was determined the Germans would not have it so easy where Norway was concerned.

Refusing to accept Dr Curt Brauer, the German Minister to Norway's outrageous ultimatum that the Norwegian people should abstain from any resistance to the German occupation, he left Oslo in search of safer pastures but not before reminding the German of his own Führer's words.

"A nation that does not resist aggression to the limits of its strength does not deserve to live." The Germans were to come to remember those words over the next five years.

During the night Von Falkenhorst received information the Norwegian King was making for Hamar. Three truck-loads of German troopers were ordered to move north and apprehend the King and his family. Word of the advancing Germans spread quickly ahead of them.

Colonel Otto Ruge received the information at his Norwegian Army Training Camp at Minnesund situated close to the main north road. At seventy-two years of age Ruge should have been enjoying a very peaceful retirement but Ruge had never been of the opinion old age was a barrier to 'action this day'. Together with his Chief-Instructor (Small Arms) Captain Rognes, he gathered up a number of his more competent trainees and skied off to deal with the German incursion.

It was a bold plan against what he knew would be a heavily armed unit not to mention ten times the number of his men.

The first of the German trucks took the full force of the two machine-guns sending it spinning off the road and bursting into flames. Its occupants, those who had survived the initial onslaught, were shot down by the rifles of Ruge's trainee marksmen. The rest, in the remaining two trucks, thinking they were under attack from a large number of Norwegian regular troops made an abrupt about turn and made off back the way they had come. Ruge immediately ordered a change of positions and set his men the task of erecting another ambush some kilometres nearer the town. Fortunately for Ruge and his men the Germans had had enough for one day and didn't attempt to return that night.

The King and his Ministers meanwhile had arrived in the small town of Elverum some ninety miles north of Oslo. In the middle of the night the town was bombed. It was obvious the Germans knew he was there. Not wishing his presence to put his people at more risk the King together with his son the Crown Prince Olav drove to the Swedish border. Enquiries on the border soon made it clear that any Norwegians entering Sweden would be interned, regardless of their standing. Unsure of Sweden's continued neutrality the King turned about and drove back across Norway. They headed west and towards the advancing German forces.

'Eidsvoll' 20miles north of Oslo. Akershus Fylke. Central Norway.

On the first day of the invasion everything was in chaos. Most of the Officer Corps of the Norwegian Army had been on leave in Oslo when the Germans attacked. Only the Norwegian 1st Division was able to offer immediate resistance. Badly mauled, they had been pushed back over the Swedish border where the Swedish authorities had interned them. This left only the Norwegian 2nd Division ensconced north of the capital to stem the onslaught of the German invader. The 3rd, 4th and 5th Divisions were still trying to mobilise. The 6th Division already mobilised but in the north of Norway and without any roads of any description connecting northern and southern Norway could offer no assistance to their hard pressed compatriots in the south.

The 2nd Division front line troops were mostly made up of part-time volunteers. The Norwegian General Staff Headquarters was now situated in the small town of Eidsvold and under the command of General Huinden Haug. Information on his own armies' dispositions, let alone the Germans, was sketchy to say the least. Facing his front the German guns had kept up a constant barrage but fortunately were having little effect with many of the shells landing in deep snow. For now they were holding their own. But it could hardly remain that way for very long, given the forces being brought against them.

Gen. Haug's Temp. H.Q. Nr. Eidsvoll.

"The Germans are advancing through the suburbs and have ranged our positions almost along our entire front. Fortunately those ridiculous grey uniforms they are wearing make them perfect targets for our men -." Haug grinned satisfyingly at the man alongside, Major Arne Ording.

"I've received a dispatch from the Minister for Defence. They've appointed Ruge as the new Commander-in-Chief -." Major Ording's face broke into a wide smile.

"Good. Now perhaps things will get moving -." Then Ording suddenly remembered to whom he was speaking. "Opps! Sorry Sir. No disrespect Sir. I didn't mean -." The General gave a hearty chuckle.

"Mouth before brain Arne. Will you ever change my friend?" The General slapped the Major playfully on the shoulder. "Well here's some advice – Don't! People like me need people like you. If only to serve to remind us of whom we are. The trappings of power sometimes get in the way of our common sense. As for 'General Ruge' – Yes Major, he has also been promoted. Can't have the C in C bearing the rank of a Colonel - . I'm delighted. Ruge may be old but he's nobody's fool. The General picked up a paper from the desk.

"I have his first orders. Everyone not at present in the line and within range is to be sent to Lillehammer. You Major are to take charge of them. All volunteers and equipment not already sabotaged by those Quisling arseholes are to go with you. Your job is to sort them out. Make them into soldiers. Equip them as best you can, then send them back down to us for the line. Ruge is staying at Minnesund until it gets too hot. The idea is to pull back slowly until we can muster sufficient reinforcements to block any further German advances. The Allies have promised help. All we need. Providing of course they can get here in time. Meanwhile the more men you can muster and put into the fight the longer we can forestall any collapse. Whatever happens there must be no rout of our forces. Every officer on the line will have to act on his own judgement, his own assessment of the situation in his sector. We shall need some units to act as 'firemen', good men we can send to bolster up any weak spots -. " Haug paused and touched Ording again on the shoulder. "- We shall be relying on what you can send us -." A shaft of bright daylight broke through the claustrophobic gloom as the door opened. The General turned.

"Ah – Good. Captain Olsen. Just the man." The new man also wore the uniform of the Norwegian Second Division. He was pale-faced, serious looking and in his early forties. He nodded.

"General. - - Council of War Sir?"

24

"Indeed Johan." replied the General. "Orders from the new C in C General Ruge."

"Ruge! Well that's one up the square backsides of those German's for a start. When is he sending us some reinforcements Sir?"

"Immediately – or as soon as Arne here gets his carcass to Lillehammer. But as for you Johan, Ruge wants you to pick three good men, officers, Lieutenants. The General says you are to pick your own men and hotfoot it to Minnesund. Pick them out and have them report here to me, meanwhile you yourself are to leave straight away. I will send the men on as soon as I have replaced them in the line. Olsen threw a smart salute.

"Yes Sir. Will do Sir." He turned and, "Er – if Major Ording is taking over at Lillehammer Sir, perhaps he should send the 'cherry boys' over to us. We could give them a lick and a promise before we send them back?" Olsen smiled. Ording grinned widely.

"Just be sure you don't kill them off before the Germans do – We might be glad of them before this lots finished -."

'Lillehammer'. Opland Fylke. Central Norway. 05-40hrs

Standing on the steps to the bank the hastily assorted convoy of trucks and vans were met by Lillehammer's Chief of Police and the bank's manager. The journey from Oslo had not been without incident. Some of the smaller vehicles had suffered from the weight of the gold bullion bars throwing them erratically around the roads icy surfaces with the result that some no longer had any suspension left. Every time one of the vehicles had gone out of control the convoy had to stop whilst the cargoes were redistributed. North of Hamar a German Me.110 dropped from the clouds and peppered the valley road in a hail of machine-gun bullets. A Post Office van slid into the truck in front and disintegrated killing both the driver and his mate and scattering bullion boxes all over the blood stained snow. This together with negotiating the dozens of refugees making for the north had made the journey long and arduous.

By dawn, Olaf Larsen, one of the drivers chosen to ensure the golds safety, could make out the cluster of grey buildings in the mist ahead. A welcome sight knowing them to be their final destination and thankful in the knowledge the convoy was well ahead of the invading Germans. The line of vehicles circled the square. They were too many. Thirty seven in all, half of them trailing back along the road into the distance. The bullion, mostly in gold bars packed into small wooden boxes, weighed in at eighty-four tons.

Unloading the vans began immediately. It was becoming light. The less people to be aware of the operation the safer the job itself would be. The police escort was ordered to return to Oslo before they were missed. It was vital no suspicion should fall on them which would allow the Germans or the hated Quisling elements to discover the gold's whereabouts.

Come 08-30 hours the last of the vans was unloaded and left the square to return to the capital. Olaf Larsen along with four others elected to remain in Lillehammer. They had designs on joining the Norwegian Army forces mobilising further to the north.

By now they were all exhausted. Olaf himself almost physically sick and with a feeling of abject despair now the operation was over. Like most of his fellow countrymen, he had never expected his small inoffensive homeland would become a target for the Nazi's. Someone put a cup of coffee in his shaking hands. A man, well into his fifties and with a face that had seen considerably more than one as young as himself.

"Don't look so damn cheerful." The man smiled. "Get that down you – make you feel better." Olaf took a sip of the scalding liquid. Somehow his throat rebelled. He had difficulty swallowing.

"Take your time son," said the seasoned eyes smiling concernedly down at him. "Drink it slowly. Then when we have all had a little rest we will figure out what it is we should do next – OK?" Olaf nodded. There were tears in his eyes. He hadn't realised. The tears were as a result of his pent- up frustration. How dare those jumped up, jack-booted stooges set their filthy black hands on his beautiful land? What gave them the right? Who did they think they were? A single tear wound its way down his cheek and froze before it reached his neckline. He knew one thing? Today the Germans had had it all their own way. But not tomorrow. Norway might be a small country and her people few in number, but the Germans would come to regret the day they treacherously despoiled her sacred soil. Of that he promised.

Central Oslo.   Southern Norway.

Gram watched the antics of the German Brass Band from the corner of the park. Several hundred of Oslo's populace had arrived to watch the performance, more probably from idle curiosity, before moving on as others ambled in to take their place. No one stayed long. It was as though to do so might give the impression they somehow approved of the Nazi presence in their midst's. Few wanted to be thought of as collaborators. But a small number were, without any doubt. How else had the Germans managed to take the city so easily?

On the Tuesday just a few German troops seemed to be in control. No concerted effort had been made to dispose of them. The people, Gram and his fellow students included, had half expected these few smiling Teutonic forerunners to have been ousted by the morning. Only morning had come and they were still there. It was on this day that the full mental process began.

The Germans had invaded and they meant to stay. Now the full realisation that the people were about to loose their neutral status and along with it their freedoms began to sink in. It showed on his fellow inhabitant's faces. Today many faces wore harassed lines and eyes that were troubled and afraid. War had come to peaceful Norway – Like it or not. Stories abounded that the city was about to be bombed. That the King and his Government had fled the country and everyone should get out as quickly as possible. What had begun as quiet peaceful mid-week day was turning into confusion and panic.

As Gram surveyed the crowd from his office window watching the German band, which had continued to play through the morning and well into the afternoon, numbers grew thinner. By three-o-clock the boulevard was all but deserted.

"Isn't it time you were going?"

Gram's employer stood in the doorway. Normally his boss worked in his shirtsleeves and was rarely seen without a bundle of papers latched under one arm. Today he was fully dressed. Jacket, tie, trilby hat.

"But it's only three-o-clock!" Gram replied.

"Yes I know. But isn't it time 'You' were going?" The inference was all too obvious. His boss didn't mean going home. A General Mobilisation Order had been proclaimed the previous day. Gram, like most of his fellow students, was exempt from military service, which didn't mean to say they couldn't volunteer if they so wished. Norway had for so long been neutral the thought of 'conscription' had never been a serious policy.

"Where do you suggest?" asked Gram.

"You should go north. My brother has a cabin near the Rena. Here are the directions -." He handed Gram an envelope. "Leave tonight whilst the trains are still running. Find some of our people. If I know the Army they will be organising something. The British are bound to come in now." He turned to leave and had gone but a few paces when he stopped in the doorway. "Two more things. One – leave your parents a note. Just say you're going away for a little while. They will understand -." He paused and remained quiet for a time. Gram finally broke the silence.

"And two?"

His boss turned, there were tears in his aged eyes.

"Come back alive – If you can -."

'Handelson's Cabin'. Stange. Nr. Hamar. Central Norway. 18-30hrs.

During the late afternoon the sun paled and with it came a sharp north-easterly wind. The seasons here in these more northern climes had a habit of intermingling without warning.

The man stood near the edge of the clearing just inside the tall firs. His breath, short but unhurried, crystallised in the thin air. The sudden drop in temperature had made the going easier leaving the snow dry and powdery. The cabin stood out clearly in the half-light. He needed somewhere safe to rest up. Tomorrow he would continue north again. His contact would be coming south to meet him. With luck he could return to Kristiansand before his employers became too concerned with his absence. His papers gave his name as Josef Brun. It wasn't his real name, not that it mattered. Over the years he had used so many. He searched the ground ahead. There were no ski tracks. Nothing had passed this way in at least the last forty-eight hours. His own tracks led back the way he had come. They shouldn't pose a problem, careful as he was to have used other skier's tracks on the way whenever possible. Only the last mile or two could his single track be followed and that through dense, unused forest. A light snowfall would have been a welcome asset.

Brun unclipped the telescopic sight from his rifle and scanned the opposite tree line for anything out of the ordinary. Seeing nothing, save the movements made by the biting wind, he pocketed the scope and pushed off towards the cabin.

The door was unlocked. Unsurprising. Such was the common practice in these parts. It was expected these isolated sanctuaries be used as a night's stopover by skiers and hunters caught unaware's by the regions unfathomable weather. Snowstorms often blew up without warning and could last for days. Life in Norway's high mountain ranges was tenuous at best and now with the events of the last few days it would soon become even more so. So much Brun already knew from the papers he carried about his person.

A chord of stika logs lay in a pile against the stone fireplace alongside some stripped sapling branches. Such a pity! A fire would have been most welcome, but the smoke a 'dead give away'. He turned. The door held a wooden closure stay. Strong and sturdy. Brun swung it shut and fastened the stay down with its locking pin. Only one way out. Likewise, only the one way in. The windows, two of them, had shutters both inside and out which, after a closer inspection, satisfied his concern. The floor was of boarded timber. Brun moved slowly across testing each one for its strength. The weakest part was around the base of the fireplace. Removing his knife he knelt and began to pry between the joins.

An hour later he had removed enough of the boarding and sufficient mounds of earth to pass his lean frame under and beyond the wall of the cabin to the outside. It had been tiring work but vital should the need arise. Outside was now night. No moon and dark for the time of year. The mountains whose snow lined slopes and from whose reflected moonlight one could usually read by, tonight, were barely visible through a haze of moisture-laden cloud that had suddenly rolled in as if from nowhere. A rise in temperature of one or more degrees and by morning the snow could be six feet deep. Brun mouthed a silent prayer. Nothing must slow him down, but it would have been dangerous to attempt to go on through the night. He was tired. Barely six hours sleep in the last two days had left him exhausted. He must sleep. If only for a short time. The single bunk beckoned. He pushed his skis and the rucksack down the hole and returned to the bunk where he lowered himself slowly on to the coarse blanket. His system had shut itself down long before his head hit the straw filled mattress.

Early Days.   April 9th – 10th. 1940.

The Fuhrer and Supreme Commander
Of the Armed Forces.   Berlin. 3/1/40.
                                                        9 Copies.

'Directive for Case Weser-Exercise'.

The development of the situation in Scandinavia makes it necessary to prepare for the 'occupation' of Denmark and Norway by formations of the Armed Forces. (Case Weser-Exercise).
This would anticipate English action against Scandinavia and the Baltic, would secure our supplies of iron ore from Sweden and would provide the Navy and the Air force with expanded bases for operations against England - - - - .
  The basic aim is to lend the operation the character of a peaceful occupation designed to protect by force of arms the neutrality of these northern countries - - - .
Any resistance which is nevertheless offered will be broken by all means available - - - .

  It was usual for Hitler to number all his 'directives'. The fact that Case Weser-Exercise was not, gives credence to the belief that the occupation of both Norway and Denmark were as a result of unforeseen events and not part of the German dictator's overall European strategy -. *(For full text of Directive, 'Fall Westerbung/ Case Weser-Exercise- See - End Notes).*

  On the evening of Tuesday 9th April, General Von Falkenhorst sent a short, to the point, signal to OKW HQ in Zossen near to Berlin, which read: 'Norway and Denmark occupied. As instructed.'
This was far from the case. It would be a number of weeks before the German invader could rest a little easier – not that it would totally ever be so. As for the cost? It would be one of the few times in the 'Wolf's' earlier ventures when events would bring him close to the edge of near despair and total collapse and

show him not to have been the 'great' genius of a commander his people believed him to be.

Germany's Naval Commander (Kreigsmarine) Admiral Raeder, had warned Hitler of possible heavy losses to his already inadequate naval fleet. In forcing the approaches to the Norwegian fjords, his newest heavy cruiser 'Blucher' had been sunk. Near Bergen came the loss of the cruiser 'Konisborg'. 'Karlsruhe' another cruiser was sunk by British submarines and at Narvik, ten destroyers, eight U-boats and a number of ancillary vessels were also eliminated from the invasion by British naval forces. After Norway, the German Navy could truthfully say it was no longer a strong efficient entity to be reckoned with and for the rest of the war never again ventured forth from its bases in German waters to do battle as a cohesive force.

On land there were problems also. The assault parties, detailed to take Oslo and arrest the King and his Ministers, foundered in the Oslo fjord with the sinking of the 'Blucher'. The troops of the 7th Air Division who were to take Fornebu airfield were delayed by a pea-soup of a fog. Thus only a token force reached the Norwegian capital that first day. In fact less than one thousand troops in total.

But with no standing army and the suddenness by which the Germans had appeared the Norwegian authorities could do little but look on in dismay.

For the first twenty-four hours German bombers frequently buzzed the capital. The show of force was intended to intimidate rather than terrorise. No anti-aircraft fire was returned. At 15-00 hours in the afternoon the first German occupation troops entered the city, led, incredibly as it may seem, by Norwegian policemen sent to clear away the traffic.

By the Wednesday, the day Gram left the city, German paratroopers had encircled Oslo and were in control of all the main arteries. All road and rail links were under German control by the evening of the 10th April. At Sola airfield near Stavanger on the West Coast a further assault by German paratroopers of X Fliegerkorps secured the airfield against little opposition and troops from the 69th Infantry Division were soon arriving. The battle, when it came, would be for Central and Northern Norway, amidst the melting of the cold winter snows.

'Handelson's Cabin'. Stange. Nr. Hamar. Hedmark Fylke. Central Norway.

Brun woke with a start. Something had disturbed the dead silence. He listened. There was nothing. Not at first. It was as he began to lay back the faintest swish of ski on snow penetrated the walls of the cabin. Instantly he gained his feet. It could be nothing. Another lone skier, lost, looking for shelter. The owner of the cabin perhaps? Whoever, they would certainly expect to gain access. A locked door would arouse some concern. If not suspicion!

The door latch moved just the once against the wooden stay then slowly returned to its former position with a barely audible 'clunk'. If the visitor was 'a friend' Brun expected the movement to be followed by a 'knock' and a voice making enquiries. He waited. Then when nothing happened he sprung into action.

The space he had dug below the cabin was barely sufficient. Slowly, stopping every few seconds to listen' he forced his way through the frozen barricade of snow and finally surfaced at the rear of the cabin. The visitor, whoever he was, had made no effort to announce himself. The distance from the cabin wall to the trees was about twenty metres. Assuming the visitor was not alone and was standing at the far edge of the clearing his, Brun's movements, would be observable for the better part of half the distance from the cabin to the woods. It was a risk he would have to take. He fixed his skis and with one determined lunge was skimming rapidly for the tree line. There was a shout followed almost instantly by the 'crack' of a rifle shot. Something buzzed passed his face and splintered off against one of the trees as he flew into them. More shouts. At least two. Norwegian. He couldn't be sure. Another shot. This time he felt something smash into his thigh. There was a sharp pain. Bastard. The man's aim was getting better. Mustering his strength he plunged down the narrow pathway between the trees. Whoever the men were they were anything but friendly. Distance. He needed to put some space between himself and these 'shoot first ask questions after' merchants who didn't seem to be in the mood for talking. Two more rifle shots. The bullets clipped branches above his head sending down streamers of icy flakes. Not German. NS more than likely. Norwegian Nazi's. Sent to pick up his trail. Locals who would know the area. Even more dangerous. If that were the case he would never outrun them. The pain in his leg was getting worse. It wouldn't be long before they would begin to gain on him, which would bring him into range for a shot that would finish him. The decision was made. In a wall of leaping ice particles he slewed to a halt and dropped to the snow his rifle already poised. There wasn't time to make adjustments to the scope. He aimed through the barrel sights. They wore white snow-suits and but for their faces and rifles slung over their backs would have been indistinguishable from the frozen backdrop. The first shot would be the decider. The man went down without a sound. One minute he was rushing onward at breakneck speed the next a ball of limbs and cascading snow. The second of his pursuers seeing his friend fall seemed undecided for he slewed away then changed his course again fumbling to unhitch his rifle. Brun's next shot took him through the head sending him crashing away. The body slid for a good hundred metres before coming to a crumpled heap against the base of a tree where one of the man's legs, its ski still attached, swung high off the ground and hitched itself to one of the trees lower branches. Brun waited. Half a minute perhaps a little more before lowering his rifle to the snow. Neither of the crumpled heaps moved. Two shots. Two bodies? It seemed too good to be true? He never considered himself a marksman. But he was lucky! As past events had shown. He winced. The pain, which in the heat of the moment had gone from his mind, returned. He looked down. A large red stain covered the space in which he was lying. At this rate unless he could do something to staunch the loss of blood he would soon be joining his two 'kills'. The surrounding landscape offered nothing in the way of sanctuary. Return to the cabin was an option. Providing always his two midnight visitors hadn't friends following on. The wound was too high to effectively staunch the blood supply, too close to the groin. A lucky shot, or unlucky depending on your point of view, but one that didn't bode well for planning a long term future. Brun removed his belt and folding his snow-cap into the wound pulled on the belt as tight as it would go. The pain was excruciating. Then why hadn't he cried out in pain? There was no one to hear. Instinct? Silence. Just one more survival technique. He scanned the tree line, more in hope than in any expectation. What now? He shook his head. This was a fine state of affairs and no mistake. The best laid of plans - -!

Lillehammer.

Major Ording stopped the car and pulled aggressively down on the edge of his tunic. Milling squads of men mostly dressed in winter white clothing and shouldering rifles besieged the building opposite. Small clumps of brightly coloured ski's sprouted like artificial flowerbeds from the mounds of snow piled along the roadside. Yesterday Ording had spent most of his precious time organising the transfer of men and materials along the valley roads from headquarters. Twice they had been strafed by German planes. The area was alive with rumour that the King was hereabouts.

"Officer present." Some of the men straightened up and made an effort to shuffle backwards as Ording entered the building. An elderly figure in soldier's uniform rose from behind a flag draped desk. He raised his arm and saluted. Ording stepped forward and squinted focusing his eyes in the darkened interior.

"Bugger me! Broch?" The elderly soldier swayed back on his heels and broke into a huge grin.

"Begging your pardon Sir. But if you don't mind I'll pass on that one."

Colonel Ole Broch was sixty-five if he was a day and a soldier of more than forty years. When the call from the Royal Palace was issued for the populace to arm itself Broch had donned his old uniform and skied the fifteen miles to the Recruitment Offices in Lillehammer. Finding the offices closed he searched out the caretaker and set up 'shop', advertising his presence with a large bill-board set atop one of the frozen snow-mounds which read: 'Soldiers Wanted. Only Loyal Norwegians Need Apply'.

Ording returned the salute.

"Yes – Sorry. Took me unaware s. I thought you had retired?"

"Well – Yes Sir. I had. But when I got here there wasn't anybody doing anything, so I thought I'd open up, so to speak. I might be passed it Sir but I've taken on over six hundred volunteers since yesterday morning. Six hundred and twenty one to be precise Sir."

"Passed it? I'd like to meet the man who told you that. Is he still alive?" Ording looked down at the register on the desk. "Bloody good show Broch. Splendid. With you back in harness the bloody Huns would be better off getting out now whilst they're still in one piece – eh? Are they all armed?" Ording looked around the hall. Most seemed to have at least a rifle apiece.

"Rifles Sir. But I haven't been able to give them any spare ammunition. The key to the Armoury. The Chief of Police has it. He was snatched by some of

Quislings arseholes. We don't know where he is."

"Snatched!" Ording's face darkened. The traitorous bastards were piling out from under their stones now they thought the Germans were getting the upper hand.

"Take some men and go and shoot the locks off. Blow the bloody doors off if you have to. This is war Broch. Not a bloody exercise." Broch beamed. "With the greatest of pleasure Sir." Broch moved from behind the table and grabbed the group nearest to him.

Ording glanced at the vacated chair and dropped his hat onto it. A man in his early twenties detached himself from a nearby group. In his hands he held a cup of something steaming which he raised aloft.

"Ringe Sir. Carl. It's good to see you Sir."

Ording took the proffered cup. It was hot and sweet but as for the taste -? Still, it was perhaps better not to comment.

"Just up from the front are you Sir?" Ording nodded. "Coffee Sir – In case you were wondering. It's not too clever Sir. Best they can do apparently. Er – What's it like down there Sir?" Ording took another sip and did his best not to grimace.

"Cold – Bloody cold." The young soldier shuffled his feet nervously.

"Yes Sir. But I mean -."

"I know what you meant– Ringe –is it? You meant how are we doing?"

The Major searched amongst his vocabulary for the right words. It would be nothing short of a brilliant stroke of good fortune if they could stop the German advance, a miracle if they could turf them out of the country. Norway's two or three fully mobilised divisions were no match for the massive German army.

"It's stable for the moment. There's lots of easy game for those of you who can shoot straight. Don't worry Ringe, you'll get your chance. The arseholes are in no hurry to leave us just yet."

Norway Central Bank. Lillehammer.

Suddenly there was a heavy knocking on the outside of the main doors. Olaf Larsen jerked awake and fumbled blindly for his rifle. He shook his head and tried to focus. It was the first time in many hours he had taken the chance for some sleep.

"Who is it?"

"The manager." came back the reply. Larsen moved from his seat amongst the avalanche of wooden boxes.

"What do you want?"

"For the black wolves to die." came back the strange reply. Larsen smiled to himself. It was the correct response. A little bit 'cloak and dagger' but he was sitting on some eighty tons of gold bullion. Larsen pulled back on the two heavy wrought iron bolts. The bank manager squeezed his pinstriped suit through the narrow opening.

"Any news?" Larsen asked.

"Nothing. There's confusion everywhere. It isn't safe to use the telephones any more. The Germans are listening in. Our army is here in town mobilising what's available. But it's difficult to know whom to trust."

"Damnnation! It's been two days. Three since Oslo. Surely they can't just have forgotten about all this -." Larsen threw both hands out towards the pile scattered across most of the bank's main floor. "Oh yes – now, let's think, where did we leave that two billion crowns in gold bars? Clue anyone? This is ridiculous – bloody ridiculous."

The bank manager cast his gaze over the mountain of boxes. He had quite often in the past felt it was his duty to the bank to be as responsible an employee as he could. But there were limits – or at least there should have been -?

"Yes -. Well -. Look. You're worn out. You need to get some proper sleep and something decent to eat. Sandwiches and black coffee are all very well but -. Look. I will take over for a few hours. Where can I contact you if I need you?" Larsen looked at the man's clean- almost angelic features. Was it a face he could trust? Certainly not a face you would expect to find guarding a 'mountain hall' full of gold. Still. He was worn out and consequently too tired to bother to argue.

"Karre Bergstrom's." Larsen replied.

"Bergstrom! Yes. A good man. Are you a friend of the family?" Larsen nodded.

"Yes. His sons. We've skied together many times. Here – take my rifle just in -

." Larsen was interrupted by a loud knocking on the outer panels of the door. The two men looked at each other. The bank manager reacted first.

"Hello -?" he called. Almost timidly.

A man's voice came from beyond.

"Good morning. Tell me-is the bank open today?"

"What is it that you require?" replied the manager, skilfully avoiding the direct question.

"I need to draw some money. Some travelling money."

Larsen shook his head vigorously. The manager shrugged.

"I'm sorry sir. We are awaiting proper instructions from head office. Maybe you should try again tomorrow?"

Larsen had moved swiftly to one of the shuttered windows. He peered out. The owner of the voice was a tall thin man, pale faced and sporting a small goatee beard. He wore civilian clothing. As the man descended the stone steps leading up to the front doors he turned and eyed the doors suspiciously. Larsen kept his eyes on the man. "He's looking. Not happily. Now he's turning. He's going away. Yes. He's gone." Suddenly he felt weak. The last few days had been very worrying. His country's gold reserves mustn't fall into the hands of the Nazi's. The King would never forgive him.

"He's gone. God I feel fucked -." There was a silence. Larsen looked up. The bank manager was grinning. It wasn't often he heard such language in his bank. Larsen smiled back.

"Stop grinning you swine. I am. Tired that is. All this waiting around is killing me. Have you got any cigarettes?"

The bank manager fumbled in his pockets and extracted a packet. "Here. Keep them. You look as they will do you a heap more good than they will me." Larsen caught the packet. The packet was new, the sealing paper still in place. Larsen put a hand in his trouser pocket. He fumbled for a moment or two then - . "Sorry. I don't seem to have any -." he mumbled. The bank manager grinned some more, then allowed himself the luxury of a little chuckle.

"Oh I shouldn't worry about that." He gestured to the mountain of wooden boxes. "Personally –I'm not without a crown or two you know-."

Stange. Nr. Hamar. Central Norway.

Beauty has the habit of becoming banal after a time. A scene that changes only marginally and then at the flick of a switch can become a killer only holds one's admiration for a limited time.

All this Gram was running through his mind as he skimmed expertly between the tall firs, one eye on the ski tracks ahead, the other surfing for the merest hint of approaching danger.

The first man had been shot through the heart. Dead centre. Clean. If one could call the ragged hole between the man's shoulder blades by such a description. The second body looked for all intents and purposes to have been 'downed' from the tree from which its right leg was rigidly suspended. A head shot. Not as clean as before, the right eye socket had been pulped and a part of his skull lay some distance away. He must have skied the last thirty or more metres as a corpse.

Another set of tracks led off into the distance. Whoever it was had been wounded. The frozen pool of bright red told its own story.

Gram had reached his employer's cabin in the early hours of the morning. Finding the door locked and skirting around he soon came across the recently made excavation and the ski track leading off into the trees. It was the tell-tale bloodstains spotting the crisp Arctic snow that first change his mild curiosity to one of a wavering concern. A closer inspection had revealed not one but three sets of tracks. All very mysterious. He decided to wait until the morning light. He was tired from his journey. To venture into the unknown in this kind of terrain took courage and an alertness of mind. Not that he had ever questioned either attribute. A few hours sleep would find him in better shape.

The body of the man lay in a hollow amongst a small copse of trees through which he must have purposely negotiated. The natural lie of the land would have taken any passing visitor away in a wider arc. His wounds and lack of physical strength must have made it impossible for him to provide adequate shelter against the biting northerly winds. The body had no warmth and had been life extinct for a number of hours. Gram looked at the pale face that now glistened in the feint silvery ray's of the Arctic sun. A thin, almost opaque layer of ice covered the lifeless skin. Mid-thirties at a guess. His ID gave his name as Josef Brun, Engineer, from Kristiansand. What had he been doing so far north? The 'papers' revealed the answer. Wrapped around the man's midriff with packing tape and expertly bound up in leather and greaseproof paper. German

38

was not one of Gram's fortes. But he would have had to be mentally retarded not to grasp the significance of what lay now exposed before him. The German Nazi symbol's and the red and green arrowed maps of Southern and Central Norway, said it all. These were a copy of the proposed German dispositions for the opening phases of Norway's occupation. The invasion plan for Von Falkenhorst's troops. So that was why the man had been hunted down. His two pursuers had bitten off a little more than they could chew but not before having fatally wounding their quarry.

Gram cast a worried gaze across the surrounding tree lines. It stood to reason that whoever had given the orders for the acquisition of the 'plans' would soon becoming concerned at receiving no word of the situation. More 'hunters' would be dispatched.

At least eight hours had passed since these men had left the area of 'Handelsen's' cabin. Possibly more. Gram slipped the large 'porte-document' inside his coat and tightened the drawstring around his waist. He checked his wristwatch for the time. Ten fifteen. Almost. Burying the bodies would take some time but would also serve to confuse the 'tracker's', especially if there was a fall of snow in the next few hours. Alternatively he could put on a good few miles between himself and the cabin in the same time? Damn! This wasn't on the agenda when he had left Oslo. From Student of Economics to Student of Espionage in less than a day. And he wasn't even a proper soldier yet!

General Ruge's Temp. H.Q. Minnesund. Akershus Fylke.

"So Captain. What do you make of this?" The old General flicked the flimsy dispatch in a circular movement to land squarely on the opposite side of the desktop. Olsan bent forward.

"The Finance Minister. Proceed Lillehammer most immediate. Matter of pressing importance. -." Olsen cocked his head to one side and shrugged.

"Maybe he has lost his briefcase. Perhaps?"

Ruge snorted to suppress a laugh. It was all he could do not to break out in a huge grin. Captain Olsen was a man after his own heart. Politicians. The bane of the Military, but equally necessary to maintain a balance of the status quo.

"Yes. Maybe, maybe -." he cleared his throat. "Well whatever the problem he wants a responsible officer over there at the double – and that, I am afraid, is going to have to be you Johan. Can you leave immediately?"

"Yes Sir. No problem. I will need to draw some petrol first."

"Good. Fine. Take what you need. If you keep to the main road and a weather eye out for enemy aircraft you shouldn't have any problems. There are some reports filtering in about German paratroops. Stragglers mainly. They shouldn't pose you a problem. Our men are picking them off slowly but surely. Still. Best keep a good eye out. You know the drill. Get in touch as soon as you arrive – OK?"

Olsen snapped off a quick salute. Trust the old man to play down the dangers. Anything could happen with so many of the Quisling's now abroad not to mention the lack of good intelligence on the German's intentions. It was unlikely the enemy had yet managed to infiltrate in any great numbers into the interior – but there were no guarantees.

'Cubs & Pups'.

Although he went by the codename 'Wuff'. MI6's prime mover in Norway was in fact one of the 'Lion's' personnel. His real name, Major Francis Edward Foley, a man whose inoffensive mild mannered looks and nature belied one of Britain's most courageous and successful 'intelligence agents' of the twentieth century.

Foley had arrived in the Norwegian capital of Oslo in August of the previous year. His 'brief'! To arrange for the removal of the 'heavy water' in production in Norway, whose use was for 'atomic energy', safely to Britain, in the event of the material being compromised by an enemy incursion. This amongst the multitude of tasks already 'in house' for a 'diplomat' of the British Embassy.

Previous to the German invasion of April 9th 1940, Foley had successfully recruited a number of European nationals into his 'cell'. One such was Paul Rosbaud, a German national, who would go by the codename of the 'Griffin'. It was Rosbaud with the assistance of another by the name of Hans Mayer who compiled the later named 'Oslo' Report. This 'report' contained details of the German military's work on the acoustic mine and torpedo but most importantly of the work taking place at a small sea port on the Baltic Sea by the name of Peenemunnde, on the 'V' (Vergeltungswaffen) rockets. This 'report' was 'dropped' (in a small package) outside the British Embassy in Oslo on the Drammensvien in November 1939, less than two months after the outbreak of the war. Although discussed at great length in London, with the exception of one of the British government's advisors R.V.Jones, the 'reports' contents were seen as an Abwehr 'ploy'. (Abwehr – German Intelligence) and was for the most part discounted.

Foley was reported to be 'furious' with his London colleagues as he was convinced of the veracity of the 'reports' contents and that such a decision put the 'veracity' of his own recruited agents in doubt. Still, as was his nature he refused to allow it to interfere with his continued work for MI6.

On April 9th 1940, Foley activated his 'emergency' plans and left Oslo for Hamar to avoid the German incursion. His orders were now to assist with the removal of the Norwegian Royal Family, the Norwegian gold reserves and the 'heavy water', to the safety of the British Isles and to act as 'go-between' for the Norwegian Armed Forces and British Intelligence. No mean feat considering the small unit of loyal Norwegians he had at his disposal and the lack of any military advantages.

41

Travelling by way of Hosjbor on Lake Mjoso he managed to keep ahead of the German paratroops arriving eventually at Otta by way of Gudbransdal and Lillehammer where he stayed overnight. The following day (the 10th April) he went on to Dombas and then Andalsnes where he put up for the night at the Hotel Bellvue. The Hotel's roof was an ideal point from which to contact, by radio, his 'station' in London. It was now he learned of Josef Brun's mission.

Meanwhile:

The 'Wolf' was herding his 'cubs' in a vain bid to pacify the troubles now brewing in his proposed 'new Scandinavian kingdom'.

On April 10th, as Foley was traversing towards the West Coast of Norway, the German dictator saw the collapse of any meaningful negotiations between his representative the German Ambassador Hans Braur and the King of Norway's government advisor's. Hitler was furious. He ranted at his Foreign Minister Joachim von Ribbentrop to rectify the ragged holes torn through his planned 'peaceful' take-over of the country. Things were not going at all to plan. Ribbentrop searched frantically amongst the leading representatives still ensconced in the Norwegian capital, noticeably one Paul Berg the Chief Justice to the Norwegian Supreme Court. Hitler wanted his 'puppet' Quisling to head up the New Norwegian government. Paul Berg and his fellow compatriots on the other hand thought that might bring more than a few 'problems', in light of the present events and played for time.

On the 11th April Hitler had had enough. He sent for his favourite Reichleiter Martin Bormann in whom he felt the greatest security and in whom he would later confer the whole conduct of the German Nazi Party and its war machine – and the 'future' of his new 'Greater German Reich'. "Find me a solution to this – Norway-." He ordered -.

Lillehammer. Oplandflyke. Central Norway.

Some of the bullion containers had suffered badly in the headlong flight from the capital. A number of them were split and broken so that their precious glittering cargo now lay strewn about amongst the jumble mountain of hastily stacked boxes.

"Now you see Johan just how important was the Finance Ministers despatch." Ording slapped the stupefied Captain playfully on the shoulder.

"You my dear Captain are to – and I quote – organise and supervise its safe removal into the hands of our allies."

Olsen had arrived in the town that morning having perilously negotiated the icy journey up the valley from Minnesund and gone immediately to Ording's temporary headquarters for instructions. But this was certainly something he hadn't anticipated.

"How the hell am I to get all this lot to the coast and onto a ship when nobody knows at which port the Allies will land – or come to think of it – if they ever will land?"

The bank's manager thought any suggestion at this juncture worth the effort. The last thing he wanted was for the 'goods' to remain in his possession.

"The Oslo Police used vans. Once you're away from the town and out of the area you could hide up somewhere until you receive word from your headquarters or the Allies." He put a hopeful smile to the end of his statement by way of encouragement to the worried frown on the Captain's face.

"Oh Yes! How many vans?"

"Oh. About thirty I think. Maybe thirty five."

"Thirty five vans -!" Olsen exploded. "Thirty five -! And where do you suggest I hide thirty five vehicles from the whole of the German army. The Nazi's are not stupid – Or blind. Every bloody Hun spotter plane in Norway will be on my arse within hours." Olsen walked slowly around the base of the wooden pile. He stopped then bent down to examine a number of the loose gold bars. "And what the hell are these for – loose change?"

The gold bars had dropped from an opening in one of the crates. They had fallen one after the other in a line on the dark stained floor. Olsen took hold of one of the bars and felt its weight then ran his fingers over the embossed mark on the smooth silky surface before replacing it exactly where he had found it. He tapped it lightly with his fingers. Then began nodding to himself a smile creeping into his face.

"Of course. Now that makes much more sense."
Major Ording and the bank manager both nodded in agreement before looking at each other totally bemused. Olsen remained silent.

"Er – what does?" asked Ording after a time, unable to contain himself any longer.

"A train." Olsen pointed to the gold bars lined up on the floor in a gentle curve at his feet. "A Goods Train. If one can be found. Much more sensible. Less likely to attract the German's attention providing we make it look innocuous enough."

"Brilliant." replied Ording, meaning it.

"Yes, yes. Quite brilliant," parroted the bank manager not caring if it was or not just as long as the bullion mountain left his bank sooner than later.
Olsen fastened the top button of his tunic.

"I'd better get back to HQ, the General needs to know about this. If anyone can get this moving Ruge can. How's the area for enemy paratroopers?"

"They dropped about a hundred of the little bastards near Elverum early this morning. We've got most of them but there are still bound to be the odd group hiding out in the forest. Just don't stop for any strangers. What can I say?" said Ording with a smile. In the circumstances it was the best and only advice he could offer.

German HQ. Central Oslo. Southern Norway.

From a military point of view the problems besetting General Von Falkenhorst's troops were, to his mind, far less critical than the panicky chatter emanating from Berlin's Chancellery would have one believe. Or for that matter the hallowed halls of OKH (Wehrmacht HQ.) in Zossen.

To the far north of Norway at the port of Narvik, the Kreigsmarine had successfully landed two thousand of his troops. At Bergen, Trondheim and Stavanger a similar number had been invested, a completion of the initial directives in the 'Occupation'. The battle at sea off the Norwegian coast seemed to be preoccupying the British and French with no reported landings of Allied forces having taken place. Events were moving satisfactorily, considering the debacle; partially the responsibility of the 'creature' now standing before him and who had the audacity to be now haranguing him in his, the General's, own office. Damn cheek of the man!

"This is not a social call Herr General -," scowled Quisling following the General's effort to persuade him to take a drink. One glance at the bottle showed it to be of Polish origins. Polish brandy? Whoever heard of such a thing! "I must protest most strongly the interference of your people in the city's civil administration. I was given an absolute guarantee that - -."

"My people?" General Falkenhorst's eyes blazed anger. "What do you mean – My people? My people for your information Herr Quisling are soldiers. Perhaps you have entered the wrong building by mistake!"

The leader of the Norwegian Nazi Party took a step backwards as the General reared up from his desk.

"With – With the greatest of respect General. These people arrived with your forces. I therefore must assume you have some degree of control over them. The whole situation is outrageous. A betrayal – A betrayal that I can assure you General will be most pointedly reported to the Fuhrer himself -." General Falkenhorst fixed the man with a stare and held it for an inordinate amount of time before slowly sinking back into his seat. He ran his eyes around the rotund figure whose pouting jowls still quivered from the strain of his defensive riposte. With a flick of his fingers the General indicated for his aide to pour out the drinks.

"My dear Major Quisling. You really should take things more calmly. There is nothing – absolutely nothing to become alarmed about. It is simply a question of timing, that is all. Norway is not yet under your government control - or that of my government if it comes to that. There is at present a state of flux – for the want of a better description. There are still substantial Norwegian forces facing both our southern and northern fronts. Yes, they are retreating, even as we speak, and it is only a question of time. But it is not – Herr Major- what you led us to expect? Is it?"

"Is it my fault you failed to secure the ports before your government issued the Norwegian government with the Führer's memorandum -?" Von Falkenhorst took the drink from his aide's proffered hands. He gave a quick grin and took a sip of the clear liquid.

"Touché Herr Major. Touché. Alright. So we admit there have been mistakes made on both sides. Nothing in war is ever perfect. I shall if you wish contact Berlin and see what can be done on the matter. Although I must warn you. I might well be told to mind my own business."

At that the Norwegian Major seemed to relax a little. The glass of brandy, Lindauer, the General's aide, had been holding out, broached the conversation with a well-timed pause. Von Falkenhorst threw the remaining alcohol to the back of his throat then rested both arms on the desk.

"So Major. What news have you on your governments gold reserves?" Quisling forced another small sip of the foul tasting liquid between his lips. Brandy! More like gasoline. He cleared his throat.

"None I'm sorry to say. But it cannot be long before we get some tangible leads. We have arrested all the Police Chiefs in the area. They are at present being questioned. One of them must know something. We shall have the information we want – before too long."

"I'm sure you are correct Major. Let's hope so. We would look complete fools in Berlin if we were to allow such a precious haul to evade us. Fall into the enemies hands -?" Quisling searched for some form of response.

"I'm sure General that will not be the case. The – er, carelessness of one of your officers? Regarding the file on 'Westerbung'? Quisling was referring to the invasion plans lost in Oslo Fjord. "I have sent some of my people to recover them. A very unfortunate occurrence. Don't you agree General?"

"Yes Major. The officer in question has been dealt with." Falkenhorst raised both eyebrows. "Not recovered them yet I assume?"

"It's in hand General. Well in hand."

"Well I have some better news. Your King. His party have been spotted on the road to Alvdal. I have given orders for a unit of paratroopers to be dropped to cut off their route of escape. This time Herr Major. There will be no mistakes - ." The General gave a toothy smile. "There have been enough of those already -."

Loten. Hedmark. Central Norway.

After hiding the three bodies under a light covering of snow Gram checked his bearings. North was towards the far ridges straight ahead.

It was impossible to know for certain how far the Germans' had by now penetrated the interior. Before leaving Oslo rumours of landings on the coast and the airfields had been rife. They couldn't be discounted. The German use of paratroops made landings of large, lightly armed units possible almost anywhere apart from some of the highest mountain ranges. Something crossed in Gram's mind. 'He who dares -!' Then almost as quickly the thought was shrugged off. Few, if any, of the invading Germans would be experts in Arctic conditions. The chances were the majority would stick to the valley and the main roads with perhaps a few alpine-trained 'specials' combing the vast tracts of wilderness in-between. Gram would need to stick to the forests. Keep heading north. Avoid any enemy outposts until he came across his own people, wherever that might be? The 'Westerbung' plans now made for infinite more urgency. Every hour passing would detract from the usefulness of the information to the Norwegian and Allied forces. The Germans may have changed the 'plan' following the loss of the documents? Who knows?

There was one by far more important problem. Gram sat back on his haunches. The edge of the tree line was perhaps a hundred metres away. Beyond that two maybe three kilometres of flat open plain before the forest edge came back into play. He would be a sitting duck for any good marksman. Certainly to begin with. He sighed heavily. But in truth that wasn't the only problem on the agenda. Food and water. Gram had sufficient to last the rest of today. After that he would need to forage. Habitation? Come the night the temperatures dropped rapidly to ten sometimes twenty degrees below zero. But habitation meant people. The men who had hunted down Brun. NS. Quisling's thugs. How was he to know who were friends and who the enemy? His enemies could be almost everywhere -. Gram glanced nervously over his shoulder. Nothing. He slapped himself on the face. Idiot. He was getting paranoid. But then this was a very unusual situation for a student of Politics. What he needed most was a fall of snow. An obliteration of the ski track that snaked obligingly back the full way he had come. Ridiculous! He might just as well left a note for any would be pursuit – This way Quisling assassins -? There was one thing for sure. He had to keep moving. At least for the rest of the daylight hours.

Later as the ice coloured sky grew steadily darker Gram noticed the far slope of the valley clouding over with a light mist, a burn-off from the sun's ray's. It was becoming colder. The going becoming easier as the ice formed a crust over the powdery surface beneath his feet. He didn't see the gully made by a stream until it was much too late. His attention had been taken by a number of tiny dark figures traversing across the opposite slope. Germans. They had to be. Silhouetted against the pure whiteness of the background in their heavy dark coats and moving slowly, very slowly, amongst the tall white firs. No self-respecting Norwegian would be abroad in these parts without a white or light coloured ski-suit. He hadn't seen a German paratrooper before and therefore only assumed such by the semi-automatic guns they carried instead of rifles.

The gully was less than a metre wide but he lanced both skis through the tenuous surface of the drift and flew forward face first. Thankfully the icy cold water was a mere few millimetres deep. But it was sufficient to douse his face and soak rapidly into the loose folds of his ski-suit. Gram was an experienced country skier, as was almost everyone in Norway, and instinctively moved slowly to untangle himself from the rocks and snow ridges overhanging the gaping hole he had opened up in the hillside. One wrong move might result in an injury. If that should happen he was certainly a dead man.

He lay for a time face down in the snow. It wasn't the most comfortable of positions. From just over his eye-line he could see the German troops still moving, singly spaced out amongst the tall trees. None it seemed had spotted him. Which again to his way of thinking said these men were not trained for operations in this type of terrain. He breathed a long sigh of relief. There was no pain. All he felt was the cold damnpness of the water to both of his feet and down the sides of his jacket collar. His rifle lay where it had fallen, across the width of the gully and pointing slightly skyward. He cursed. Damn. Quietly, but with a fair spluttering of venom. Wet feet were the last thing he wanted – well almost. An enemy bullet up his rectum certainly wasn't anything to wish for – come to think of it. He chuckled. It was good to find he still had his sense of humour. It was perhaps as well. More than his humour was going to be tried over the next few hours and days. This was only the beginning.

'Minnesund'. Akershusfylke. S. Norway.

As Olsen drove into the camp it was obvious there was a 'flap' on. Men and vehicles moving everywhere. General Ruge was busy cramming handfuls of papers into the belching mouth of the pot-bellied stove as the Major entered his office. The old man's serious demeanour changed abruptly.

"Johan -." he smiled. "Good man. Got through alright then." Olsen snapped off a moving salute. The General turned back to his work.

"We are moving back on Hamar. The Germans have broken out on the line about five kilometres to the south. How are things in Lillehammer?" Olsen gathered up a pile of the loose papers from the floor and waited an opportunity to feed them to the flames.

"Ording is gathering as many volunteers as he can muster. About a thousand men when I left. And you remember Colonel Broch. He's re-enlisted. Carrying on as if he had never retired."

"And the job? Had the Minister of Finance lost his briefcase? Ruge beamed, something of the usual twinkle to his eyes returning.

"Some briefcase Sir. Eighty-five tons of gold bullion from the Central Bank in Oslo. It's in Lillehammer now. They want me to keep it out of the hands of the Germans." The old man's face didn't move a muscle. If he was surprised by the news it didn't show.

"Eighty five tons you say? Hm. More than the odd car-boot full then? Did they suggest how?"

"There was no one there to ask Sir. I thought a train. A goods train? Find the quickest route out to the coast and haul it aboard the first friendly ship that comes along Sir." Ruge pursed his lips. His brow line furrowing deeply.

"Hm. Just like that eh! I can't see our German friends not having such a prize already in their sights. They will have planned to get their hands on it somehow." The General thought for a moment. "Our Allies haven't landed yet. You can't just hang around in Molde or Andalsnes whilst something appropriate comes along -." The old man stuffed the remaining fist-full of papers into the mouth of the stove then crossed to where the situation board hung on the wall. A large map showing the whole of Norway served its purpose.

"The best thing would be to keep moving. It might be several days before it's safe to move to the coast. There are a number of small branch lines you could take. Nothing much will be moving on them at present. But that itself is a danger. You won't want to draw attention to yourselves. There are German paratroops everywhere. They very nearly got the King and his party this morning -." Olsen's jaw fell open.

"Oh it's alright. We gave them the 'chop'. Every last one of them. Teach the little bastards to keep to their own country. Still -. It's not nice work. War never is." Ruge paused, staring off into the distance. "Bloody business. Hell of a trade for a decent man to get into. Anyway. The king is safe. They had some trouble. The party became separated on the road to Rendal. The Crown Prince went on to Alvdal. The King is resting at a place nearby -." Ruge tapped the map with his pencil. "Here. He's at a farmhouse owned by a man named 'Wolf' – very appropriate – it's about five kilometres north of Rendal. I am sending Major Ording and some of his men to escort them on – as a precaution."

"Should I tell Ording that when I get back Sir?"

"Yes. I was about to suggest you do just that. Who knows who is listening in on our radio traffic these days. Tell the Major his codename for the King will be 'Magnus' and seeing as how you also have important work to do for our country, your codename from now on will be 'Fridtjof'. You are to use them in all future communications. Best not trust anyone from now on. Least of all our own countrymen – especially anyone offering you easier alternatives. Quisling's arseholes are everywhere." The old General threw the pencil down on his desk.

"You'd better not waste any time. Get something to eat for the road." Olsen gave a quick salute and tried to think of something positive to say. Nothing that didn't sound emotional or jingoistic came to mind. General Ruge fixed him with a smile. The way a father might a son.

"Be careful out there Johan. Watch your back –"He extended his hand.

"We shall meet again – that's a promise."

Lillehammer Railway Station - . Later - - -.

Although on the main Oslo to Trondheim railway line, Lillehammer Station was rarely a hotbed of activity, unlike today.
The platforms and surrounding buildings bustled with a frenzy of pimpled, pasty-faced volunteers. Hundreds of them. Coming and going in a continuous stream of loud chatter and ribald remarks. Those with orders making to join the front lines those arriving looking excited and wondering the prudence of this next step in their, as yet, young, inexperienced lives.
Olsen, with old Colonel Broch at his side searched amongst the tangle of bodies for sight of the station master's dark blue uniform. The goods train that was to take Norway's precious haul of gold stood stark and peaceful looking in a

nearby siding. A pair of legs and a rather large pair of attached buttocks jerked tantalisingly from inside one of the two open wagons.

"What are the floors like?" asked Olsen steeling himself from the urge to give the mountainous wobbling flesh a swift jab with his boot. The stationmaster struggled from within his face crimson with exertion.

"Looks OK to me – You must be Olsen -." Olsen nodded. A phone call from Ruge had put a 'shot' up the rear end of the regions 'Permanent Way Supervisor'. Where there hadn't been the remotest possibility of an engine and wagons for days, suddenly there had been spirited into existence a locomotive, fuel tender and two functional box cars for the 'use of'.

"Can you find a couple of flat-cars? And the name is 'Captain' Olsen." said Johan. The stationmaster blinked, both eyebrows shooting arrow-like over his bulbous cherry-red nose.

"Flat-cars? Flat-cars?" As if unsure what they were.

"Yes. You know the kind of thing. Bogeys. Wooden floor. No sides. No roof. Flat – very flat -." Olsen looked at Broch and rolled his eyes.
It turned out there was an abundance of flatcars in a nearby siding.

"Two on the end Broch. And machine guns and plenty of ammunition."

"Yes Sir." replied Broch. "And the men and supplies Sir?"

"A dozen. Besides the driver and myself. We shall need food and cigarettes. Enough for a week. I don't want anyone wandering off foraging for supplies unless it becomes absolutely necessary."

"Bedding Sir. Medical kits?"

"Yes. Let's hope we don't have to use the latter. Do you think you could come up with some brandy or schnapps or something? Purely medicinal of course."

"You're expecting that much trouble Sir?" asked Broch smiling.

"Good grief man. It's not for us. We might need it for the German wounded. Every man is entitled to some small comfort before he dies."

The locomotive stood cold and sullen, glistening in the late afternoon sun. It's polished brass works reflecting a deeper yellowing glow across the crests of the adjoining snowdrifts.

"Do we have a driver?" enquired Olsen of the stationmaster.

"He is having his break Captain. There are very strict regulations regarding the number of hours a driver can be on the foot-plate." the stationmaster replied adjusting his hat with a flourish.

"You mean there were – until a few days ago." said Olsen annoyed. He turned to his old Colonel. "Broch. Go and find this engine driver. Tell him he is to be ready to roll in one hour -.""Broch turned to go.

"Impossible. One hour. Impossible." The stationmaster's eyes popped from their sockets like a gaffed halibut. "Don't you know anything about trains? These engines need a terrific head of steam to get them rolling. With the weight of your cargo. What is it? A hundred tons plus men and materials. You are going to need three to four hours stoking." Olsen looked the man up and down. The look he received in return from the reddened face was obviously very serious. The man was right of course. What was a Captain in the Norwegian Armed Forces supposed to know about trains? It wasn't in any of the training manuals.

"Alright then Broch. Tell him he's got two hours. After that we leave without him."

"Impossible. Two hours. Impossible. You have to load the cargo as well?"

"We can load the cargo whilst the engine is warming up." Olsen replied irritably.

"Impossible. Impossible. You have to get the engine to the loading bay to do that -."

"Then we will push the bloody thing there." The stationmaster opened his mouth to reply. "- And if you say 'impossible' one more time I will personally give you to the first German troops we come across -." The man's open mouth clapped shut with a snap.

"But Captain -. Please. Listen to me. Your job is fighting the enemy and to know how that is done. My job is to move trains around and to know how that is done. You can't push a hundred ton locomotive to shunt on wagons then push the whole lot into the station. Even should you get it moving you will never stop it manually. It will end up ten kilometres down the line – in a bloody great heap -! Isn't there something else you could be doing like organising the trolleys and men to bring your cargo to the loading ramps – Hmm?" The stationmaster put on his best grovelling face and sucked both protruding eyeballs back into their sockets. Olsen found it most disconcerting. Perhaps he was being a little unreasonable. In the days to come he would sorely need the good graces of these railway people.

"Hmm. Yes. Most unsatisfactory -." Olsen turned to the amused figure of his septuagenarian second in command grinning in the background.

"Colonel Broch. Whose crazy idea was it to use a train anyway?" Broch flashed his set of sparkling false teeth in a wide smile.

"No idea Sir. Couldn't possibly have been one of ours could it Sir!"

Nasjonal Samling HQ. Oslo.

Pride of place amongst the portraits hanging from the walls was that of Adolf Hitler, the German Chancellor. His own, somewhat smaller in size, hung over the open fireplace and flickered nervously with every carbon fusion from the logs crackling in the hearth beneath.

Vidkum Quisling, like the dancing reflection on his portrait, was in a similar mental state.

"What now!" Quisling's aide de camp slid timidly through the crack he made in the door.

"We have the reports from German Wehrmacht headquarters Sir. They are a little more detailed than those from Von Falkenhorst's offices."

"Yes, yes. And -?" snapped the troubled NS leader.

"The road block at Hamar. It failed Sir. Trainees, led by 'Ruge' ambushed the convoy before it could reach the Royal party - ."

"And the paratroops the General sent to Rendal?"

"Failed also I'm afraid Sir. The Luftwaffe reported the main road clear of traffic. There haven't been any signals or radio transmissions received since they 'dropped' Sir. It's beginning to appear as if they didn't make it – Sir."

"Imbeciles! What damn use is sending a paltry 'detachment' with the area swarming with 'Ruge's' men? Of course they didn't 'make it'. Sitting ducks. The lot of them. So much for the great German General's plan." Quisling lashed out angrily at the burning logs at his feet. A shower of golden sparks shot skyward and bounced joyfully across the tiled hearth cracking and spitting as they went.

"The –er- pilot of the German plane did make one unusual observation Sir."

"Oh! And what was that? There was a lot of snow in them there mountains?" Quisling growled sarcastically.

"Here Sir –." The aide crossed the marble floor and stabbed a finger at the map open on the desk. "Tyre tracks Sir. Fresh tyre tracks. Here and here -." He tapped the map. "To the east of the main road." Quisling dragged himself away from the heat of the fire.

"So?"

"Well Sir. I know this area. I lived near Rendal for a time. Most of the roads are nothing but tracks once over the lower slopes. If the King and his people are looking for a short-cut to the Swedish border – from here they could be across it in a matter of hours."

Quisling squinted at the map.

"Only a fool would take such a chance of finding a clear route through at this time of year."

"Quite Sir. Only a fool or – a desperate man." replied his aide.

Quisling murmured quietly to himself as he pondered over the suggestion. Eventually he appeared to have made up his mind.

"No. No Colonel. It's possible he might still be somewhere in the region. But my guess is he will go for the coast. West. To the Allies. His friends – the British. Who have we got in that area?" The Colonel thought for a moment. "We have our special unit near Hamar."

"No! No, no, no. Getting the Germans their precious plans back will give me something to stuff up the great General's arse – and besides it would take them all of a day to get there. Have we no one else? What's happened to our thousands of dedicated NS members? Expect the German's to do all the dirty work do they?" The Norwegian Colonel resisted an impulse to say 'yes' to the party leaders question. The truth was the majority of Norwegians who had joined the 'Party' came from the disaffected and disenchanted who's political views could change on a day to day basis depending on who was offering 'jam' that morning. Getting killed wasn't part of the main stream's agenda. Getting rich and powerful without too much danger was much nearer the mark.

"There is a man in Lillehammer. He's a mercenary. Works for whomsoever pays the most."

"And who might that be at the moment?"

"The Germans Sir."

"Really! Good. Contact your opposite number at the General's HQ. Have him send this man east to scout out the area and west between Rendal and Alvdal. He's to report anything suspicious. Tell your contact to double the man's blood money. We will take care of it from this office."

The Colonel gathered up the map and made for the door.

"What's the man's name? This – mercenary?" asked Quisling.

" Kraft Sir," replied the aide. "Fredrick Kraft.

Temp. HQ. Norwegian Forces. Lillehammer.

"So -!" Olsen sat back. "You're the young hero I've been hearing so much about?"

The scene in the theatre foyer was lit by a single light bulb sending grotesque distorted shadows out over the threadbare furnishings. The Captain looked the 'boy' over. Barely could he have been in his twenties and if he was yet shaving it certainly didn't show. The immature, impish face looked nervous.

"A bit jittery was it? Looking after all that gold?"

"Better now that you're here Sir," replied the young Larsen conjuring up a feint smile from beneath the tightly drawn hood of his jacket.

"Good. I could do with men with guts to keep the Germans away from it. Fancy doing something like that do you?"

"Have to Sir. The Chief of Police said he would 'throw me down a hole' and toss away the key if I didn't. Said I wasn't to let it out of my sight until it was safe Sir."

"Right then. You had better do as you were told. Don't want to get the wrong side of the Chief of Police -. So. You're in charge of the loading. Go with the first sledge. Tell the stationmaster at the railway station I want to leave the second the last of the boxes are stowed. Can you do that?"

"Absolutely Sir" Larsen saluted and wheeled away.

A bull of a man, wrinkled and wearing the uniform of a Norwegian Army sergeant burst in through the snow encrusted swing doors. As he slammed to a halt before the long counter Olsen was startled to see a huge white moustache, not the result of icing up or un-brushed snow, protruding from beneath the man's ageing eyes.

"Borg Sir. Sergeant. I have the men the Captain requested inside ready for your inspection Sir." Olsen stared at the man in disbelief. This one had to be older than Broch – if that was possible.

"Er -. Yes. Right. Well why don't you lead the way Sergeant."

"Officer Present!" Olsen shied away as the man's white moustache flew out at right angles to his chin. The sergeant's bellow must have been heard on the outskirts of Olso. It certainly had the desired effect. All the men inside the auditorium were standing at attention as the two of them entered.

"I'm looking for a dozen good men Sergeant. For a very important and dangerous job. Is there somewhere we might use as a temporary office?"

"Yes Sir. Managers Office Sir. A dozen men Sir. Very good Sir. Sir is going to need a very reliable Sergeant to knock them into shape Sir. Would Sir think of taking me along with him Sir? I'm useful to have around Sir." Olsen juggled the question around for a moment then;

"Don't you think you should know about the job first Sergeant?"

"About the job Sir? Hopefully it's killing Germans Sir. If the job is that important Sir, you will need a good Sergeant along with you Sir, to ensure its success. Won't you Sir?" There was no doubting the man's determination to be included, nor for one second did Olsen doubt the man's courage, but he was so old. He must have been seventy-five if a day. Olsen adjusted the nib of his hat.

"Alright. Borg is it? You're on. Now. Can you recommend some good men for me? Someone with your experience and need I say 'longevity' must know a few in this neighbourhood?"

"Yes Sir." replied Borg drawing himself up with a renewed vigour.

"You will first be needing a good officer Sir. There is one Sir. Not commissioned as yet but a cracking good officer just the same Sir. The men trust him Sir. They will follow his orders to the letter Sir. Olsen smiled to himself. The wily old sergeant knew the score well enough. A local officer, one the volunteers had good knowledge of. Always better than the 'new-boy'.

"Right. I'll see him first. Where's this office you spoke of? And one other thing Sergeant. Just between you and me. It really isn't necessary to 'Sir' me every other sentence. Once or twice will do very nicely."

"Yes Sir. I will bear that in mind Sir. If you would follow me S- Captain S-." Borg fumbled the end of his long moustache "Damn." he mumbled under his breath. Olsen chuckled loudly. If one good thing could be said of this 'Nazi nuisance' it was there hadn't been a single dull moment from the minute it had begun.

Loten. Hedmark. Central Norway.

It had grown steadily colder. The way forward was hardening to a solid sheet of undulating ice. Then it began to snow.

Gram had long lost the feeling in both feet. Waiting around for the German paratroopers, whose ungainly, excruciatingly slow traverse of the opposite hillside had gone on forever, had slowed down his planned objective, the railway line from Hamar to Elverum, which lay north east of his present position. He dissected the Germans knee-deep footprints in regular succession as he clambered slowly up the high valley slope. The Germans were heading north-west, towards Lake Mjosa and the town of Hamar. Gram wasn't sure what that meant. Where the Germans already in possession of the town or was the unit part of a forthcoming planned assault? The 'plans' strapped around his middle may have held the answer, but now wasn't the time for a 'research' session. He needed to find some worthwhile form of shelter. His feet needed attention; frostbite was a sure result if he didn't change the wet articles for something dry. He carried a spare pair of boots in his rucksack but would need to dry his socks before changing back into them.

It was well into the night when he stumbled upon the half-buried remains of the hut. The hut was built of turf, two long sloping sides and a hole in the roof where the smoke from the centre hearth escaped. It had seen better days. Turves were missing in a number of places but with a little effort Gram was able to plug the larger gaps with branches and some hard-packed snow. Regardless of the dangers he made up a fire. Chords of fir branches lay cross-sectioned against the rear wall. For a time it was pretty miserable, but with constant rubbing and some measured heat from the burning embers of the fire, his feet began to return to normal. Outside the falling snow had covered his tracks. For the first time since leaving Handelson's cabin he felt relatively safe, but all that could change in an instant. The dried socks and replacement boots gave him a new sense of well being, feet being the most important item of survival out here in this wilderness. His gaze fixed itself on the green and yellow flames curling greedily along the glowing fronds of fir needles in the fire hearth. It was peaceful here -.

Gram awoke with a start. Falling asleep had not been a conscious decision. The intention had been to doze, one ear cocked for signs of anything out of the ordinary. Stupid really. He was exhausted. What should he expect to happen? He struggled to expose his wristwatch. Dawn was still a couple of hours away. He smoothed down the cuff of his jacket and threw another of the more substantial logs on the black-red embers of the dying fire. The biting Arctic wind still found its way through the many exposed patches bringing with it small bursts of powdery snow particles that whirled gracefully upwards in the rising warmth, free at last from their frenzied sub-zero torment beyond.

Gram slumbered awkwardly for a time, then slept, fitfully.

Railway Station. Lillehammer.

Everything but the locomotive. The boxcars and flats could be covered with white canvas tarpaulins. But how did one camouflage a steam engine?

"Bit of a teaser that Sir!" Olsen could do no more than agree with the sergeant. She, the engine that was, could easily be blended in with the surrounding countryside whilst she was at a standstill. Canvas. A few branches. That sort of thing. But on the move? That was another question entirely.

The sergeant moved away. The stationmaster had appeared at the base of the footplate.

"The Captain wants to know how things are coming along?" The stationmaster wiped his brow with the segments of an oily rag and looked down the rake of vehicles to where the last of the bullion boxes were being loaded aboard.

"I've been checking the pressure. If you can get one of your men to give her a good stoke she should be ready in about thirty minutes." he replied, wiping the black smudges from the clean whiteness of his hands and checking through his fingernails with obvious disapproval. That he considered such work not in the province of one of his high status didn't go unnoticed. Borg ignored the man's theatricals.

"Where's the driver?" Borg asked.

"The driver? In the signal box. He's not due on until midnight. You're not thinking of asking him to stoke up are you?"

Borg fixed the man with a stare.

"Asking? No. Not asking. Whatever gave you that idea?"

Bjerklund's next recollection was of flying. How that equated with the sumptuous breasts the young woman had been about to offer his outstretched hands didn't seem to fit snugly with the unfocused scenario. The jolt as he hit the floor was even more unwelcome. Then there was something cold, something metal, tapping at his cheekbone. He squinted through sleep filled eyes.

"Wake up you useless tub of whale grease." growled a grizzled voice in the half-light. "Your services are required. Your King and your Country need you."

Bjerklund blinked and made out the white hair of the sergeants moustache waddling irritatingly in front of his gaze. He struggled up on his elbows and reached for his wrist.

"It's only – Christ man. It's only ten past eleven. Piss off. My break isn't over until midnight. Push off and leave me alone – what the hell."

Borg glanced over his shoulder. Larsen who had accompanied him to the signal box hitched his rifle under his chin and sighted purposely down the barrel.

"I could shoot something off Sergeant. Some bit he wouldn't necessarily miss – in the long term?" Borg turned back to the driver's widening pupils.

"Well?"

"Look. I don't know who you are or what you think you are doing. We have rules. Set shifts. If we don't get our rest periods it can be very serious. We have to stick to the rules. The Union. I'm not allowed to exceed my set hours. It can be very dangerous." growled Bjerklund.

"So can my friend here. With his rifle – but. I am a reasonable man. So people tell me. What say we negotiate? I will be the 'boss' and you can be the 'union representative'. Now! For your part of the deal – You – will get up off your fat arse, stoke up your engine and get the train under-way. I, as your employer, will order my young under-manager here not to shoot your balls off. How's that for an agreement hmm?"

"Shoot my balls off!" Bjerklund shrank back up the floorboards a good half a metre.

"That's correct. Your balls. Your ding-a-ling too if he's slightly off the mark."

"My ding-a-ling!"

Bjerklund scrambled hurriedly to his feet and made straight for the door. Larsen lowered his rifle, swinging it back over his shoulder and watched as the engine driver made off at a gallop down the wooden stairway. Borg retrieved the man's cap from the bed and popped it gingerly over the snub of his grey machine pistol.

"What bit had you got your sights on then young Larsen?" asked Borg.

Larsen grinned.

"None really Sergeant. Apart from which I never keep my rifle loaded. The old man you see. Never put one up the spout until you are certain you are going to use it." Borg nodded. A sound enough policy in peacetime. But now, things had changed. And very much for the worse.

"Well get it loaded now. Your old man was right. But now, for the duration, I'm your old man – and that's an order soldier. Got it? What would have happened had I ordered you to fire?"

"Oh I don't think that would have been necessary Sergeant. He was already well convinced – even before you got to his ding-a-ling."

The platform was bathed in pale blue lighting, the usual yellow sodium bulbs replaced now under the emergency regulations. Olsen was overseeing the last of the gold bullion loading onto the train when Ording hove into view. The Captain could see the news was not good as the Majors grim countenance came towards him.

"Johan -." said the Major in greeting. Olsen stepped away from the loading ramp and out of earshot of the men loading the gold.

"Arne. How are things?" Ording removed his gloves to rub some warmth back into his numbed fingers.

"The Germans have broken through. Ruge is regrouping. We are mounting a new defensive line around Hamar. I've got orders to make for Rendal. The King. He needs to know the situation."

"The King? I thought he would be safe across the border by now. Better than the Germans getting their dirty paws on him. So. Where will you take him?"

"North. I'm going to try for Andalsnes. An Allied ship." Ording pushed the gloves back on. "And you?"

"The mountains. Hjerkinn. I will try and find some cover for a few days. Maybe the Allies will have some help on hand by then. I hope so. If not – I don't know how the hell I'm going to spend all this lot. What the hell is there to buy out here?" He grinned. Hoping some of the ridiculousness of the situation might infect some of the Majors obvious concerns. It worked. Ording stared hard for a moment then gave in as the corners of his mouth turned up slightly.

"Yes. OK. I know I'm a miserable bastard. It's just that -." Ording knew it would have been useless to try and infuse his friend with any more of the seriousness of the situation. Norway couldn't win through this lot on her own. She needed help. Huge amounts of it. It was doubtful the British or the French could bring such forces to bear in the time it would need to push the Germans back out of the country. They were going to loose. Norway would be occupied. At the beck and call of the traitor Quisling. And all this 'friend Johan' knew. What the hell made the man so damn positive and cheerful all the time? Bastard.

The slamming of metal on wood and the echoing trundle of empty luggage trolleys signalled the beginning of the next phase of 'Operation Fridtjof'. A long tunnel of scalding steam roared from beneath the steel framework of the hissing locomotive. The great metal monster was impatient to be off.

Loten Region. Hedmark. Central Norway.

The nights were becoming appreciably shorter. With the passing of each day now, the land of the 'midnight sun' swung ever closer towards its fabled reputation. In peacetime the lack of night often proved beneficial. Now, with the desperate need of the nights cloaking security no longer available, local knowledge and the use of terrain and camouflage would become vital.

It was still snowing. The winds from the north had eased slightly giving more quarter to the forest's sounds. The crack- snapping of ice laden branches, the sudden rustling and cascading thud of water-laden snow. But this was different.

Gram pulled himself towards the cover a nearby tree. He scanned in the direction of the noise. There it was again. Too distant and not in keeping with one of natures usual displays. Gunfire? A mortar? Friendly or unfriendly? Not that it really mattered. Shellfire meant only one thing. Whoever they were, they were blocking his line of direction. Had the front line moved so rapidly in so short a time? Or were the sounds of battle an out of theatre skirmish. Norwegian loyalists and German paratroopers? He adjusted his rucksack to ease the ache between his shoulder blades. A trickle of cold sweat ran sensually down his spine and came to rest where the wadding holding the 'plans' closed tightly up against his skin. The 'gunfire' was on a line north-east. Elverum or perhaps a little further south. Gram checked the webbing on his skis and began to traverse up the slope. The first people he wanted to meet required they wore Norwegian or Allied Army uniforms and if possible have more knowledge than one like himself as to the present military situation -!

The high buzzing noise was a 'Fiesler Storch' only Gram could not have told anyone that at the time. A German reconnaissance aircraft, unarmed, with two hawk like wings supported on thick membrane trusses and sporting the unmistakable evil black crosses on their grey-green camouflaged underside.

The pilot came in to land, on skis attached to the wheel struts, tracking along a narrow plateau that graced the forest edge. Gram ducked for cover behind the trees. He thought it highly unlikely he had been spotted on the planes single fly-over and was astonished when the Luftwaffe pilot turned the aircraft about and began taxiing towards his place of concealment waving at him to come out. Gram took to his skis. Vertically downhill. Uncaringly casting aside the two hours it had taken him to ascend from the valley floor. Something clipped a notch from his ski-stick and rattled a tingling sensation up through his left arm. He deviated away. Whatever it was wasn't friendly. The German must have been a good marksman to make a moving target over such a distance. On the other hand it could just have been a lucky shot. Gram wasn't waiting to find out. He sped on a further hundred metres before ducking for safety behind an over hanging outcrop of rocks and throwing himself sideways into the deep snow.

The outcrop sloped gently skywards with a frozen drift of snow capping the ridge. Gram scrambled up on all fours and peered cautiously over the top. The German pilot was nowhere to be seen. There was nothing but the trees, the folding snowdrifts and the tell-tale zigzag of his own trail leading down through the frozen landscape. It was to be hoped the German had no designs on following him. One never knew with these damn Nazi's. Strange creatures the lot of them!

He waited and listened. Presently he heard the planes engine increase in velocity and disappear into the distance. The German had gone. The trouble was where? It had been a close thing. There was one valuable lesson to be learned. It wasn't sufficient just to keep ones eyes on the surrounding terrain. He hadn't seen the German planes approach until it was almost on top of him. From now on it had to be one eye on the ground and one on the sky.

Thankfully the engine noise from the plane continued to fade into the distance and made no attempt to return over the valley. Had the pilot been looking specifically for Gram? In which case it stood to reason the bodies of Brun and his two hunters must have been discovered and his movements tracked. There could soon be men on the ground looking for him.

Gram removed his goggles and rubbed at his eyes. He checked the wheel of his compass and turned it back and forth wildly.

"Hm! Well then – Go on. Pick a bearing smart-arse." he growled to himself shaking his head.

Hjerkinn. Oplandfylke. C. Norway.

Olsen eased the door to the boxcar open by a few centimetres and peeked out. The train had come to a stop on the side of a tall escarpment. Ahead the track curved sharply away from sight. There was nothing with the appearance of the train, to the casual observer, that would give the impression all was not as innocent as it seemed. The guns and the men who operated them all lay out of sight behind the white canvas cover sheets. Olsen scanned the forest and the wide plain beyond. Why had the driver stopped?

Bjerklund's face projected from the footplate.

"What is it?" demanded Olsen angrily. This engine driver had yet to earn his spurs if the sergeant's report on him was a fair assessment.

"Hjerkinn Station. It's just around that next bend." Bjerklund wiped nervously at his hands with a disgusting scrap of blackened material.

"We shouldn't stop in the station. It's too open. If the Germans are there or some of the NS -? There's a siding. Cuts into the forest about half a kilometre further on -?" The Captain looked away in the direction Bjerklund was pointing. At this distance the station was completely hidden by the mass of trees. Sergeant Borg's opinion of the man, indolent and a bag of nerves, may have been a little rash. His nerves, if they were such, erred the man towards caution. Wisely in this instance.

"Fine. Let's take her on through then." Olsen replied. Larsen had come forward to see if he could be of some assistance, no doubt in his capacity of reserve engine driver, hopefully, from the eager glint in his eyes. Not this time thought Olsen to himself. But he could still be useful.

"There's a siding. Beyond the station. We will hold up there -." Olsen lowered his voice. "See this guy keeps her ready to roll at a seconds notice. Don't let him out of your sight." Larsen nodded and hopped aboard the bottom step of the footplate. Bjerklund scowled down at him. Possibly the memory of the 'ding-a-ling' incident still fresh in his mind? Larsen returned the look with a beam of a smile and hitched his rifle up over his collarbone exaggerating the movement in the process. Bjerklund growled something that was lost in the escaping gush of steam from the locomotive's pistons as he opened the throttle. Olsen returned to the boxcar.

"Sergeant! Two men. On the double." Inside the wagon there came the sound of scrambling limbs as half a dozen bodies tried to make for the narrow opening in one rush. Olsen suppressed a grin. From the gloomy interior came the sergeants' snarl.

"As you were - -. You limp excuses for a palace guard -." Slowly the wheels of the train began to roll.

"We'll come into the station from behind. Larsen will keep the train moving. Keep the men quiet. If anything happens, you're to be assistance to the Lieutenant and get the whole lot out of here. Understand?" Borg's face appeared in the doorway.

"Yes Sir. Will do Sir. Good luck Sir." Two bodies apparently propelled from the rear shot from the open doorway towards the snow.

"Schwartz and Astrup Sir." The door snapped shut before either man had hit the ground.

For professional skiers of international repute, Olsen would have expected both men to have gained the ground in a daintier fashion. He shook his head. There was still some way to go before some of them would be truly ready for serious combat. Still. For the time being he would have to make do.

"Shall we gentlemen -?" he suggested quietly.

The half-glazed door shot inwards as Astrup leapt into the room. The interior was warmed from a pot-bellied stove standing centre stage. Otherwise the room was devoid of any human presence. A pleasing aroma of brewed coffee assailed his nostrils. Astrup waved the barrel of his rifle menacingly about.

"No one here Sir. The stove is lit and there's coffee on the boil -." He sniffed the air again, his mouth watering in anticipation.

"A good soldier never lets a good drink go to waste soldier," said Olsen entering and beckoning Schwartz to follow. "See if you can find something to put it in." Schwartz made for a cupboard at the rear of the dimly lit interior. There was a desk and a single high backed chair that looked anything but inviting. Olsen crossed the creaking floorboards and rummaged amongst the papers strewn across the open top of the desk. He extracted a tattered map showing the regions railway network.

"Shit – Ow." Astrup let fall the lid of the coffee-pot as it seared into his over eager fingers. "Damn it. Sorry Sir. Christ – there's enough coffee in here to satisfy half a division."

"No. Not quite young man." The voice came from behind. Astrup wheeled about his rifle already at waist level. "And you can put that thing back where you got it. Children shouldn't play with guns. It can be dangerous."

The man wore a station master's uniform. No doubt the coffee was his personal property and he wasn't too pleased to witness what he was seeing.

"I usually make enough to last me three or four days – Hm. If I can." The stationmaster turned his attention to Olsen. "I see you have found my old railway map Captain. It does show most of the disused sidings – judging by the way you have hidden your train – I should imagine it would be invaluable to you -." He paused and looked down at the splintered remain of the door. "It er did have a handle on it. One that you turn and 'glory be' the door opens. Quite easily actually. It wasn't locked you know. Did you know that? No? Never is. God in heaven – I don't know!" The stationmaster stood shaking his head at the debris and bouncing his fingertips stiffly against one another. Olsen tapped his fingers along the edge of the desk then scratched at some imaginary irritation on the side of his face. The door hung drunkenly off its top hinge and wallowed disjointedly around the man's shins. It would need more than a single tube of wood glue to fix it all back together. Olsen coughed apologetically.

"Yes. Well. Yes sorry about that. We don't normally go around kicking doors in. The er manual suggests a grenade through the window. But that would have ruined the coffee. I do apologise. Really. But we had to be sure there were no Germans using it."

"Germans?" The stationmaster seemed genuinely surprised.

"Yes." Olsen replied. "There are a few wandering about the country. Haven't you heard about it?" The stationmaster knew sarcasm when he heard it and straightened his back authoritatively.

"There is very little chance of that Captain. We have our people out. I knew you were coming half an hour ago. There are no Germans in the immediate area. Not live ones anyway."

"Your people?" Olsen frowned.

"Yes Captain. Our people. Farmers. Most of them. Each farm has its own lookouts. Where there are no telephones we pass the word by heliograph. That's how I knew you were coming. The latest reports have the Germans moving inland from Trondhiem. It will be three or four days at the earliest before they can get anywhere near here in sufficient numbers -." The stationmaster paused and stepped into the room over the debris. "I have a brother in Storen. He will telephone immediately there are Germans sighted in the region. You have nothing to worry about for the present – Captain."
Olsen was impressed. The man would have made good officer material.

"Excellent. Well done. In that case. Sorry again about the door. Does that mean there is no chance for a cup of your excellent coffee?" A shrill blast of a locomotive whistle interrupted the conversation. Olsen ran to the door. He listened.

"Are there any more trains in the area?"

"No. Only a passenger train. But that's not due for another two hours." replied the stationmaster frowning.

"Come on -." Olsen flicked the snub of his machine pistol for Astrup and Schwartz to follow him. Regretfully the coffee would have to wait.

Dombas. Oplandfylke. C. Norway.

During the night Generalleutnant Geisler's paratroops dropped across the cold grey plains between the townships of Dombas and Dovres in the north of the region having failed to locate the King and his retinue in the area around Alvdal.

Some distance to the east and moving cautiously under the cover of darkness, Ording's cavalcade, with the Norwegian King and his ministers, were slowly negotiating the almost impassable mountainous terrain, using roads and pathways known only to the loyal Norwegian inhabitants in whose region they crossed. Ording, with the help of information passed on by the Kings loyal subjects had thus far managed to evade the large number of paratroopers dropped to bar their progress. Latest reports regarding the townships of Dombas and Dovres were confusing. The Major had therefore decided to make for Hjerkinn unaware that here to was Olsen and his gold train. The German push from the south, the west and now the north was rapidly reducing the odds and also the area of country in which it was safe to travel undetected.

Vangsas. Hedmark. C. Norway.

Three bodies found near Stange. One, that of the British spy Brun, took Kraft back towards Lillehammer. Nothing of the King and his family was to be found in the Rendal area. As Kraft had suspected it was almost certain the King had not gone east to be interned in Sweden. He knew the Kings loyal subjects would find ways and means to keep a route open to the west and the hope of salvation from an Allied rescue. As for the Germans and their uncoordinated attempts to capture him. It was laughable. Far more troops would be needed than already available, if their casualties and slow progress across the country were anything to go by. Reinforcements if not already under way would be vital if the Germans were to win the coming battles.

But none of this troubled Kraft. The ten thousand crowns. The reward for the Kings apprehension muted by his German contact and a further five thousand for the capture of an unknown man carrying vital secret documents was all that interested him. Who would ultimately win all the battles springing up in all directions of the compass he could care less? Norway would be Norway regardless of who ruled her craggy snowbound landscape. To his mind it wasn't worth the fighting for in the first place.

Kraft removed his skis and rammed them home into a snowdrift. There was gunfire in the direction of Hamar. The battle drew nearer. He would have to decide to stay put until the outcome had been decided or leave for Dombas. To stay on the valley floor would be dangerous. That's where all the major fighting was taking place. Along the main road networks. The Germans preferred to take out the towns turning each into a mini-fortress and ignoring the vastness of the forests and plains beyond. Securing the main arteries and the airspace above would give them fluidity of movement through which to then channel the mass of reinforcements that would comprise the 'occupying' forces. Land mass wasn't important. Blitzkrieg tactics. Von Kalkenhorst's plans called for speed, with consolidation to take place at a later time. All quite new to the art of modern warfare.

But of this Kraft knew very little. Nor did he care. He mounted the steps towards the door of the café. He would eat first then fill a 'bergen' with sufficient supplies for a week, then take a course north. Towards where the bodies of the three men had been discovered. His quarry was now two fold. He had confidence both could be secured very satisfactorily. With careful planning.

Vang. Hedmark. Central Norway.

Only a mere ten kilometres separate the two Norwegians. Kraft moving along the valley checking constantly with his numerous contacts for any signs or rumours of his quarry. Gram heading across the Hedmark plain in a north westerly direction, worrying about his food rations now dangerously low and unsure of finding suitable cover for the coming night.

For Gram, when leaving Oslo, the idea of joining the Norwegian Volunteer Reserves to fight the enemy on the front line, had not been his intention. The thought of offering himself up as some old General's cannon-fodder didn't sit well in his educated mind. The odds had always been heavily in favour of any invader and when his employer had offered his brothers cabin the idea had been to spend a few days thinking over his options. Gram had always been interested in the 'politics' of the conflict and believed strongly in Norway's exposed position, more could ultimately be gained through the use of propaganda and subversion to gain ones freedoms than hoping to win militarily against overwhelming odds. Not that he was a coward! Afraid to risk his skin in an open fight. Or at least he didn't think he was? But to lose ones life hopelessly wasn't the intelligent way of doing things. Nor come to think of it was getting lost in the middle of nowhere and starving or freezing to death?

Gram pushed on through the deep carpet of snow. The deep tracks in his wake were a dead give away. But there was nothing to be done about it for the present. The name of the game was to keep one step ahead – and hope for the best.

Hjerkinn.

The whole scene looked slightly ridiculous. But Olsen strongly believed that idle hands created the devils work.

The sounding of the locomotives whistle had been an accident. Larsen had pulled the wrong lever. Bjerklund had been sleeping. Something about 'working hours and contracts'. Uncharacteristically Olsen had lost his temper. Which was why the engine driver was sat polishing machine-bullet casings on the engine footplate whilst Larsen and the rest of the men were being put through a series of parade ground drills in a clearing of deep snow? Borg stood centre circle using the foulest language this small area of forestry had ever experienced in its life.

Olsen cocked his ear. The sound of a train whistle. Distant but clear. The passenger train the stationmaster had mentioned.

"Sergeant Borg. Stand everyone down. Get under cover. I want absolute silence. You and Larsen come with me."

A while later, from his vantage point in the branches of a large tree, Olsen watched as his Lieutenant and two of the men came scurrying back from the direction of the station buildings.

"No Germans on board Sir -." reported Lieutenant Ringe. "-Just locals. She will be taking on water and fuel. She is due to go on to Kongsvoll in the morning. The driver. Union man. It's the rules. Eight hours duty only."

"Really? Eight hours eh! Why does that not surprise me I wonder?" Olsen shook his head despairingly. With all that was now happening, nothing but nothing it seemed had changed for many of his fellow countrymen. It was to be hoped they survived all this and lived to tell their children how useless they had been in 'the war against the Nazi invaders'. Arseholes.

It was later and well towards daybreak when the pencil stabs of hooded headlights could be seen heading in the direction of the country station.

Olsen decided to position half of his men to the side and rear of the buildings, the rest to remain with the train for a hurried departure should anything go wrong -.

'The Lion, the Eagle and the Wolf'.

April 10th – 15th 1940.

The German 'Occupation' plan of the small Scandinavian countries of Norway and Denmark called for landings both from the sea and from the air. Denmark, whose only land border was with that of Germany, possessed no standing army and was therefore easy prey. The occupation of this small inoffensive country was doubly infamous in that she had been the only Scandinavian country to sign a non-aggression pact with Nazi Germany in 1939.

At 04-25hrs on April 9th 1940 the first of the German 'occupying' forces crossed the Danish frontier at Krusaa in Jutland. Shortly thereafter Danish Naval HQ reported German units had landed and were coming ashore at Assens, Middlefart and at Nyborg in Funen. By 05-00hrs more incursions had been logged in South Zealand, then Copenhagen with paratroops dropping on Masnedo.

The Danes were completely unprepared for the German 'sneak' attack and could bring only a few units to bear against the sudden onslaught before being 'bulldozed' by the sheer weight of enemy troops into surrender. The Danish government had no choice but to capitulate before the onslaught and did so within a few hours.

Norway however was geographically more secure and would, as time would tell, provide the Germans with a much more difficult 'nut to crack'.

It was known by Norwegian Army Command that landings had taken place along Norway's West Coast by various German units. What wasn't clear was by how many in number, had they been reinforced and to what extent had they penetrated the interior. Paratroops had been reported at various locations in the south of the country and at points behind the front lines in central Norway. To the north the mountains made a serious German penetration almost impossible but nevertheless a danger that could not be ignored. Only to the east and the border with Sweden was there a lack of serious German intent. But for Norwegian forces to pull back on their eastern front would place them up against internment by the Swedish authorities should they cross the border. The Swedes were in no mood to antagonise the Nazi's or risk a battle on their borders that might lead to a German invasion of their own country on some concocted German pretext of securing their battle lines.

In London meanwhile, the 'Lion' had at last raised itself from its lethargy for on the 12ᵗʰ April the British War Cabinet agreed to send an 'expeditionary force' to Narvik in northern Norway. The intention to make contact with Norwegian forces there and to cross Norway into Sweden to destroy the iron-ore installations at Gallivare. On the 17ᵗʰ April the British also landed 13,000 troops at Norway's western seaports of Namos and Andalsnes. These troops, after a series of inexplicable delays, began to move slowly inland and down the Gudbrandsdal valley towards Dombas.

In Berlin, the 'Wolf' Hitler, hearing of the British landings and the destruction of half his northern battle fleet at Narvik and numerous points south, ordered the evacuation of his forces from Narvik and northern Norway. The 'Wolf' was getting the jitters, alarmed now the 'Lion' had decided at last to bite back. This was one occasion his orders were ignored.

Meanwhile, the 'Eagle' was spiralling down from his lofty mountainous heights, waiting and watching and hoping for an opportunity to strike back against the wanton aggressors who would rape his beautiful lands. The fight was not yet over – not by a long way?

Hjerkinn Station. Oplandfylke. C.Norway.

His relief hadn't arrived. Which came as no surprise, things being as they were. The stationmaster was pouring himself another mug of steaming coffee when the door opened and the uniformed figure of a man entered.

"Good morning Stationmaster. Major Ording. That train -." The Major pointed to the track, "I'm afraid I must requisition it." The stationmaster finished pouring the coffee. The speaker wore the uniform of an officer of the Norwegian Army but going by its dishevelled appearance hadn't changed out of it in over a week.

"Must you indeed -," the stationmaster replied, "– And where are your requisition papers - Major is it? And on whose authority do you claim you can remove vital government property – especially in a time of great emergency?"

"Will mine do?" came the soft reply from the Major's rear as the King stepped into the room.

The coffee-pot fell with a crash to the wooden floor. It would have been most unusual for any Norwegian of average age not to have recognised the sovereign's features immediately. The stationmaster was no exception. He began to hop nervously on the spot.

"I er, Oh my god, I mean-. Your Majesty, won't you -, Good gracious me. Oh dear -."

Ording smiled. He had seen a number of similar reactions to the King's presence throughout their journey over the past couple of days. It was most refreshing not to have to argue the situation around to ones own benefit at every twist and turn of events. Instant compliance. Wonderful.

"You were saying -?" Ording watched the man scrabbling to retrieve the scalding coffee-pot from under his feet.

"Yes your Majesty, I mean Major, I mean – Yes. Straight away Sire, I mean Sir, I mean – Oh dear -."

In the chill of the early morning air the sounds of busy movements muffled Olsen's approach. Most of the King's retinue were aboard the train when Johan descended the slope to the platform.

"Arne. I see you still have 'Magnus' safe with you?"

"Johan -!" Ording sprang round in surprise. "Where the hell did you come from? I thought you long gone from this area?"

"So do the Germans – hopefully. But what are you doing here?" Ording looked around the almost deserted platform. If nothing he was constantly security minded.

"It's a bloody mess, between me and you. An awful bloody mess. Ruge has lost Hamar. We've had word the Germans have dropped paratroops all over the Dombas-Dovre region. We have to get off the roads. Ruge is falling back on Lillehammer - - ." Just then the train's engine driver made towards them. Ording stopped speaking.

"Excuse me Sir. I must contact my wife. Let her know I'm OK and where I will be. Can you tell me where we are going -?"

"Lesjarverk." replied Ording. "When will you be ready to leave?"

"Five minutes Sir. I will just phone my wife first." The man nodded and moved away in the direction of the stationmaster's office.

"Lesjarverk? But that will take you through Dombas. I thought you said there were Germans there?" Ording pulled a quizzical face.

"Did I say Lesjarverk? How very astute of me -." He paused. Then brightly. "And what about you. What are your plans?" Olsen feigned a look of innocence.

"Me? My plans? Do you think I ought to tell you?" The two broke into laughter. Anyone viewing from a distance may have assumed them both mad for a quick observation of the scene would have shown nothing the least hilarious to draw any comfort from. It was very cold, very grim and with a snow laden cloud cover echoing back the sounds of heavy gunfire in the distance. But then war did breed some very strange situations, not to mention people.

Telephone Exchange. Dovre. Oplandfylke.

Of the one hundred and thirty six paratroopers falling from the sky over Dovre some eighty three finally made it to the town boundary. There they met a withering sniper fire from some of Ruge's Lillehammer volunteers and after a short battle took control of the town's telephone exchange and a number of buildings surrounding it. For a short while the Norwegian volunteers withdrew to regroup and await reinforcements on their way down from Dombas.

For the German Oberleutnant in command, things were not looking too good. Two of his best engineers had taken over the telephone switchboard from their Norwegian operators and were handling the incoming calls as if nothing untoward had happened, but for the rest of the 'operation' it was a bloody mess. The Norwegian snipers roaming the countryside had picked off dozens of his comrades. His commander included. He was surrounded on all sides by an enemy who could be easily reinforced whilst he himself could expect little assistance in the short term. If that assistance didn't arrive within the next few hours his command and the tenure of the centre of the town was in grave doubt.

The telephone call when it came through was couched in the most innocent of terms. A railway engine driver informing his wife his train had been requisitioned and was heading for Lesjarverk with the Norwegian Royal family aboard.

"But that's miles from here -?" replied the German operator.

"Yes I know darling. They will have to change trains at Dombas. I can come home then. There will be a relief driver to take them over to the western line for the onward journey. Sorry sweetheart. Must dash. The King and his small bodyguard are waiting -."

The revelation of the King's whereabouts reached Oslo within minutes. Both Quisling and the German General Von Falkenhorst now had exact information barely minutes old. The first good break in news from the hinterland in days. Word came back from Oslo. 'Get him alive'. The German Oberleutnant looked at the message then at the street outside where he knew dozens of Norwegian crack-shots had positioned themselves, waiting. His reply was unprintable.

Vang. Hedmark. C. Norway.

Two buildings. A logging camp of sorts. Both well constructed and joined by a narrow corridor made from the same notched and pinioned timbers in the traditional style.

The previous night had been spent huddled inside a makeshift 'wicki-up', a shelter made from branches of fir, not the most salubrious sanctuary. Gram took in the scene from the cover of the thick forest. There was still many hours of daylight left, but before moving on it would be folly not to check out the area for anything he could find. Especially food.

It was still very cold. But that had made the going easier. The thought of wasting good travelling time irked him regardless this was an ideal place to stop and rest up for awhile.

The buildings were empty. The camp had not been in regular use for some time. No food. Not even the rusting remains of cans in the shelved larder and judging by the black foetid liquid floating a chemical scum across its mirror surface the 'privy' hadn't seen a posterior for maybe a year or more. The lamps still contained fuel oil and lit instantly shedding a warm inviting feel to the darkened interiors.

The first building was a bunkhouse. Six doubles and each layered with the remains of what had once been canvas palliasses now shredded in places by the teeth of various nocturnal beasties, or so they appeared. At the far end of the darkened corridor closed off by a split log door was the larger of the two buildings. An office, a cooking and eating area and the privy. The privy must have been an afterthought set beyond the walls of the main structure and sprouting a straw covered floor through which various forms of flora had advanced their opportunities. It nevertheless looked inviting. Gram threw off his pack and rifle and placed them side by side across the dust-laden table. It would be the first time he had seen to himself properly in days. A hole in the snow not being his first choice for ablutions.

It was a mistake to drop one's guard. To assume because everything was going well it would continue that way. His father had often told him. 'Expect the unexpected'. That way bad surprises are never too traumatic and never leave one vulnerable. Gram should have spent more time listening and less time thinking the 'old git' was mouthing off for effect. Then he would have heard them coming. Heard them enter the room and found time to hitch up his trousers before the door flew in and flattened him back across the pine boards housing the cess pit beneath.
Unceremoniously he was dragged from the small room and flung headlong halfway across the boarded floor.
"Who are you?" snarled a less than friendly voice. Gram curled up into the foetal position and took a tight hold of the waistband of his trousers.
"Speak. Who are you?" Gram peered around. They were four. NS armbands decorated the right sleeves of their tunics.
"Nobody." Gram replied, hitching the seat of his pants back into place, less to cover his modesty than to ensure the leather wrapping around his lower chest remained out of view.
"What are you doing here? What's your name?" The man snapped angrily. He lowered the point of his rifle towards Gram's face. "Where are you from?"
"Finse – Originally. I'm taking a couple of weeks – hunting. Travelling. Seeing the valley." Gram searched the man's face. It wasn't a kind face. Not one you might take too readily.
"Your name. What's your name? Don't you know your name – idiot?"
Gram saw no reason to lie. If these men had stumbled upon the camp accidentally, as had he, no harm could come of it.
"Gram. Gregers. I'm a student at Oslo University. Economics."
You have an ID?" Gram unbuttoned the flap of his top pocket and pulled out his wallet. One of the men reached down and snatched for it. The man read the

front cover then nodded. The one Gram took to be the leader relaxed visibly and took a step back.

"So Gregers. And where did you think you were going. Haven't you heard there's a war on?"

"Hamar. I was making for Hamar. I thought I would stay the night here. Start out afresh tomorrow."

The man, whose nose flattened sharply to the right the result no doubt of a bad break not having been treated, hauled his massive bulk upright. There was a look of scepticism to the rest of his features. He looked at the others then back to the floor.

"Hamar. Alright. Then you won't mind if we go along with you. Just to make sure you arrive safely – so to speak. There are a lot of people running around out there with guns. No doubt you will have seen one or two – perhaps?" Gram shook his head vigorously. "No! Hm. Pity." The man looked at Gram's backpack and rifle then to one of the men. "Check that lot out and put our friend back where you found him -." To Gram.

"I'm sure you won't mind sleeping on your own. I'm sorry we can't be more accommodating but until we have confirmed your identity and what it is you are doing out here we must insist you remain our guest." He turned. "There's no need to tie him up. Just make sure you secure the door properly." He turned back and grizzled a sort of sideways smile the upper row of teeth crooked and dotted with holes where the gums had retreated away. "We don't want our guest to go sleep walking in the night and loose his bearings now do we?" he added menacingly.

Hjerkinn. Railway siding. Hjerkinn.

It reminded Johan of something from his youth. His childhood, given he didn't yet consider himself to be middle-aged. Like a snowman when the figure tried to regain its feet.

"Better give him a hand one of you." Bergstrom raised himself from his haunches and ploughed off through the snow.

The stationmaster had been in such a hurry he had tripped and rolled down the long slope gathering speed and snow as he went. Now he was finding it almost impossible to extricate himself from his ice prison.

Ording's train and the royal party had left hours ago. Nothing untoward had been heard or reported until now. Ording's face must have been grim for the stationmaster hastened to reassure him it was good news he was bringing.

"The line to Dombas has reopened. Norwegian volunteers under a Colonel Broch, I think he said, have secured the town. He had a message. The message was for 'Fridjtof'. The message was, 'The eagle has flown'. He said, You would know what it all means?" Olsen smiled. That was Broch alright.

"Bergstrom. Find the Sergeant. Tell him we are moving out in five minutes. Now -." Olsen held out the railway map towards the stationmaster. "We shall need cover at Dombas. How well do you know that area?"

"There -." The stationmaster tipped at a point on the map with the thumb of his glove. "A siding. It's deep amongst the trees and very much overgrown. But the track is still sound. You'll be alright there." Olsen pocketed the map.

"The Germans. When they come. They will want answers. Don't be a hero. They will just as likely kill you if you hesitate or try to bluff them. Tell them what you know. With luck we shall be one step ahead. We shall out-run them. Take my word for it." The stationmaster replied with a weak but well-meant smile. "Perhaps we shall meet again. Sometime. When this is all over. Remember. No heroics. And – thanks for the delicious coffee. Best I've had for ages. Take care." Olsen ploughed off through the deep drifts to where Borg was stood waiting alongside the boxcar. A hiss of pressurised steam and the ponderous wheels of the metal monster slipped momentarily then finally gripped along the rusting metal lines. Slowly the train began to pick up speed. The stationmaster hunched himself against the cold until the buffers of the huge engine slid effortlessly by. Then he remembered the coffee and turned in the direction of the station lights and his warming stove.

Dovre. Hedmark. C. Norway.

"Citizens of Norway. I have something to tell you. Your King is dead. The English have killed him. Their troops have landed as we warned you they would and tonight they reached Dombas. A German pilot watched the King's car being blown up by our mutual enemies. Norwegians. You are leaderless. Lay down your arms and unite with your brothers against the English. Our beloved Fuhrer will - - -."

A loud bang. A grenade ended the speech by the German interpreter. There was a flash of flame and three of the buildings windows flew upwards and cascaded down amongst the remains of a farmer's cart whose horse, unfortunately shot through with grenade fragments from an earlier upsurge in the fighting, lay stiff and cold still in its leather harness amongst the debris laden snow. Ording allowed himself a satisfied smile. So the Germans had bombed the Kings car. Now perhaps they would all get some peace if they thought the King dead. He was pleased to have confirmation the Allies had finally landed and were advancing down the valley towards Dovre. The Norwegian 2nd Division, having done battle like tigers, were falling back before overwhelming German forces. It was only a matter of time before they became too fragmented and would lose their defensive posture. The English must hurry.

Ording had arrived at Dovre looking for a route through to the west. The Germans held the centre of the town. Colonel Broch had arrived with his two hundred volunteers from Dombas in the nick of time. After a vicious fire-fight, in which both sides lost heavily, Broch secured a passage through for the King and his family who were now secure in a safe house on the outskirts of the town. Tomorrow they would try for Lasjerverk. This time by road. With luck they would meet up with the British forces coming inland.

Vang. Hedmark. C.Norway.

Not to put too fine a point on it, it was bloody freezing. Gram grabbed more straw from the floor and pushed it inside his jacket. In the darkness bright shafts of daylight pierced through the unevenness of the timber walls. Gram had thought them a possible way of escape then changed his mind on determining the thickness of the logs. Around the perimeter the earthen floor was frozen concrete. Or at least it might as well have been. His belt buckle made hardly an indentation. The only way out of his prison was the way he had come in and 'that' had one of the NS men guarding against it on the far side of the wall. Gram cursed his luck. Together with the fact he was cold, hungry and thirsty into the bargain. None of his captors had offered to feed him when the smell of their own food preparations had permeated the slatted slabs of the timber door. And in addition he was angry. Angry with himself for his stupidity. And it rankled!

It was some hours later when the muted conversation ceased. One of the men remained behind to guard the prisoner. The others, Gram heard moving away towards the bunkhouse along the adjoining corridor. After a while all was still.

A heavy snoring filtered through the ice particles glistening on the wall, a result of the condensation from Grams breath. The snoring came from the bunkhouse. The men were asleep save the one in the adjoining room whose restless sighs and odd movements Gram could hear the other side of the door.

The 'privy' was built to accommodate a long wooden bench seat down the one side on which Gram was lying and the boarded 'thunder box' of a toilet, at right angles and up against the outer back wall. Gram began to formulate a plan in his mind. He waited until the restless movements beyond the door ceased and changed to a heavy laboured breathing. The man was dozing. The floor in the centre of the room leading in from the office area was malleable, unaffected by the hard frost and protected by its straw covering. Gram removed his belt and began to carefully scrape away at the surface half a metre in from the door. After about an hour he scooped out a fair sized hole. Gram covered the hole lightly with a layer of straw. If his plan worked, all would be well. If not, these Quisling thugs might very well kill him on the spot. Once they discovered the German plans he carried his execution would be automatic. Norwegian loyalists they didn't like. Norwegian spies even less so. No one had prepared him to make these kinds of decisions. It most certainly wasn't on the syllabus at the University. He thought the matter over and it was another hour before he finally made up his mind.

"Hey. Hey out there. How about something to eat?" Gram tried to control the strength of his yell. He didn't want to awaken the others. The man grunted. There was a growl of sorts then everything went quiet again. Gram curled into a crouch in the corner of the bench.

"Hey. Dozy. Hey you. I need something to eat."

Another grunt and this time the sound of scrapping boots on the boarded floor.

"What is it? What do you want? Go to sleep can't you? Idiot!"

"When do I get something to eat?" shouted Gram. There was no reply.

"Well at least give me a drink of water. I'm dying of thirst in here."

Another growl and the sound of a heavy weight lifting off a creaking chair. The man was moving. Gram tensed himself as the sound of the man's footsteps move across the room to where the canteens were hung then carried on towards the door. The door opened inwards.

He was a big man. Not as huge as 'crooked teeth' but half as big again as Gram himself. He suddenly toppled forwards, face first towards the box like structure, as the ground beneath his feet disappeared. Gram leapt up and landed both feet between the man's receding shoulder blades. There was a sickening smack as the man's chin ricocheted off the edge of the hole and disappeared down inside the box followed by a gargled scream that cut off almost instantly as something snapped or gave way under Gram's weight. The man sagged and went limp. Quickly Gram jumped off. He listened for the sound of rushing feet, an indication the others had heard the commotion. Nothing. The man's head jerked and turned upwards as his limp frame slipped nearer the floor. The one eye Gram could see was popped outwards. There was a startled look of surprise on the ashen blue face. That had been far easier than Gram could have wished for. He had never considered himself a 'killer' of men. Animals? That was different. Through the sights of a rifle and at a distance. Easy and not at all wasteful. But this was something else. He fell back and stared at the death mask glaring accusingly back at him from the lip of the toilet seat. He remained crouching for a full three or four minutes, fixed by the one eye and the curl of the snarled lip from which drops of dark, almost black blood dripped intermittently into the foul pit below. Drip. Drip. Drip. The man's neck was obviously broken and no doubt his windpipe crushed to oblivion in the process. It had all been too easy. Damnn. Now he was feeling sorry for the man. Gram shook himself together. He wasn't safe yet. Snap out it idiot, he told himself.

Three grenades of the 'egg' variety came off the man's belt. Gram would need two, the other he placed carefully in his pack. The three men, all fully clothed and waving their arms wildly in all directions, staggered from the smoking doorway towards the light. Gram shot the first one squarely through the chest, the next through the head, a lucky shot if the truth be known and the last one through the back as he was running away. The grenades had done well shredding through their clothing evident by the numerous ragged patches dotting the men's tunics. Gram congratulated himself on his foresight to shout the men awake three or four seconds before he lobbed in the grenades. Had they been protected by the straw palliasses the damnage wreaked might have been far less. As it was, everything was very satisfactory. And now? - Now there were none! Gram scanned the horizon. It was time to move. Regardless of priorities. Four very dead Norwegians shot full of holes would be difficult to explain away regardless of who it was asking the questions. They being Quislings made no difference to many people. Not yet anyway.

Oplandfylke. C.Norway.

"Rubbish! How can that be? Has the idiot been on the juice -?" Larsen tried the best facsimile of acute exasperation he could muster. "- And why are we stopping? What's wrong with the man?" growled Olsen.

"Germans sir." Borg's heavy white moustache bristled in the gap of the doorway. "They still have the station Sir."

"What!" Larsen banged the stock of his rifle hard on the floor.

"That's what I have been trying to tell you. There is a German machine-gun position at the end of the station sir. Bjerklund swears to it. He saw it as we approached."

"Christ! Don't tell me our people forgot to check it out. God Almighty. It's a damn good job the driver was on the ball otherwise -." Olsen forced the vivid picture of what might have been from his mind. "Tell Bjerklund to continue on to Rauma - - And Larsen -." Larsen who was already clambering back across the boxcar roof. "Tell Bjerklund. Well done. Quick thinking. Not stopping."

"Oh! Well. Yes Sir. Only – the reason we didn't stop sir was because we couldn't. No brakes sir."

"What!"

It was like being trapped in an avalanche and waiting for the rescue dog to find you. You wait for hours and hours then three of the smelly beasts turn up together.

The journey down from Hjerkinn couldn't have been more peaceful. The countryside was beautiful in the semi-darkness as the train rumbled gently towards their destination and a successful completion of their vital mission. It was perhaps as well he hadn't known of the air-brake situation also that Dombas Station stood on a small incline that had slowed the train down considerably as it rumbled in.

"What the f - - -?" The train was coming to a stop. Olsen stuck his head from the open doorway. Larsen was jogging towards him.

"Bjerklund says it's a no go Captain. Not Rauma. Can't be done."

"Can't? What does he mean can't?" Olsen kicked the side of the door angrily. "God damn the man. I'm getting fed up with his bloody whinging. Can you drive this train Larsen? Please say yes then I can go and shoot the miserable bastard." Olsen jumped to the ground and moved rapidly towards the engine. Ringe and the sergeant were already there.

"The man says we are on the wrong line sir." chimed in Borg seeing his Captain was in a potential mood for a showdown and hoping to diffuse the situation.

"Wrong line! What's wrong with the line? Not enough of them are there? How many bloody lines does he want?" Bjerklund peered over the panel of the footplate.

"Just the one set Captain. But not this set. This set is on the Lillehammer-Dombas circuit. We need those that are on the western branch and that means waiting until it gets light."

"Gets light? Are you off your blasted head man? You saw the Germans back there. Do you want them come crawling all over us? Get this train moving now and get us to this western line." The engine driver sighed heavily and as if to make his point adjusted the beak of his cloth cap.

"Not possible boss. With no lights, no railway staff, she's likely to de-rail. If that happens a couple of dozen Germans will be the least of your problems." Olsen stared at the man. Now he really did feel like shooting him.

"Of all the damn - - . Well we can't stay here. We're sitting ducks - . Sergeant Borg! Take a couple of men. Walk your way back through the trees. Find out if you can how many of them there are throughout the station. We shall just have to blast our way through."

"Sorry boss. But you can't do that either." said Bjkerlund before the sergeant had time to react. "If you're thinking of fighting your way through with this train you can forget it." For a moment or two Olsen thought he had misheard the man.

"Forget it! What do you mean forget it? What the hell are you talking about?" Larsen sniggered. He couldn't resist. "Probably thinks he's off duty again sir."

"No young man -." Bjerklund scowled straightening his shoulders. "It's my watch alright. But for your information it's not my fight. I'm Swedish. A neutral. So is this train. She belongs to a Swedish company – also neutral Captain. So you see young man. No fighting with this train if you please gentlemen." Olsen's jaw had dropped open. He had another vision of the three mountain dogs before snapping it shut again with a bang.

"Sergeant. Wake me up please. I'm having a very bad dream. It's turning into a bloody nightmare - - ." Now he really, really wanted to shoot this engine driver, this stupid excuse for a man. "You are Swedish? You are a neutral? You saw all the gold being loaded and all the guns and ammunition? The flat cars being attached to your neutral train with my troops on board? Just what the fuck did you think we were going to do with it all? Play monopoly and go for target practice in the mountains in the middle of winter. What sort of a brainless arsehole are you?"

"I assumed Captain that the weapons would be for self-defence only." said Bjerklund aware the Captains temper was slowly rising.

"So you suggest we stop here until the Germans come and find us so that we can then use our weapons in self-defence -?" Olsen roared angrily. "This train is a rolling arsenal you idiot. Too many bullets in the right place and we could all be blown to hell. If you are a neutral, what the hell did you come along for in the first place?"

"Money boss." Bjerklund had shrunk down for the protection of the metal wing of the footplate. "I was promised by my office in Lillehammer I would be well paid for my services." Borg raised his rifle.

"So you're nothing but a stinking mercenary. Shall I shoot the swine for you now sir? You can't trust neutrals sir. You never know which way they will jump in a tight spot sir. Better I shoot him now sir. Save a lot of trouble later."

"Brilliant. That's a splendid idea Borg -." Olsen pointed the snub of his machine pistol at Bjerklund's bobbing head. "What say I let the Sergeant here shoot you Mr Mercenary Neutral?" Bjerklund blanched. Even in the darkness his change of pallor was evident.

"It's not a good idea boss. The Germans will hear the shots and come running. And who's going to drive the train for you – eh boss?" Olsen put a hand to his chin.

"Sergeant Borg -." Borg hitched up his rifle. Bjerklund disappeared down behind the protection of the footplate. Only the whitened tips of his fingers showed above the metal rim. "He's right you know. The Germans will hear the shots. We don't want to alert them unnecessarily – best use your knife." Bjerklund sprang up like a 'jack-in-a-box'.

"Please boss. Captain sir. I'm the only competent driver you have. Please tell him to go away." Bjerklund wriggled his fingers in Borg's direction his face twisted in abject terror. Olsen cradled the barrel of his machine-pistol in his arms. He scowled.

"You miserable little shit. You gutless excuse for a human being. Now get this and get it straight. From this second on you will not only do everything I tell you, but you will do it immediately, willingly and as if your very life depended on it – because it does. One more argument from you after this. One whinge of discontent and you are going to be 'wolf bait'. Do I make myself clear Mr Swedish man?" Bjerklund almost collapsed with relief.

"Yes Sir. Yes Captain. Certainly Sir. You're the boss. Whatever you say Captain Sir."

"Right then. To start with, give me your consignment papers." The sheaf of pink papers almost jumped from Bjerklund's pocket. Olsen looked them over then began writing in some of the blank spaces.

"These say – You are carrying ammunition for the German Army to a secret arsenal on - - the West Coast. Your train was commandeered in Lillehammer and the original cargo of dry goods was substituted for ordnance. Got that?" Bjerklund nodded. "If necessary. You will show these papers to the Germans. If they question you too much you will look annoyed. Show them your Swedish ID. That should get rid of them. Understand?" Again Bjerklund nodded. "Now. You will move the train back towards the station. How are the brakes now?"

"Fine boss. A disconnected hose. Nothing Major."

"Good. Stop just short of the platform. That way the Germans will have to come to us -."

"To us? But, but what if they don't believe me. Don't accept my ID or something like that. What then."

"Then? Then I suppose they will shoot you. Saves me the trouble." Olsen took in Bjerklunds look and snorted a laugh. "Don't be stupid man. Just do as I say and all will be well. Now get the train moving." Bjerklund faded away into the gloom. Only the sudden bright orange glow from the firebox showed he was already at the task. Olsen looked about.

"Sergeant Borg. Take some men and move up on the blind side. Get near enough to listen in to what is being said. One false move from Bjerklund, put a bullet between his eyes." Borg saluted and vigorously waddled his moustache.

"That sir would be my pleasure." he growled as he walked briskly away.

Asmark. Hedmark. C.Norway.

His presence of mind to strip one of his captors of his NS armband, that and his decision not to turn away from the German paratroopers, probably saved his life.

Gram had made good headway but had become lost in his own thoughts as he skimmed the undulating slopes almost majestically, like a bird in flight, serenely engrossed in a sense of well-being and careless freedom. He didn't see the Germans bivouacked amongst the trees until it was far too late and he was almost upon them. Their camouflaged smocks and alpine caps told him instantly he was amongst an enemy to reckon with. His decision to ski on towards them was less foolhardy as he spied the skis and the rifles with the telescopic sights in the hands of the two Germans out-posted on the perimeter of the camp. He sliced to a halt the nozzle of the German's rifles sighted distinctly in his direction. They only need pull the triggers and it would be a nineteen years wasted, his age and one he wished to make additions to. One of the Germans got to his feet.

"You, come here." snarled the man in Norwegian. Gram nodded and released the pressure on the side of his skis.

The Oberleutnant spoke only German. The guard with the sniper rifle translated. Who was he? What was he doing in this area? Your papers please! Gram answered all the Germans questions. He was a member of the NS. He had orders to search the region for the whereabouts of a British spy who had escape custody from Oslo the week previously. His superiors in Hamar had ordered a thorough search between Vang and Asmark. So far he had found nothing. Had the Oberleutnant or his men seen anything suspicious? The German Lieutenant gave a snort of disgust. Suspicious! Seven of his men were already dead and another two wounded. Why hadn't the NS leader Quisling got things under proper control? He hadn't expected his men to be hunted down and murdered. They (the Germans) had come to Norway to help the Norwegians stave off the British Imperialists, stop them from occupying the country and subjugating its people. The German High Command would be informed of all these murders. The population would suffer greatly, if they continued. The Lieutenant ceased his tirade. Gram wished now he hadn't asked the question. Had he, Gram, seen anything of a Norwegian military convoy? A large party of people, some civilians with a military escort? Gram shook his head. There were no decent roads hereabouts. Sledges and skis were the only possible mode of transport. A large party travelling in such a manner would leave lots of signs along the way and would be easy to track.

At length the German Lieutenant seemed satisfied. His second in command, an Unterfeldwebel Holtzbar, asked to inspect Gram's backpack which after nothing more than a cursory peek he handed back. It seemed the NS armband had done the trick into lulling the Germans into a false sense of security.

Not wanting to push his luck further Gram replaced the pack and pulled on his gloves. The Germans he knew, from the conversations between the NS men at the logging camp, were in Hamar. How far up the valley they might have penetrated since was anyone's guess.

"Good hunting." growled the Oberleutnant in Norwegian and smiled, no doubt pleased with himself knowing at least the two words in Gram's own language. Gram responded with the same, in German, which pleased the dour looking Teuton all the more. Not all Grams' time at the university had been spent reading 'dirty magazines', nor was it learning the German language. He just happened to know the German for the verb 'to hunt'.

Dombas Station.

"Papers." The German paratrooper had kept his machine pistol trained on the cab of the locomotive until the train had come to a halt. Bjerklund handed over his consignment papers.

"Swedish? Long way from home aren't you?"

Borg crouched behind a rise in the forest floor listening as Olsen squeezed in behind.

"He's checking Bjerklund's papers sir. There are three of them. The other two are just below the big drift to the right." Olsen beckoned one of his men. It was Lerdal.

"Go out over the other side and keep your eye on the track. There must be more of them somewhere." Lerdal crept away. Olsen inched forward trying to hear the German's words. He didn't altogether trust the Swedish engine driver.

"And where did you say this place was on the West Coast?"

"I didn't." replied Bjeklund. "What I said was – It was a secret location – and that is what it is – secret."

"We were told you had the King on this train."

"King! Which King?"

"How many King's do you Norwegians have?" The German was getting quite annoyed. So was Bjerklund.

"It's not just the Norwegians who have a King you know? What makes you think any King of any standing would travel on a goods train. Are you mad?"

"Be respectful when you address a German officer." snarled the German.

"I might be, if he was to ask me sensible questions. King indeed! I have never heard anything so ridiculous. What's biting you Lieutenant? You know you are not supposed to badger neutrals?"

Just then one of the Germans hiding behind the snowdrift ambled up and towards the flatcars. He stopped, lifted the canvas cover to eye level and peered in. Olsen fingered his machine pistol tightly. Inside and behind the stacks of ammunition boxes Eriksen crouched low over the sights of the machine gun. One accidental movement now by any of them would have set the ball rolling and all hell breaking loose. The German frowned and fingered the faded black lettering on the boxes. He yawned put one hand behind his head and stretched before slapping the canvas fold back in place and moving away.

"Fine! No more 'ridiculous' questions Swedish man. You are free to go." The Oberleutnant stepped back from the cab of the train and raised his hand high in the air.

"Thank you Oberleutnant. My papers please?" The German shrugged his shoulders and handed them back. "Oh. Yes Oberleutnant. I nearly forgot. Think you could lend me some men and a railway lantern -?"

"Men? Lantern? Why?"

"I need to change over the points to put her on the other line. Two or three men ought to be enough." The Oberleutnant frowned then after a moments thought signalled his men to his side.

"Stay here. Help the driver. I will send another man to you with a – lantern -." The German scowled at Bjerklund.

"Thank you Oberleutnant – Er. Heil Hitler. As you people say." smiled Bjerklund. The German Lieutenant scowled even more. Was this civilian neutral mocking him? Deciding it not worth the trouble he saluted and walked away.

Half an hour later and the train together with its German helpers was on the west line. The German sergeant with the lamp swung by the cab.

"A drink driver? Before you go?" Bjerklund cringed, as much as he would have liked to accept the Germans offer.

"Sorry Feldwebel. It's against regulations. I can't leave this train with all this ammunition aboard."

"Nonsense. Don't be such a misery. The train is not going to walk away. Come on down man. The Oberleutnant would not like you refusing him. When

85

does a good Swede refuse a beer or schnapps for that matter? Come on. Get down from there." The sergeant's last words had a ring of finality about them, almost insistent. Bjerklund tapped the throttle and inserted the locking pin before checking the brake lever. One small drink shouldn't matter. He didn't want to antagonise this German. He didn't have a kindly look about him. Bjerklund nodded and began to dismount the footplate.

"What the hell – What does he think he is doing -?" Olsen had been too far away to catch the tail end of the conversation. Borg slid down by his side breathing heavily.

"He's gone for a drink with the German sergeant. The idiot let himself be talked into it sir?" Olsen whacked the barrel of his gun in anger.

"Bloody fool." He signalled over his Lieutenant. "Ringe. Go down and tell Astrup to keep his machine-gun trained on the track below the platform. If anything goes wrong he is to wait until they are off the platform before he opens up -."

"Yes Sir -." Ringe turned to leave then hesitated. "You mean – just mow them down sir?" Olsen stared at him.

"No Lieutenant. He's to invite them over for tea."

"But sir. A machine-gun -?" Olsen's eyes flared.

"What's the matter Ringe? Unsporting of us is it? Rather they kill some of us instead would you? War isn't a bloody game Lieutenant. It's a bloody obscenity, a massacre. You massacre them before they massacre you. We didn't invite them here to carve up our country. Kill our people. Destroy our homes. Now get on with it. And Lieutenant – don't ever question my orders again." Ringe snapped to attention and saluted.

"Yes Sir. Sorry Sir. Right away Sir."
Sergeant Borg who had witnessed the performance followed Ringe's retreating back. He sighed, then.

"He will learn sir. He's a bit young, but I'm sure he will come good when it matters sir." Olsen knew he was right. All the same -?

"He better had Borg. Our lives may very well depend on it."

The sound of laughter from the station area filtered back into the trees.

"How many of them did you manage to count Sergeant?"

"Ten sir. There may be one or two more we haven't seen as yet. Probably the remains of those sent over yesterday towards Dovre to nab His Majesty. It's as well Major Ording Sir changed his mind. They would have rolled right into them."

An hour had gone by. The Swedish driver was still 'toasting it up' with the Germans. Not a good sign. The more the man consumed the more likely he was to 'give the game away'.

Down behind the machine-gun Astrup thought his backside was on fire.

"God it's bloody freezing. I think my balls have frozen to my ankles!" Ringe pulled his gaze from the station building to Astrup's rear end.

"Then just try to remember if you can to keep your bum pointed in their line of fire. With an arse like that the German's will never hit us." The Lieutenant moved position, more to keep the blood flowing through his legs and ease the cramp to his freezing joints. Cautiously he peered around the flap of canvas.

"God I hate this waiting around. What the hell is that thick headed idiot up to?" Almost as if on cue the door to the station building opened bathing the track and the side of the train in a watery yellow light. Bjerklund, supported by three of the Germans emerged into the crisp air. The big Swede was singing, Swedish and German with snippets of harsh Norwegian thrown in as he was manhandled slowly down the station platform. The three Germans, after a few minutes of guiding him in the right direction, decide they had had enough and propelled the swaying engine driver forward down the tracks. They stood watching his progress their breath clouding up the air in huge pockets of vapour. Olsen remembered clasping a hand over his eyes.

"I knew it. I bloody knew it. He's tanked. Full to the eyebrows. Useless bastard." Bjerklund staggered on a few steps then turned around.

"Hey. Hey you. You German guys. You don't know what I know. You don't know – anything, nothing about what I've got on – on my train. Nothing. Do you. Eh? You don't know – Do you?" Bjerklund stood swaying and bent over from the waist down his nose almost scrapping the railway sleepers. One of the Germans detached himself and went to Bjerklund's side. The big Swede was making conversation in a low whispered voice and waving both arms around sweeping the fingers of his hand towards his lips in loud 'shhhhuuushhhing' noises that under another circumstance might have been mistaken for the trains steam release valve. Olsen caught one of the words, 'Gold'. He watched in horror as the German detached himself from Bjerklund and walk back towards the station platform. Bjerklund resumed his staggered swaying towards the train. For what seemed a number of minutes nothing happened. The Swede managed somehow to haul himself up into the cab of the engine. Then the door of the station building flew open again and the German Oberleutnant emerged followed by a number of his men.

"Christ. I think we're blown. Sergeant -." Through the frosted window of the station wall Olsen caught sight of one of the Germans lifting the telephone and shouting into it.

"One of the bastards' is on the telephone. Larsen! See if you can pick him off." The bullet from Larsen's rifle crazed the subzero glazing. If it hit its mark was impossible to tell? The second shot from Larsen's rifle was lost as Ringe opened up with the machine-gun. Three paratroopers collapsed across the snow like disjointed marionettes, the rest threw themselves franticly aside to avoid the hail of bullets. Two more collapsed as they tried to reach the cover of the ditch the machine pistol of one spitting bullets to the heavens in a flowering spray of death. A bullet thwacked the stile against Olsen's head and splintered off into the night. There was a shriek. One of the Germans had been tattooed across the stomach the bullets press-studding his smock into his flesh. He staggered to his feet hurling obscenities and was attempting to ram another magazine into the chamber of his gun. A single rifle shot from Larsen took the top of his head off. He collapsed rolling head over heels to land upside down against the wheels of the locomotive in the form of a letter 'Y'. There were two more Germans still to be accounted for, four, if the two who had helped carry Bjerklund were now lying somewhere under the train.

"I count six down sir -." came the sergeant's gruff voice from out of the darkness. Another burst from the machine gun shattered the air. A scream, then quiet. Borg raised himself up and stared through the gap in the boxcar door.

"Sorry sir. Eight sir." Olsen pulled back from the cover of the wooden planking.

"Pass the word. No more firing. I want absolute silence. Fire only if you can see a target." The order was almost unnecessary. Conserving ammunition and shooting only on a good mark was a Norwegian tradition. Bullets cost money – in peacetime.

"I can hear something. Under the train." whispered Larsen eyes popping like a surfacing Arctic seal. Olsen listened.

"The bastards are using the track to move down to the machine gun. Larsen. You and you three Bergstroms. I want you to carry on talking as if nothing was wrong. Krefting. You take one of the lamps. Go up top and make your way to the front of the engine. When you hear me whistle, lower the lamp down between the tracks. You Schwartz. Take Storm with you. Make your way down to the back end. After you hear me whistle, count to three, drop down onto the track and let the swine have it. When they see Krefting's lamp they will turn to fire at it. They should have their backs to you. Don't hesitate. We have no time to be gentlemen. Here. Take my gun. Leave your rifle." Schwartz frowned.

"Yes Sir – but what if they don't fall for it?

"In that case we shall soon see who are the best shots – wont we?" Schwartz thought about the Captain's reply but only long enough to realise he had no choice in the matter.

"Humph. Come on Theodore. Let's go get our balls shot off shall we?" Theodore Storm smiled and hitched up his trousers. His reply would have made a 'street walker' blush.

North West of Asmark.

There was blood, frozen, all over his right shoulder and down the side of his coat. The bleeding had stopped some time ago and the furrow across his cheek smarted in its frozen congealed state even though he had pulled up his hood for the maximum protection.

He was one man, fast on his skies and an expert shot with his rifle. The bullet had grazed Grams face at a distance of over two hundred metres. The assassin had fired from the cover of the trees. Whoever he was had enough sense to remain under cover. All Gram saw was the shadowy outline, a flurry of snow and he was gone. Had there been more than one Gram felt sure they would have taken him on and set off after him in pursuit.

For most of the early daylight hours he had headed west. That should bring him down towards the floor of the valley in the direction of Lillehammer. If the Germans were in the town he would have to skirt their positions and head off north, perhaps try his luck nearer to the coast.

The man or at least Gram assumed it was, had thought him the enemy and had a propensity to shoot and ask questions afterwards. It was either that or his trail had been tracked from the logging camp. In which case it was most probably one of Quislings thugs. Whatever, it was imperative to put some distance between himself and the rifle at his back. Somewhere he would need to take stock of the situation. Lay a trap or loose him. The main road? Grab a lift from a passing vehicle? The road would be alive with German military and ordnance. Some could still be under fire? Part of the front lines? It was a very big risk. But no less so than a bullet in the back without warning. There was approximately another ten hours of daylight left. Gram gave another kick with his skis. He had to keep moving.

Dombas Station.

Through the semi-concious haze the distinctive outline of a German helmet began to take shape. Olsen snapped awake and went for his revolver.

"Whoa. It's me sir. Schwartz sir." Olsen blinked wide his eyes and made them focus.

"What the hell -? Are you stark raving mad Schwartz? I could have killed you – you blithering idiot." Schwartz grinned back impishly from under the rim of the steel helmet.

"Not a chance sir. I'm very fast. As you know." Olsen snorted a grunt. Schwartz had indeed proven himself to be fast on the draw. There had been four German paratroopers hiding beneath the train and not two as Olsen had assumed. Schwartz had riddled all four with three short bursts from Olsen's machine pistol, the last of them as he attempted to escape by making a break for the trees. Schwartz had killed the man with a single shot through his steel helmet, the one he was wearing at the moment. There had been twelve Germans in all. The other two, he and Borg missed, had come from the machine gun position Bjeklund had spotted on their approach to the station. Olsen tried to remind himself that although the man was a liability he did have some good points.

"Jesus. You lot are bloody dangerous. I nearly had a heart attack -." Olsen swung his feet from the bed. "Is there anything wrong?"

"A spotter plane sir. Been circling overhead. Lieutenant Ringe had us put these uniforms on. In case it decides to come back for another look."

"Good thinking." Olsen stretched himself. Six hours. According to the time on his watch. He could have slept a good deal longer. His nostrils twitched involuntarily.

"Is that coffee I smell? If so I would like a cup if you will."
The door opened. Ringe walked in wearing the uniform of a German Oberleutnant.

"Christ Almighty – Try giving some warning before waltzing in dressed like that -!" Ringe froze. Then looked down at himself.

"Oh! Yes. Sorry Sir. Didn't Schwartz tell you?" Ringe clicked his heels together smartly and threw out his arm. "Heil Hitler. Oberleutnant Richter reporting spotter plane still circling Sir. Does the Hauptmann have any orders for his men Sir?" Ringe ended with a wide smile and a quick twirl for effect. Olsen remained stone-faced. The Lieutenant came to attention slowly. "Ah. Yes sir. Sorry sir. Not funny eh Sir?" Just then the door opened and another German helmet appeared inside. It was Astrup.

"Spotter plane Sir. Coming back this way Sir." Olsen raised himself from the bed and waved his fingers at the Lieutenant.

"Take your clothes off." Ringe pulled back.

"Pardon Sir?"

"Your clothes. Take them off. I want to take a look at that plane. Give me the hat and the smock – and the boots. Hmm. Incidentally what size are they – the boots. Look OK to me -."

The German Storch droned in slow and low over the buildings the pilot clearly visible in his fur-lined headgear and goggles.

"Give the little bastard a wave all of you." snarled Olsen through the wide smile of his clenched teeth. "He's supposed to be a friend of ours."

The pilot of the plane waved back and attempted a waddle of his wings as he droned away lazily into the distance. Olsen kept a watch on him until the aircraft was but a dot on the horizon.

"Stupid swine fell for it." he said lifting both clenched hands onto his hips.

"Hardly surprising Johan. You look all the part of German Teutonic manhood in that get up. What is it? Fancy dress?" Olsen spun about. Now it was his turn to be surprised as Ording appeared around the end of the building a drawn revolver clenched menacingly in his hand.

"Arne! What the hell? Where did you spring from?" The Major slipped his gun back into its holster and stepped down onto the platform.

"I nearly put a hole in one of your boys. What the hell are you playing at?"

"Yes. Sorry. German spotter plane. Wouldn't go away. Had to convince the bastard somehow. Make it appear they still held the station – which they did until a few hours age. What about you? Is 'Magnus' safe?" Ording nodded and did his usual quick survey of the area before replying.

"For the moment. It's not good news I'm afraid. The Germans have by-passed Lillehammer. We were getting penned in. It's all total confusion at the moment."

"We were told Dombas was safe. That Broch's men held the town. But when we got here - . Well you can see for yourself." replied Olsen.

"Broch's men were called to Dovre. The Germans hold the telephone exchange but Broch got us through. It's been a hell of a night." Ording frowned, then gave his junior the once over. "Er - Just a suggestion Johan. But do you think you might get rid of those clothes for the present. I keep having this peculiar urge to shoot you. If you wouldn't mind?" Olsen laughed and slapped a hand to his thigh.

"Lieutenant Ringe! Get everyone out of those uniforms. Put them with the ammunition. We might have use of them again." He turned.

91

"Und nun Herr Major. Eine kafe ja?" He ignored the look of disapproval on Ording's face.

"Wissen? Was? Unglaublich. Du bist ein dummer. Wo ist dein offizier – fallschirmjager idiot." Ringe put his hand over the mouthpiece of the telephone receiver.

"I think our friend is getting a little upset sir. Seems to think he is speaking to an idiot."

The telephone had rung in the station masters office. It was the exchange at Dovre. The German officer in command was demanding an explanation. Ringe put the receiver back to his ear and removed his hand.

"Herr Oberleutnant. Herr Oberleutnant. Telefon - ." he roared loudly. There was a distinctive howl of pain from the other end. "Eine moment bitter" purred Ringe in satisfaction. Olsen took the receiver.

"Ja. Oberleutnant Richter -?"

"What the hell is going on up there Oberleutnant? Why haven't you contacted me?" Olsen cleared his throat.

"I beg you pardon sir. I have tried a number of times. But the telephones in this god-forsaken place are most inefficient Sir."

"Tried! Then you should have tried harder. High Command takes a dim view of sending out spotter planes to locate missing units who are not missing Oberleutnant. Now. You have the Swedish train? It's cargo. Is it gold or ammunition?"

"Ammunition sir. Like I reported last night. The driver was drunk sir. We have searched the train from top to bottom sir. Nothing but ammunition."

"Have you discovered the drivers' secret destination yet?"

"No sir. He was very drunk sir. He's still asleep sir."

"Asleep! Asleep! Get the bastard on his feet. Wake him. Immediately. There are new orders from Oslo. As it seems impossible to discover where your driver got his orders, we have decided to use the ammunition for ourselves. You are to proceed to Andalsnes. A large drop has been organised to occupy the port before the Allies reach it. Our troops will need the extra ammunition you have. The drop will take place at exactly 1400 hours this afternoon. You and the ammunition will be there at precisely ten minutes after then 1410 hours. Do you understand Oberleutnant? Is all that clear?"

"Ja herr Major. Das ist selbstverstandlich. Heil Hitler." Olsen slammed the telephone receiver back on its cradle. "Damnn-." He glanced at Ording. "The slimy little bastards are planning a drop on Andalsnes this afternoon. We must warn Colonel Hagan -." He turned to Ringe. "Get the men aboard the train. Tell them to stay out of sight. And see if you can find the station master – On the double." Ringe moved smartly away.

"So. What do you plan to do -?" Ording asked. Olsen made for the desk and some of the stationmaster's writing material.

'Colonel Hagan. Andalsnes. Enemy paratroops. Your area. 1400hrs.
Objective. Harbour installations. 'Fridtjof'.

"How's that?" Ording nodded.

"Good. I'll inform His Majesty. I must go now. The latest reports we have are the British are moving down from Molde. Let's hope they are correct." Ording reached the door. Before leaving he turned.

"Best of luck Johan. If the worst comes to the worst dump the lot in the deepest hole you can find and make sure nobody sees you. Oh – and don't forget to leave me a note as to where it is –"Ording grinned. "Well somebody should know for when we kick all these arseholes out of here. The King might need it. And I am sure he would show his appreciation. I'll mention your name, in passing –."

Olsens reply was unprintable.

The stationmaster proved his worth. The message for the 2nd Division commander reached its destination within the hour.

Olsen knew it was time to move. The Germans now had knowledge of the train and would soon put two and two together when nothing appeared on the outskirts of the inland port of Alsdalsnes to supply their men.

"Where's Bjerklund?" From the darkness of the boxcar Astrup got to his feet.

"Still out Sir." Bjerklund lay curled up in ball at the back of the wagon.

"Get the lazy bastard on his feet. He's needed." Olsen cast about in the darkness at the eager young faces looking back at him. "Schwartz. You and Sergeant Borg get back into German uniform -." From the corner came the dull clunk of glass on wood. An empty bottle, previously full of schnapps, rolled away out of sight. Astrup bent down over the prone form of the engine driver. "Shit-." Astrup stood up. "Sorry Sir. He must have found a bottle from the supplies. He's out cold -." Olsen felt his temper begin to rise. Stiffly he walked away from the boxcar until his progress was in danger of being impeded by a large snowdrift. Once there he proceeded to give the silent innocuous white powder the best kicking it had received since the beginning of the winter. It was perhaps better than using Astrup's head. For one thing there was a plentiful supply of snow and Astrup only had one head.

"Larsen --! Get the f - - - out here. Now!" he roared, loud enough to be heard on the train but not across the surrounding countryside. Larsen almost fell out into the snow.

"Can you drive this blasted thing?" Larsen nodded eagerly.

"Absolutely Sir. Just say the word Sir." Sergeant Borg eased himself down from the doorway.

"He's alright Captain Sir. I watched him for a while last night. He can handle her. Of that I'm sure."

"You seem very confident of that Sergeant?"

"Well sir it's not just that. I was a railway guard myself for a time. At a pinch I could drive her – but, well you see sir, Larsen is younger. I think he might be quicker. In an emergency, so to speak."

Olsen was impressed. One minute nothing, the next everything.

"Is there anything you lot can't do?" he said, a smile rising to his lips.

"Alright. Larsen. Get rid of the uniform. Take Bjerklund's jacket. And then gentlemen. What say we get the hell out of here?"

Brottum. Hedmark. C. Norway.

Descending to the bowels of the valley was a big risk. The Germans would be making every effort to control the main road. He still wore the NS armband and his cover story had proven it would stand scrutiny from all but the most zealous of inquisitors.

It was mid-afternoon of the fifth day since the Germans had come to Oslo. The German Military plans Gram carried would have already lost some of their value. But who was to say they couldn't still be very useful to the Allies. Gram had to make contact with friendly forces. And soon.

The Red Cross pennant and the fact the car carried local Norwegian number-plates prompted him to break cover. The most efficient way to ensure the car stopped was to stand full square in it's way but be ready to leap for it should the driver appear less than friendly. Gram raised his ski sticks in the air to indicate he had no intention of moving. The car came slowly to a halt. The driver was a local doctor from Hamar called to assist residents injured in the fighting that had been taking place in small groups in and around the valley.

"Our Army seem to think I have no patients in my own district -?" complained the doctor. "Ridiculous. But I go where I am told." The doctor, greying and in his mid-fifties, eyed the blood on Gram's smock.

"And so what happened to you then?"

"I slashed my face on a branch. Clumsy of me. I should have been more careful." The doctor nodded and gave Gram a look of scepticism.

"Indeed young man. You should. It would make my job a great deal easier if you young people thought more deeply about a number of things." He glanced down at the NS motif on Gram's armband. Gram thought for a moment then decided it would be worthwhile to take a chance with this fellow countryman. Nothing the doctor had said indicated he was anything but a loyal Norwegian?

"This -." Gram flicked the edge of the armband contemptuously. "Isn't what it seems. It stops the Germans asking too many questions. I'm not interested in helping anyone occupy our country." The atmosphere in the vehicle changed almost instantly. The doctor smiled. The first time he had done so since agreeing to give the lonely skier a lift to the next town. But there was caution in his reply.

"Yes. Well it's all a very bad business. War. Stupid. Nothing good will come of it. It should have been avoided - . Somehow!"
They drove on in silence.

On the outskirts of Lillehammer stood a long line of traffic. Many of the drivers were out on the road. A group of white smocked youths displaying NS armbands were checking all traffic. The doctor slowed then chose a turning off towards the trees. The driveway to a large house.

"Remove your hood. Let me take a look at that cut on your face." he said when the car came to a halt. Gram didn't argue. The doctor retrieved his bag from the rear seat and squinted at the deep red furrow running in a parallel line above Gram's lip and along passed the lob of his ear.

"Hmmm. A very clean branch fortunately. No tearing. No infectious bearing material. You were lucky. I would say an accident in a million – under different circumstances." The doctor knew the path of a bullet on a surface wound when he saw one. Gram made no comment.
Five minutes later and the wound had been drawn together with a couple of sutures.

"Keep the padding on. Change it at least once a day. I will give you something to put on it to ward off any infection. It would be better to keep your hood up otherwise the scar will not heal properly. You don't want to spoil your good looks." The doctor thrust a handful of pads, some sticking plaster and a small bottle of liquid into Gram's hands.

"You paint it on. On no account drink it. It will make you violently ill." He replaced the bag back on the rear seat. "And now I suppose you will be leaving me – for – wherever it is you are going?" Gram gave a nod. He had intended to do so when he spotted the NS checkpoint. Here was ideal.

The ageing doctor turned the car around and slowed as he came level with Gram at the entrance to the driveway. He smiled and gave Gram a long parting look that said 'Good luck and be careful'. Gram tried a look of what he hoped was reassurance and a thumbs-up. Whether or not it was successful he couldn't be sure. It was the best he had to offer under the circumstances.

Hvitby. Dovrefjell Mtns.

It wasn't the most salubrious accommodation yet the warmth from the firebox and the tarpaulin cover made the coal bunker an ideal spot for Olsen to keep an eye on the terrain up ahead. He snaked the map from under his smock and studied it closely.

"Borg. You must know these lines pretty well? What we need is a suitable siding. Somewhere easy accessible where we can bolt for cover if need be." Borg took the map and fished a pair of spectacles from his pocket.

"Only for reading sir – ," he said flourishing the bronze rimmed glasses. "Otherwise my eyes are perfect – well almost Sir." He scanned the map. "Would the Captain mind moving onto a branch line – here." Borg jabbed the map with his finger. "Trollheim. The track cuts north into the Dovre Mountains. If we could join the Trollheim line at Hvitby we could be off the main line and away into the cover of the peaks in minutes."

"Trollheim? Why there?"

"Because there's this siding I know. Just here -." Borg pulled the map nearer Olsen's face. It runs into a quarry. The track goes clear into the mountain. Sheer rock walls. Both sides. If we wanted we could spread our tarpaulins from one face to the other. It would be impossible for the Germans to spot us from the air Sir."

"Sounds brilliant. How far is Hvitby?"

"About another four and a half miles Sir."

"Good. Then I suppose the best thing to do is - - - -." Olsen never finished the sentence. With a squeal the locomotive jerked violently and began to buck from side to side. Then came a long pronounced judder, as its massive steel wheels gouged a thin layer of metal from the protesting tracks below.

"What the hell - - ?" Larsen stuck his head inside the covering.

"Up front sir. A blockage. Across the line."

As the rake of wagons ground slowly to a halt, Olsen peered around the flank of the footplate. Trees. Half a dozen or more were stacked across the track. Recent and to Olsen's guess, deliberate.

96

"Could be trouble. Larsen you stay put. Schwartz. In with Borg. Keep quiet. No shooting unless we have to - Shit -." Borg peered out; the spectacles perched precariously atop his huge moustache.

"I take it that wasn't an order Sir. The last bit?" Olsen nearly smiled and was pleased he hadn't when half a dozen or more German troops left their hiding place behind the barricade and began advancing slowly towards him.

"Germans. Not paratroopers. Not Wehrmacht either. German Police troops. Gestapo at a guess." Borg fingered his rifle tightly. Gestapo! Not a good omen he thought to himself as he withdrew from sight.

"Oberleutnant Richter?" The call came from one of the advancing Germans. From the insignia on the lapel of the man's tunic beneath his elegant grey topcoat the man was a Captain like himself.

"Yes -." Olsen tried to make his voice sound as irritable as he could.

"What is it you want? Why have you blocked the line? My train is on an important mission by a direct order from Wehrmacht High Command. I have an almost impossible schedule. I cannot be delayed."

The German Hauptstumfuehrer came to a halt alongside the footplate. He was young. Perhaps not more than twenty years of age and sported a small duelling scar beneath his left eye. His lip curled sarcastically when he spoke, regardless of his mood or at least so it had seemed to Olsen when he recalled it later.

"The Gestapo have no wish to delay your journey Oberleutnant. If you co-operate it will not take long."

"Co-operate? Take long? What won't take long? What is this?"

"My orders Oberleutnant. We all have orders. Some tasteful, some not so. I have orders to search this train. And I always obey my orders Oberleutnant." The reply was meant to put Olsen in his place. The Gestapo man outranked him in his German Lieutenant's uniform. Olsen tried again but with little confidence he could distract the man from following out his superior's commands.

"Search the train! What's the matter with everyone? This train has been searched twice already. Once when your people were looking for the Norwegian King – only God knows why such a person would choose to travel in a goods train – and again for gold bullion. What is it this time? The Crown Jewels?"

"Yes, yes Oberleutnant. All that I know. The Army may well be satisfied there is nothing hidden on this train but we of the Gestapo are not."

"No! No I am sorry Sir. We haven't time to waste. Do you realise how many boxes there are aboard? A top scale operation is under way and this cargo is vital to that plan's success. You must clear the line immediately or I will have

97

no choice but to inform High Command of this inexcusable delay." The Gestapo man sneered.

"Absolutely Oberleutnant. You can inform whomsoever you like. My orders come direct from the Reichsfuehrer Himmler himself. The whole of the Norwegian gold reserves are missing from the Norwegian Central Bank in Oslo. This Oberleutnant is the only train so far unaccounted for. You may have searched it yourselves, but have you searched thoroughly? Some of these types of wagons have double boarded floors for example. The boxes of ammunition? Have you checked those boxes right at the bottom or – as I suspect – just those at the top? You do see what I am saying here Oberleutnant? Now. My men will execute a thorough search. The sooner they start, the sooner they finish. Your men by the way – where are they?"

The German was leaving Olsen no choices. He had hoped to avoid any trouble.

"Around –. I wasn't sure who had blocked the line. It could have been Norwegian loyalists?"

"Very wise Oberleutnant Richter. Very wise indeed. I can see now why they chose you to take over the mission to get through to the coast with these supplies. The –er Swedish driver, Bjerklund. He is with you?" Larsen stepped forward to the edge of the footplate. "Ah! Good. You will come with me," the German said in Swedish. Larsen got down and followed the man for a few paces before the man stopped and turned about.

"So. You are Bjerklund. Swedish. Neutral. Ja?" Larsen nodded. Larsen spoke very little Swedish and even less German. The Hauptsturmfuehrer's eyes flashed angrily. "I would prefer you answer me properly. You are Swedish are you not?" Again Larsen nodded, this time with a smile on his face. The German exploded. "What is the matter with you? Are you stupid?" Then to Olsen. "What is wrong with this man? Is he Swedish or isn't he – idiot -?" Olsen leaned out.

"Yes. I'm sorry Hauptsturmfuehrer. He is a little simple-minded. Not surprising doing this sort of job." The Gestapo man tried again.

"Bjerklund. You don't have to be afraid. I like the Swedish people. We Germans have the greatest respect for your Germanic culture. But Herr Bjerklund, not when they assist our enemies. You must have seen our Norwegian friends exchange their cargo at Lillehammer. So. Where did they hide the gold?" Larsen didn't move and kept his gaze riveted on the ground at the man's feet. He hadn't understood a word the man had said. Suddenly something smashed against the side of his head. He staggered. The German's face was now a twisted image of the former condescending half smile with the mouth now emitting an animal like roar.

"Fucking swine. Indolent pig. Where is the gold?" The German raked Larsen's face a second time with the side of the raised pistol. A cascade of brightly flashing stars and a crushing blow from behind sent Larsen tumbling towards the ground.

"Stop that." Olsen was off the footplate with a burning desire to put a bullet between the eyes of the cowardly Gestapo soldier whose rifle butt had felled the young Norwegian from behind. He checked himself.

"Can't you see the man doesn't understand what you are talking about? Bjerklund -?" Olsen bent over his young recruit. "Bjerklund?" he shouted.

Inside the boxcar, the real Bjerklund heard his name being called through his alcohol fogged stupor and got to his feet. He was almost out the door when the elder of the Bergstrom brothers gave the big Swede a belt to the stomach sending him back almost to the far side of the wagon where he slid silently to the floor again. Rolf Bergstrom peered through a crack in the planking. None of the Germans it seemed had heard the small commotion, concentrated as they were alongside the hissing locomotive.

"Get him up." ordered the Gestapo officer savagely. Olsen and one of the Germans helped Larsen to his feet.

"Here. Let me. You won't get anything out of him that way. He's not all there -!" Olsen tapped the side of his head to enhance the point. He waved the Germans back and took Larsen by the shoulders.

"Bjerklund. Bjerklund. Now listen to me -." Larsen raised his eyebrows and took his next cue from Olsen's face.

"Now. When the train was loaded at Lillehammer Station – You know the station -?" Larsen gave a slow nod. " The boxes of gold must have been put aboard first -. You show me the first boxcar the army people loaded first. Understand - ? I know it's difficult. Just concentrate. The first boxcar. The first boxcar to have boxes put in -. Show me -." Larsen tried to look knowledgeable and lolled his head as if in agreement and pointed. "That's it. Show me." said Olsen eagerly.

The boxcar door was still slightly ajar when Larsen, followed by Olsen and the Gestapo officer, appeared in the gap. Behind the stacks of boxes Ringe and the Bergstom brothers held their breath.

"You think it's this one?" Olsen shook Larsen by the shoulders. "This one? Good. Now. Fetch me a metal bar from the toolbox on the flatcar. Understand?" Larsen grinned stupidly and nodded as he ambled away.

Beneath the cover of the tarpaulin over the flatcar Astrup and Eriksen had been keeping a keen eye down the barrel of the machine gun. Larsen came on, stopped beside the toolbox and fumbled with the loose tarpaulin ropes.

"Be ready. Let the others get closer. Wait for a signal." he whispered.

"Come on Bjerklund. We haven't got all day." Olsen's sharp rebuke spurred Larsen into action. He fumbled for a crowbar and dropped the lid of the box with a bang. The German officer sniggered. People like Bjerklund would have found no place in his modern day Germany.

"About time too." snapped Olsen snatching the crowbar from Larsen's trembling hands. "Go back to the engine. Be ready to leave when I come." Olsen threw the crowbar into the darkened interior of the wagon and gestured Larsen impatiently away.

"You there -." Harald Bergstrom stepped forward into the gloom and enough for his German uniform to be recognisable to the Gestapo officer.

"Open some of those boxes. Come on. Quickly now." said Olsen. "The Hauptsturmfuehrer is impatient to conclude his business." Bergstrom picked up the crowbar and disappeared again into the darkness where he proceeded to give some of the boxes a few well-aimed blows as ordered.

"Not those on top you idiot. Move them. The boxes on the bottom – God! Do I have to do everything myself – Get out of the way." Olsen clambered up into the boxcar. Bergstrom began sliding some of the boxes around on the floor. The Gestapo officer moved a little closer to the gap in the door and contented himself stamping the cold from his feet in the thick layer of snow alongside the track and slapping his gloved hands together to increase his circulation.

"I'll try to get them to come in one at a time. No shooting. Use your knives." Ringe looked at him in horror. The thought of slitting a dozen men's throats didn't equate with his idea of modern warfare. It was far too personal. "Lieutenant. Pull those boxes across to form a barricade. Wait for them to get well inside. Who's on the machine-gun?"

"Astrup and Eriksen." replied Ringe automatically. He was still trying to come to terms with Olsen's first remark. Had Olsen any reason to doubt his Lieutenant's abilities it was far too dark inside the boxcar to see Ringe's face clearly. He waited until the boxes had been moved then -.

"We've found it! Hauptsturmfuehrer. It's here. At the bottom. Just as you said. Would you like to come aboard?"
The Gestapo officer slapped his hands together loudly a look of triumph smoothing away the permanent scowl on his narrow chiselled features.

"But of course." He half turned. "Some of you men. Come with me." Three of the men detached themselves from the main group and shuffled forward.

As the Gestapo officer clambered inside the boxcar Olsen's machine pistol broke the back of his neck. The crack of splitting flesh and bone echoed around the blackened interior. Bergstrom slit the man's throat just to make sure. Olsen moved in front of the prone corpse and stuck his head outside the wagon.

"Your officer wants one of you men in here. The rest of you check out the wagon in front." Olsen held out a helping hand for the German soldier. The man was halfway off the ground when something to Olsen's rear made him hesitate. He peered into the gloom. A look of surprise.

"Was is -?" he cried his face turning to one of horror. "Auflau - - ." the rest of his warning cry lost as Olsen let go the man's hand. The man's machine pistol burst into life bullets peppering the interior of the boxcar as the man himself catapulted backwards towards the ground. Olsen aimed and fired just the once the bullets from his own machine pistol stripping the flesh from the German soldier's face as the man hit the snow. The German rolled over with a groan and lay still. His comrades had been momentarily stunned by the suddenness of it all and only began to react when the machine-gun began to chatter. Eriksen at the first sound of shooting had thrown back the tarpaulin cover and was already busily feeding the smoking barrel of the machine-gun with a steady stream of bullets taking the milling Germans completely by surprise. One of the Gestapo men managed to reach the sanctuary of the railway track as the rest of his friends bucked and staggered under the hail of steel shredding blood and flesh from their bodies. Within less than half a minute only the odd involuntary jerk of a mangled limb and gargled gasp bore witness that the heap of gore had ever breathed life at all.

Olsen knelt in the doorway of the boxcar and stared out. He had always known the deadly effects of a machine-gun at long range but this was entirely something else. Another twenty seconds went by before the mound of twisted flesh became totally still. Carnage was the only word that came to his mind. For a split second he felt a pang of regret then just as quickly brushed the thought aside. These men had come to his country as murderers and thieves. Not one of them would have baulked at executing him or the rest of the 'Fridtjoft' team had they been discovered or to attain their own imperialistic ends. To hell with them. Hopefully.

Everything was strangely quiet. The one German light on his feet had disappeared into the trees on the far side of the tracks. Olsen shook himself jumped down and grabbed a refreshing handful of snow to rub across his face – having firstly made absolutely sure it was free from bloodstains.

"Bergstrom. You and your brothers keep an eye on the tree line. One of them got away. If you see anything, shoot it -." Olsen made to move away from the boxcar then stopped. Harald Bergstrom was standing with his back to the open doorway, stock still, not making any effort to move, his rifle dangling loosely from his fingertips. "Bergstrom! – Bergstrom! What's wrong with you man? What the hell - -?" Olsen clambered back into the boxcar. He followed Harald's frozen stare. Rolf Bergstrom knelt on the floor the limp body of his younger brother cradled in his arms. There was blood smeared across the young boy's face.

"Peter? Peter? Speak to me Peter. Open your eyes." Rolf was massaging the youth's pale cheeks with his hands. Three glistening dark blotches traced a line across the boy's upper chest. There was no sign of life. Olsen had seen enough. Bullets from the German soldier's machine pistol had found at least one mark with a deadly accuracy. The boy was almost certainly dead. If not he would be before long.

Sergeant Borg appeared alongside. He looked in, had been about to speak then abruptly changed his mind. He looked at Olsen. Olsen shook his head. Placing his rifle carefully down on the floor of the wagon Borg gained the interior with an agility that belied his apparent old age. Several shots. Singly spaced and distant broke the stillness of the snow-bound surroundings. Olsen looked out, nodded to Borg and swung himself down through the open doorway. The shots had come from the forest. Olsen walked the full length of the train all the while keeping a close eye on the trees and the mound of snow on the opposite side of the tracks. As he crossed before the glistening hiss of the locomotive a shout came from the forest.

"Captain Olsen? Are you and your men alright? We have your stray black sheep. Dead, I'm afraid -." Olsen pulled back behind the cover of the engine.

"Who are you? What do you want?" he replied. "Come out and show yourselves."

"Hvitby Rifle Club." cried a voice as three figures on skies emerged from the trees and slewed slowly towards him. The man in front kept his rifle across his arms with one hand on the trigger guard, quite a feat for anyone other than a very experienced skier. These men had to be Norwegian thought Olsen.

"My apologises Captain -." said the man with the unslung rifle as he panted to a rest. "Would you mind lifting your smock?" Olsen smiled. Had he been the enemy all three men would now be dead. He lifted the front of the German paratrooper smock to expose his Norwegian Army uniform beneath.

"Sorry Captain - ." said the man sheepishly, "German uniforms unnerve me. You understand. The –er- one that got away. He didn't. We snapped him before he reached the road. I'm sorry we couldn't get here any sooner. Do you have casualties?"

"One dead. There are just the three of you?" asked Olsen.

"Yes. Just the three of us on this stretch but from here on in there are a number of others checking out the line ahead of you. One dead you say. I'm sorry - ." he motioned towards the pile of bodies. "At least not as many as our German friends I see – Bloody business!"

"Yes. Thank you. I suppose all things considered we haven't done too badly. Thanks for the runaway. Good work." The leader of the group turned and signalled with a movement of his head.

"We must get going. We have quite an area to cover. Our report has to be with our HQ before dusk. Good luck Captain. Give the bastards hell eh?" The three men slewed away, caught the top of the snowdrifts and sailed gracefully down towards the lower slope. Olsen watched them for a moment, wishing he too could be as free to carry the fight to the enemy on his own terms and not tied down to the line wherever the railway tracks were taking them. He crossed over the track and moved quickly down the reverse side of the train until he came to the boxcar again. He rapped on the door. Borg's face appeared.

"Well?" he asked hopefully.

"Nothing we could do sir. He was killed instantly sir. Sorry." Olsen grimaced. It wasn't unexpected. "We are – er – covering the bodies with snow sir. Best we can do under the circumstances. What about –er-." Borg tilted his head to where the body of Peter Bergstrom lay.

"No. You can leave things here as they are for now. You had better wake Bjerklund." Olsen cleared his throat. "Corporal Bergstrom. Take three men and clear away the blockage up ahead." Harald Bergstrom touched the face of his youngest brother for the last time and ran his fingers through the boy's flaxen hair before rising to his feet. He wiped the back of his sleeve across his cheeks to remove any sign of his tears then nodded to Olsen before moving away.

"Captain sir!" Olsen looked to his sergeant. "I'm afraid Bjerklund's dead sir. He must have caught some of the same as young Bergstrom."

"Serves the Swedish bastard right -." snarled the distraught voice of Rolf still sitting with the head of his younger brother in his lap. "But for him the German's wouldn't have known about the gold – bastard." Olsen tapped the floor gently but firmly.

"That's enough. Get up off the floor, get out of here and get yourself some fresh air. That's an order." Rolf Bergstrom glared up angrily. Tears welled up afresh in his eyes. Borg stepped forward and put a hand on the sobbing boy's shoulder.

"Come on Rolf. Do as the Captain says. I will look after Peter for you. He won't be alone. Go on now. You know Peter would want you to carry on – there's a good lad." Olsen bowed his head from the young boy's gaze. It was all his fault. Borg had warned him about bringing along members of the same family, and three brothers with barely a year or two between them. God he was an idiot. Why hadn't he listened?

Sometimes events happen in the most fortuitous way. Had Olsen not sent Rolf Bergstrom off to grieve on his own, what happened next could well have been disastrous.

Rolf had seen his brother Harald and the three others moving up the track to remove the barricade. Something, he wasn't sure what, alerted his senses regardless of his somewhat emotional condition. He gave out a long low whistle that instantly sent his brother and the rest of his group scurrying for the cover of the trees. Olsen stuck his head from within the boxcar just in time to see the men disappearing from sight. His temper flared.

"Bergstrom! What the hell are you playing at now -?" Rolf remained with his back to his Captain.

"Quiet! Please sir." hissed Bergstrom. "There. Do you see it?"

"See what for Christ's sake? What's wrong with you man?" retorted Olsen angrily. Rolf raised his rifle so the butt of the stock was near his shoulder the barrel pointing down. For one horrible moment Olsen thought he had overdone it and that he was about to receive a bullet for his pains as the young man turned slowly to face him.

"The bastards have left behind a look-out -." Bergstrom gestured with his thumb then slowly turned back again. With one simultaneous movement he swung the rifle skyward and fired. For a second or two nothing happened, then came a sudden shuddering of branches from one of the tall firs and a bundle plummeted from within producing a hollow thud as it hit the ground. A mass of ice particles and clumps of snow followed in a tumbling cataract of pure white. Rolf raised the barrel of the rifle to his lips and blew away the last vestiges of the blue smoke.

"That's for Peter -." he whispered to himself quietly then. "These Germans. They'll never get the hang of flying that way – don't you think sir?" Olsen looked at him in astonishment. That had been one hell of a shot. The boy hadn't even aimed properly. Olsen went across to check on the body. Another Gestapo soldier. The Hauptsturmfuehrer hadn't been quite as incompetent as Olsen thought. Had the German officer left any more of his men hidden away? The sound of a car engine coming to life and of a vehicle being driven away broke the hitherto silence. Olsen scanned the trees. He hadn't realised the road was so close. From the forest and breaking cover near to the train came the eldest Bergstrom brother followed by his men. They ploughed a pathway through the high bank of snow up the small incline and knelt panting to a halt.

"Someone has been watching us. They had a car. They've taken off along the road. South I think. I caught a glimpse of him. Civilian." Olsen nodded.

"Probably one of the rifle club checking we are alright. I shouldn't worry too much." Olsen could see his explanation hadn't convinced Bergstrom. "Best get the barricade moved as soon as possible. It's time we got the hell out of here. The sooner the better." Bergstrom rolled away. Olsen pulled apart the German soldiers greatcoat lapels. The man had the German Iron Cross-medal laced around his neck. The Polish campaign no doubt. The man had seen action before. Well not any more Fritz or whatever the man's name was. The bullet from Rolf's rifle had cut through the man's neck and exited through the right ear of which there was nothing left. One hell of a shot or was this particular young Bergstrom just lucky? Sometimes that was all it took.

Larsen had been watching everything from the engine footplate and saw Olsen approach.

"Ready to move when you are sir. Just say the word and I'll run that lot off the track for you." Larsen pointed at the trees straddling the track. Everything alright is it sir?" Olsen pursed his lips.

"We lost Peter Bergstrom and that idiot Bjerklund." The smile on Larsen's lips faded.

"Jesus! Poor Rolf. I thought Harald looked a bit grim. Christ they must be devastated. Shit. Bastards. Bloody bastards." Olsen pulled himself aboard. It was a bad business. All of it. What the youngster failed to realise, rightly so in the circumstances, was that fifteen people had just lost their lives. Somewhere they each had a mother or brother or a lover waiting for them to return. In war there were no winners. Young Larsen was right in one respect. It was a 'shitty' business by any standards of humanity. But one they would all have to pursue, until the end. Whatever that might be.

Hvitby. Dovrefjell Mtns.

Larsen drew the train neatly to a halt before the long station building then threw the lever over towards the far end of the cab. He leaned out. Slowly the giant wheels began to move in the opposite direction. Larsen looked anxiously down his left hand stretched taut nervously tapping at the regulator handle. The wheels gave a sudden sharp burst of spin then just as suddenly gripped the steel rails. Gently the clanking wagons began to roll backwards the way they had come. Astrup stood ready track side to throw the point lever as the huge metal bulk hissed impatiently by. He waved. Larsen gave a sharp toot on the steam whistle and pulled the long lever back in place once more. He let out a long low gasp of relief then smiled. Engine driver 'first class'? Well almost!

"Look Sir -. There. Beyond those trees and the coal bunker. That's the same car we spotted in the forest. At the German barricade -." Harald Bergstrom jabbed an excited finger in the car's direction. A lone figure stood reclining against the car's rear window. He was dressed in civilian clothes and wore a trilby hat. Olsen hitched at the strap of his machine pistol and put up his hand to wave at the shadowy figure. The figure returned the wave. One of the locals. A Norwegian, from his relaxed demeanour

"There. You see. One of the local rifle club making sure we're alright. What did I tell you? You're beginning to see Nazi's behind every bush and tree Bergstrom."

Down on the road Fredrick Kraft smiled grimly to himself. That was the train with the 'gold'. He was sure of it now. If he couldn't pick up the trail of his primary quarry then the recovery of this as a secondary target would prove very lucrative indeed. There was a lot to be made in getting the information back to Dombas and his German contact as soon as possible.

Trollheim. Dovrefjell Mtns.

It was as Borg had said. Narrow, slightly curving and the claustrophobic sheer rock faces either side made it an ideal 'bolt hole'. Olsen signalled for Larsen to cut the steam.

"Just perfect Sergeant. It will be a miracle if they spot us here." Borg was pleased with himself and grinned his yellowing teeth into a wide smile; including those not his own and made from whalebone.

"Yes sir. Thought you'd like it sir. About the men sir. It's been almost two days sir. I thought I might set a guard and stand the rest down sir?"

"Two days? God – so it has. Yes. Of course Sergeant. As soon as you can." Borg gained the steps of the footplate.

"Captain Sir! Up front Sir!" Larsens' curt warning brought Olsen's machine pistol to the ready. Borg leaned out. A figure was approaching from along the tracks.

"It's alright sir. I recognise him. It's Hvaldal. The station master. He's harmless enough sir." Borg got down on the track.

"Welcome, welcome and almost doubly welcome Captain. We have been expecting you -." gasped the perspiring visitor. "– Mr Borg. Good grief. Is that you? I thought you had died. You must be the oldest ex-railway employee this side of Lillehammer -!"

"Cheeky beggar." growled Borg extending his hand and shaking the man's hand warmly. The stationmaster turned to Olsen.

"Captain. Please tell the King we have arranged suitable accommodation for him and his people in Trollheim. We are delighted he is safe and well." Olsen looked at Borg.

"Yes. Well I'm sure His Majesty would be very grateful to you for all the trouble you have gone to – But unfortunately he's not here -." replied Borg.

"Oh!" The stationmaster took a step backwards then smiled. "Ah! Then if His Majesty is not here, yours must be the gold train -."

"Gold train. What on earth makes you think we are carrying gold?"

"Come, come, Mr Borg. All the stations in the area know there is one train carrying the King and one train carrying the 'gold'. So, no King? Must mean 'gold' – Yes? Logical really Mr Borg." Borg shrugged his shoulders and looked up at Olsen.

"Logical really Captain sir." he mimicked. Olsen chewed at his bottom lip. A habit he had when confronted by a dilemma. This was getting ridiculous.

"Alright, Hvaldal is it? So we are the 'gold' train. Who else knows about us – apart from half of Norway?" Hvaldal blinked. Then smiled at the Captains little joke or at least he thought perhaps it was.

"No-one. Just the station staffs. They have to know these things. We can't not know about trains on the lines – otherwise, well, they hit each other. Don't they?"

"What I meant was, do the local population know what our cargo is or are they expecting the King?"

"Only the staff knows of your two trains Captain. We haven't spread the news about the King or yourself. Too many of those NS people on the loose at the moment. They can't be trusted. Oh. We do have about twenty riflemen stationed in the town. Would you like I send them down to you. Extra protection -?" Olsen shook his head.

"No. The fewer people know we are here the better. Less chance the Germans will get to know." Olsen got down from the footplate and made his way down the side of the train. Borg and the station master followed.

"There is something you can do. Take a couple of my men. We need a baggage car. We have a couple of dead bodies that require removal; otherwise the air in the boxcar will be getting a little strong in a few hours time. I would like you to arrange for them to be taken back to their respective homes. Do it on the railway's budget. After all, they did die in the service of their respective countries. I presume that will be in order?" Olsen stopped by the boxcar containing the two bodies.

"If anyone should raise a complaint Captain I will tell them as the King's representative your orders had to be obeyed. If they wish to take it further they had better make their complaint to His Majesty – in person. That should shut them up." Hvaldal smiled showing a full mouth of near perfect teeth.

"Corporal!" Harald Bergstrom appeared in the half open doorway.

107

"You and Lerdal. Go with the stationmaster. He will give you instructions." Bergstrom gave a nod and before leaving cast one long look back to the body of his dead brother now laid out with his arms folded across his chest. His head was covered with a large handkerchief on which had been placed his international skiing cap with the Norwegian flag boldly embossed.

"Friend of his was he?" asked Hvaldal. Olsen grimaced.

"Friend of us all. They all are. That was his youngest brother. We are all brothers here. Remember that." The stationmaster nodded and couldn't resist craning his neck to get a better view of the two cadavers.

"Yes. Of course -." he mused thoughtfully.

It was only a microsecond but enough not to escape Harald Bergstrom's keen hunter's eye as the three men made their way towards the deep snow layered skirt of the forest.

"Down." he snapped grabbing Hvaldal by the scruff of the neck and pushing him headlong into a dive.

"What is it?" asked Lerdal who on command had dropped like a stone. Bergstrom waved his hand impatiently. He wasn't sure. Something lower down the slope? His mind playing tricks?

"Do you mind young - - - ." Hvaldal was not impressed with having his head buried in six inches of frozen snow. Bergstrom slapped his glove over the man's mouth. There it was again. This time a series of bright silver flashes then a feint humming noise on the breeze.

"Into the trees." he ordered gruffly, instinctively grabbing the stationmaster by the collar and half dragging him to his feet. The distance was about six metres. Bergstrom made it in four leaps.

"Enemy aircraft Sir -!" Eric Krefting had heard the whisper of the aircraft's engine at about the same time. Olsen looked up.

"Take cover." he hollered and watched as half a dozen forms melted swiftly from his line of sight before throwing himself under the nearest wagon. Borg was there before him. There was a grunt of pain. "Sorry Sergeant. Didn't see you there." Borg looked at him in amazement. He was twice the bulk of the lean faced Captain.

From high above the rim of the rock face came the aeroplane, German as distinguished by the sharp contrasting black crosses on the underside of its grey silver wings. Olsen wasn't sure the type. A reconnaissance aircraft certainly. There was very little indication of heavy armaments.

The German aircraft droned on its set course taking it directly across the deep cutting. Half a minute later and it was gone.

"He's missed us sir. Idle bastard." growled the sergeant, relieved but at the same time annoyed. Some pilot! Lazy. It was to be hoped the British pilots were better trained. Typical of the young generation. Olsen caught the annoyance in Borg's voice and smiled as he crawled back over the stone hard trackbed.

"Well that's the first one Borg. Better have the men rig up those tarpaulins, pronto. The next time we might not be so lucky." Borg saluted from his prone position and heaved his bulk off the ice-cold ballast.

Olsen had reached the end of the train and had just turned when a huge black shadow threw the cutting into dark relief. Startled Olsen looked up. Above and coming down almost level with the rim of the cutting was the German aircraft. He could plainly see the German pilot hunched towards him; his cockpit lit up to the rear like a ballroom candelabrum. No low drone this time. Just a roar as the plane flashed by overhead and down the length of the train. Olsen stood rooted to the spot. Then it began to happen. The cutting led to a quarry that was still in operation a few of the summer months each year. The German pilot must have turned his head to observe the reaction his surprised arrival had wrought for when he resumed his place there was nothing in all directions but massive stone walls rising far up into the sky. Olsen watched in horror as the planes wings dipped frantically first in one direction then in another. The pilot attempted to pull back and turn almost at the last second. But it was much too late. There was a resounding crash of metal as the plane's nose gouged out a huge crater in the quarry face. An explosion followed instantly, blowing the pinioned debris outwards in a ball of blackened orange flames. Olsen gawked stupidly. Large ragged forms of mangled steel and flaming detritus tumbled and cartwheeled around the gaunt grey walls, a cacophony of disassembled noises echoing around and around the deserted man-made bowl. Slowly the noises ceased. Then what few pieces there remained of the aircraft's tail plane disengaged from the burning black hole and slid clattering down onto the snow-bound landscape below. The whole episode had taken less than four or possibly five seconds. To Olsen and the rest frozen in horror at the suddenness of the German plane's fate, it had seemed like an eternity.

"Good God!" said a voice at Olsen's side. Olsen pulled himself out from his semi-comatose state and looked around. He removed his hat and wiped dazedly around the inner brim his head shaking from side to side.

"Is he?" he replied. Borg glanced up questioningly. "What was all that all about then – Sergeant. Huh? Not much goodness going on there as far as I can see. Do you seriously think that poor bugger is responsible for those idiotic madmen in Berlin? Eh? Good God indeed! There is something wrong with your use of words." Borg puffed out both his cheeks and looked disconsolately around. He hadn't really meant it in those terms.

Harald Bergstrom coughed up something anti-social from the back of his throat and spat it out.

"That's one less of the bastards to worry about. Good riddance," he snarled and looked over his shoulder. "Bastard. No you bloody don't. Swine -." Lerdal looked at him askance. Bergstrom leapt into the air and plunged off running down the slope. From behind a clump of firs a lone figure was moving swiftly away.

"Erik! Up top. See if you can cut him off." Bergstrom's urgent cry echoed loudly through the deadness of the trees.

The car's tyres were already spinning for a grip on the concrete mud covering of the forest roadway when Bergstrom broke wildly from the tree line and crashed to his knees. He levelled his machine pistol and fired off a long arching burst. Splinters of mud and ice fountained a sharp tattoo around the rear of the vehicle, which for all the attention of the sharp metal projectiles leap crazily away. Bergstrom swore and raised his gun to loose off a second burst. The car appeared to gather speed then slid across the road at an angle as the rubbers on the rear tyres gave way. Bucking erratically it side- swiped a small sapling snapping the tree clean in half with the sound of a pistol shot before slewing agonisingly to a stop. Bergstrom struggled to his feet and set off in pursuit.

At the train Harald Bergstrom's cry and the sounds of firing spurred Olsen into action. Leaving Ringe in charge he gathered Borg and Astrup and set off into the forest towards the direction of what could only have been more trouble.

For Fredrick Kraft he began to realise today he had taken one too many chances. In his greedy bid to keep track of the train and its glittering contents he had been foolhardy and careless. Today's throw of the dice was not proving at all beneficial to the continuance of his good health.

Bergstrom had anticipated the driver's movements, saw him fall into the tangle of undergrowth and with a yell of triumph leapt at him from above. The two men fell backwards grappling wildly at each other for a hold. They rolled, feet, legs, knees, hands even teeth, snarling abuse as together they crashed into the bottom of the roadside ditch. Bergstrom had misjudged the man's smaller frame. He was tough. Sinewy. Unfortunately the roll had Bergstrom underneath the man's clawing hands. He felt the fingers searching for his throat and from the corner of his eye saw something swinging towards his head. He instinctively braced himself for the blow to fall when suddenly the twisted orifice of the mouth only centimetres from his face suddenly sagged loose and the wildness of the eyes changed to one of utter surprise. The hands fell away and the man pitched forward crushing the whole of Bergstroms head sideways into the snow. When the darkness gave way he found Lerdal staring angrily down at him. "You bloody idiot. You had him in your sights. Why didn't you shoot him?" Bergstrom struggled to lift the limp limbs aside and gasped for a much appreciated lung-full of air.

"I wanted the swine alive. He's one of ours if I'm not mistaken. A Quisling bastard."

"Quisling or not. He could have killed you!" snapped Lerdal. Bergstrom thought otherwise but from Lerdal's furious glare decided not to argue the point. He looked down at the prone figure. A large area of the snow was beginning to turn a bright red beneath the man's head from where the butt of Lerdal's rifle had smacked his skull. Lerdal looked at the man and took his cue from the frown that had appeared on Bergstrom's face. He bent down and removing his gloves felt under the man's collar for the side of the neck.

"Well -," he said at length, "- he's dead anyway. I must have clouted him too hard." Bergstrom gave a sigh and grit his teeth.

"Shit! Now we'll never know will we?" he snapped angrily.

"Got him have you Corporal?" From above came Olsen's voice. Bergstrom winced and made a face at Lerdal.

"Yes sir. Sorry sir. He's dead. Erik here had to give him a tap on the head – well more of a bash really. Anyway I'm afraid the swine's head couldn't take it sir, he's definitely no longer with us." Olsen slid down the slope and gave Lerdal his machine pistol to hold.

"Did he now. Well. That's the way it sometimes goes. Never mind. Let's see who he is shall we?" Olsen emptied the dead man's pockets and laid the contents out across the man's back. A small mirror, a pocket compass and a wallet. Olsen held the mirror between his fingertips and turned it until it caught the sun. A pattern of bright dancing lights flickered off the surrounding trees.

"Now we know how that German pilot knew where to find us. We have ourselves a turn-coat I do believe." He flipped open the wallet. "Kraft – Fredrick. Well, well, and what have we here-?" Olsen drew out a well-thumbed piece of paper. It was a Nasjonal Samling membership card.

"One of Quisling's people. Surprise? I think not."

"That being the case sir. The German's are bound to have us pin-pointed by now. Shouldn't we be getting back sir?" said Borg. Olsen pocketed the man's belongings and got to his feet.

"Astrup. Go back to the train. Tell Lieutenant Ringe he's to be ready to move at dusk. The Sergeant and I will go with the stationmaster. Tell Ringe if we are not back by 1900 hours he's to go without us. If the Germans come, they will have to get passed us at the station house. If you hear firing I want no heroics.

You're to leave immediately. Go hell for leather for Andalsnes. Don't stop for anything. Is that clear?" Astrup snapped to attention.

"Yes Captain Sir. Very clear Sir." Astrup disappeared in a flurry of disturbed snow.

"Do you expect they will come soon sir?" Borg's concerned features expressed his most innermost thoughts. Olsen wiped at his lips before replacing his gloves and reclaiming his gun from Lerdal's shoulder. He smiled but he knew it wasn't a smile oozing confidence.

"No Sergeant. Not if we can help it. Let's go shall we -?"

Trollheim Mountain Railway Station.

Sometimes two heads were better than one. In Lerdal's case that was certainly true.

"They were zipped in an inside pocket sir." Lerdal dropped the items on the desk. A packet of cigarettes, a box of matches, a set of keys, not belonging to the man's car and a red handkerchief. Borg sifted through them then opened the flap of the cigarette packet. He squinted at it closely.

"There's a telephone number on here sir. Dovre 295? It wouldn't be his own number. Not according to the address given on his ID card.

"Isn't Dovre still held by the Germans?" asked Hvaldal. Olsen flipped the leather closure of the wallet back and forth thoughtfully.

"Do you know what I am thinking Sergeant? I'm thinking that our dead traitor has been getting his orders from our German friends, our Oberleutnant in Dovre perhaps? The one I spoke with this morning -?" Borg didn't reply but didn't doubt his Captain's words. Olsen continued.

"If we assume our German friend wasn't overly convinced by my impersonation – it's just conceivable he sent our Mr Kraft to check up on us."

"Either that or they thought it less wasteful than using aircraft trying to find us sir." Borg brushed thoughtfully at his moustache. Sergeants weren't paid to think beyond certain perimeters.

"What say I phone this number? See who answers?" mused Olsen.
Sergeant Borg had gone beyond his brief with Olsen's last question.

"Whatever the Captain says sir. In for a crown in for a thousand sir."
Olsen picked up the telephone receiver and studied the dial.

"Quite Sergeant. Only in this case – tens of millions don't you say?"

The German telephone operator held one hand over the mouthpiece of the head set and leaned back from the switchboard.

"Herr Oberleutnant! Herr Kraft - -." The operator pulled the head set from around his neck and held it out. Oberleutnant Holst clapped one of the round cups to his ear.

"Kraft? Is that you Kraft?"

Olsen grinned a huge smile and stuck his thumb up in the air.

"Oberleutnant. You have been informed of my precise location? I expected you would be sending me my orders. Your messenger hasn't called a second time. Is there a problem?" Olsen ran his thumbnail along the hard plastic edge of the telephone mouthpiece.

"What? What is that you say? This is a very bad connection. Too much interference. Speak German. Are you trying to tell me my aircraft hasn't returned for a second search?" Olsen switched to German and continued scrapping at the mouthpiece.

"Yes. Are you saying you have sent out another aircraft?"

"What? It doesn't matter. I have the siding marked on my map. The stupid idiot has probably flown into one of the mountains up there. Cocky little strutters those Luftwaffe."

"What? I didn't catch that. Luftwaffe? What did you say?" grinned Olsen beginning to enjoy himself.

"I said – Never mind what I said. It's not important. What are they doing now?

"Now? They are going to stop here for a few days. That's what the stationmaster has been saying. After that I expect they will make a dash for the coast -."

"Good. Well done Kraft. Keep your head down but keep your eye on them. Wait until I get there – unless they make a move. Afterwards you can come back with us and the gold to Dovre. You will be very well rewarded for this Kraft. I will make sure you are mentioned frequently in my report. Good man." The line went dead. Olsen replaced the receiver on its cradle.

"He didn't suspect anything sir?" asked Borg.

"Nothing. Not a thing. They are coming for us. Paratroopers probably. I doubt they will risk it by road -." Olsen went to the window. "Unlikely they will try a drop tonight. There's snow coming. South-west looking at those clouds. No. It's far more likely they will come first thing in the morning. I know I would." The sergeant looked at Hvaldal then back at his Captain.

"Then let's hope you are right sir." he said slowly not unaware of a slight doubt creeping into Olsen's eyes.

Lomshurrungen – Gudbrandsdal Valley.

This was as far as this train was going. From the conversation below his head Gram had gleaned that and far more. They had stopped somewhere beyond Dovre on the Dombas main line. The train, of all the trains to choose from, had been stopped by German paratroopers who had blocked the line and taken over control. None of the few passengers had been approached by the German troops. It appeared all the Germans wanted was a lift further up the line where they now intended to erect another barricade against further railway traffic. Gram tried rubbing some feeling back into his lower limbs. His feet had gone totally numb hours ago. And it was snowing again.

The mountains of the Lomshurrungen reached beyond three thousand metres above sea level and ran in a winding spine first to a peak and then off down the valley to the inland port of Andalsnes. But to reach the port by its quickest route Gram would have to follow the line of the valley, the line of the German advance. To avoid this would mean travelling at a higher level. He was now on foot having left his skies buried on the outskirts of Lillehammer. Not that his skies could be of any great use from here on in.

The Norwegian driver had shunted the rake of wagons into a siding and left taking his engine with him. There were no guards. Apart from Gram himself, there was no cargo. He settled down in the corner of the last wagon next to the 'brake van' and opened a tin of pears. A kind donation from the NS Quislings at the logging camp. The pears were quite delicious, removing the pangs of hunger that rumbled alarmingly from his stomach whilst slating his rasping thirst. He must remember to cram his water bottles with some of the fresh snow now coming down like a thick blanket and in which he must somehow avoid leaving any tracks when he left.

Gram intended to wait until dusk. The night would come earlier with so many snow clouds settling across the valley. He closed his eyes and tried to remember less stressful times. There were many, indeed plentiful, but none as exciting or remotely as dangerous as now. Somehow, strangely, he felt he was just as happy now, if not more so.

Trollheim Station.

Any delay in moving the gold might prove disastrous. Olsen hadn't wanted to alarm Borg or the stationmaster but inwardly he knew the lure of such a prize for the German Oberleutnant could prompt the man to take risks he wouldn't normally.

"I will see if I can raise Hagan. We should try to move as soon as possible." The relief on Borg's face was plain to see.

"What if we can't go through to Andalsnes tonight sir?"

"Then we go into the mountains. By pack-mule if necessary." Olsen took up the telephone again. "Trollheim? This is Captain Olsen. Do you know who I am?" There was a pause then, "Yes, that's correct. I need a safe line to Andalsnes urgently. Can you do that -? You can. Good man. Call me back as soon as you have a connection." Olsen replaced the receiver. To Hvaldal. "Can we trust them?" The stationmaster nodded and added. "We have any dubious characters under surveillance."

"Good. Now. Do you know the Chief of Police? We shall need all the trucks you can find. At least twenty if not more if we are to move all the bullion. Find him and as much help as you can muster. Phone me here when you know what's available." Hvaldal nodded and made for the door. Borg waited until he had left.

"We shan't get far in this weather Captain Sir. Not by road."

"Neither will the Germans Sergeant. It works both ways." Just then the telephone buzzed. Olsen snatched it up.

"Yes? Yes, this is Olsen." A familiar voice came down the line.

"'Fridtjof'. Good to hear from you. Many thanks for your timely message. They dropped about four hundred of the bastards on the town and across the harbour. We have them bottled up. We should have them netted by the morning. How are things with you?" Olsen chose his words carefully.

"I'm being squeezed Colonel. I was hoping to come down your way tonight?"

"Tonight! No sorry. Not tonight. It's still far too dangerous. The woods are swarming with dozens of small groups of them. Give it a couple more nights with these temperatures and the cold will finish them off. What the cold doesn't – we will. Can't you wait it out until then?" It wasn't what Olsen had wanted to hear.

"No. Not really sir. If I can't come through to you, I will have to go back on the road."

"The road! Damn hell of a choice Captain! Look. The best I can suggest is you contact me every twelve hours or so. Let me know where you are. I will send help up to you as soon as I can. When it's safe I will contact you and give you my best advice. Sorry Johan. It's the best I can do – for now. Good luck." It was pointless arguing with a man like Hagan. If the Colonel said it wasn't advisable, then it wasn't. Hagan was a good commander. Often taking chances when he believed the odds might fall in his favour.

"Bad sir?" Borg had poured them both a shot of schnapps. Olsen took a sip of the cold liquid and stretched his lips. Not the best he had ever tasted but close, very close and any way there was no point in leaving it around for the Germans to plunder.

"We're going into the mountains." declared Olsen and proceeded to pour the whole of the contents of the glass down his throat in one. The liquid warmed the pit of his stomach, certainly more so than the thought of taking his men up to where the weather now closing in could swallow them whole – without trace.

Douvre Telephone Exchange.

The buildings or large parts of them displayed the end results of a major battle. Huge ragged holes pockmarked the masonry and fractures some a metre wide split one room from another. None of the windows had any wooden pieces left in them. Oberleutnant Holst was in the process of loudly castigating his sergeant, Fahnenjunker Buttner, who was now wishing it had been the Oberleutnant who had received the critical head wound instead of the Major.

"Not possible! Not possible! A German officer does not use that word Sergeant. Explain yourself?"

"The latest weather reports are just in Oberleutnant sir. Heavy snow! Storms moving in rapidly from the Jotenheim mountains sir. All aircraft are being grounded sir -."

"Grounded! Grounded! Grounded for how long?"

"For several hours sir. Probably most of the night sir."

"Most of the night? What kind of war are we fighting here? Eh? Fahnenjunker. Tell me that?" Buttner had no wish to answer. He was only the blasted messenger. The authors of the order were sitting snug and safe in their airfield barracks some kilometres south.

"A –er- difficult one sir. In these temperatures. But if Oberleutnant wants to go to Trollheim tonight we could do it before dawn by car – sir."

"Car? Car? Are you stark raving mad Fahnenjunker? Haven't you heard – half the British Army are digging in near Dombas?"

"Yes sir. But we could by-pass Dombas. If we go south, pick up the main road near Rauma. From there it's only fifteen miles to Trollheim – Sir." Holst staggered to a halt and stopped his pacing. He swung around.

"We could Sergeant? You are sure of that are you?"
Buttner crossed all his fingers behind his back and ran through a silent prayer.

"Yes Oberleutnant Sir-," he replied, "Given enough will we most certainly could."

Dovrefjell Mountains.

The new location lay five kilometres east of Trollheim. A narrow forest road gave access, well hidden from above and easily camouflaged by dragging a few small firs and undergrowth into place to mask the entrance. The snow now falling would do the rest.

At the end of the road a logging camp which consisted of three large buildings, a sawmill, a bunkhouse, a canteen and an office with adjoining tool and fuel store. Various smaller units dotted the area forming a semi-circular ring around a bark-layered forest clearing. Most of the largest trucks managed to find cover. Those that couldn't were driven into the girdle of trees and liberally layered with fir branches. Again, in less than an hour the whole area would be comfortably secreted under a blanket of new snow. There would be no tracks for the Germans to follow. Olsen was pleased with himself.

Before leaving Trollheim Olsen had left instructions with Hvaldal, the stationmaster, on how to handle the Germans when they arrived. As before there were to be no heroics. Accompanying the 'Fridtjof' team were sixteen local volunteers from the Trollheim Rifle Club. Olsen had them take up guard duties to allow himself and his men to get some well-earned rest. The weather was getting worse. High winds began whipping up the heavy snowflakes breaking them down into a wall of white that soon took on portends of a blizzard. In the darkness of the bunkhouse Olsen's thoughts went out to his friend Arne, Major Ording and the huddle of precious charges under his protection. It was to be hoped they too had kept an eye on the changing temperatures and found some adequate cover in time. From the violent shrieking sounds now penetrating the thick wooden walls the blizzard had taken on storm proportions, a condition that up here on the lee of the northern Trondelag could last for days.

Lesjaverk. West of Dombas.

Even the chains manacled to the rubber tyres seemed to be of little help as the snow on the metalled roadway grew thicker and thicker. At this high point almost vertical walls of snow coated the funnel shaped slope of the mountainsides. There was no vegetation. Nothing could take a permanent hold on these sheer blocks of rock. The biggest danger now lay in snow slides, miniature avalanches as the crust of ice packed snow overhanging the high ridges gave way under their own weight.

Major Ording saw the covered lights of the vehicle ahead come to a stop. The passenger's door flew open and a figure emerged, head cowed against the flurries of snow. The figure disappeared for a few seconds ahead of the car then re-appeared again and staggered back towards them. Ording got out.

"Roadblock sir. About fifty yards -." The young Norwegian soldier shielded his face from the swirling clouds of ice particles whipping along the walls of the ice funnel.

"Did they challenge you?" Ording had to shout to be heard above the howl of the wind.

"No sir. Nothing. I couldn't see anything other than the outline of a vehicle and the trees -." Ording gripped the man's arm and staggered forward. Whatever the problem, in this weather to stay put would be suicidal. They had to keep moving.

It was impossible to make any form of identification of the soldiers who would be manning the roadblock. For one they were nowhere to be seen and for another the driving snow was like trying to see through shimmering reams of mosquito netting. Ording decided to take a chance.

"Have the men take cover wherever possible. If they fire at us, open up with everything we've got. Put the King and the young Prince into the last vehicle and be ready to turn around. If you get a signal from me get the hell away from here, back towards Dombas. Anything happens to me you are to use your own initiative." The young soldier gulped. That he might have to be ultimately responsible for the saving of his country's King and the rest of the Royal family he had never thought possible. This couldn't be right. He was only eighteen. He wasn't even an officer.

Ording took cover behind the passenger door of the leading car and crouched down. German, Norwegian or English? He plumbed for Norwegian. There was a fifty-fifty chance either of the other languages would provoke a hail of bullets as a reply.

"You there. You at the roadblock. Identify yourselves." he shouted at the top of his voice. "Who are you?" There was no reply. He tried again.

"At the barrier. I repeat. Declare yourselves in the name of the King. Identify yourselves or we shall open fire -." At that three figures emerged from behind the vehicle and a voice came back in broken Norwegian.

"Which fucking King?"

"King Harkkon the Seventh." hollered Ording. There was a pause then a voice shouting, only this time in English -.

"Who the bleedin' hell is Harkong the Seventh?" Ording let out a long gasp of relief and began to laugh. Only a real British soldier would have given such a disrespectful answer as that. They had found the Allied front line at last

South of Dovre. Gudbrandsdal. C. Norway.

Her ski jacket covered just the one half of her pert posterior; the other was like a smooth pink marble globe. His fingertips tingled as he traced the rippling mound. She giggled and brought her knee up allowing a small space between flesh and blanket, enough it transpired to allow his hand to glide inwards and down the crease of taught flesh between thigh and groin. He felt the tips of his overly extended fingers brush the mat of velvet hair. That of which he craved lay barely centimetres away. His pulse quickened. Their eyes met in the semi-darkness. He studied her pupils closely noticing the amusement in the curvature of her eyelids and the deep anticipation exuding from the dark blue pools enclosed within. She was ready. So too was he. He had been ready for ages. Solid, hard, so hard and erect it hurt him physically just thinking about it. Her leg rose into the air the inside of her calf sliding rapidly along the exposed surface of his skin. Suddenly she snatched a clawed hand to his lower back and dragged him even closer. Now he would have her. Now was the moment he had been waiting for. A mutual meeting of desires - - -. Damnn. Why was it so cold?

Gram shot bolt up-right and grabbed instinctively for his rifle. It fell with a resounding clatter to the floor. Damnn? What the -? Hell! He hadn't meant to fall asleep. Damnn and blast it! Gram sat gulping in great gasps of the cold air. He rubbed at his face with the deerskin mittens to help clear his head. Damnn it to hell! Then he remembered the girl and felt the dull pain surrounding his lower regions. Such was distinctly out of place considering the circumstances. He took a few seconds to re-align things, realising it had been some days since he had bothered to relieve himself of any sexual urges and looking around couldn't find anything at all to assist him to assuage the problem either. No matter. In a minute or two things would return to normal and the ache in his lower region would disappear. It was better that way. He still needed all his physical strengths to deal with whatever trials and tribulations there may still be ahead. Sex would just have to take its turn in line. He sniggered to himself. There was a 'turn-up for the book'. Sex would have to wait? Things must be bad?

Outside the wind was howling a gale. A gusting flurry of ice particles tossed and twirled in the grey light seeping in through the wooden slats of the ventilators. Gram watched them for a while as he rubbed away the dullness that had etched itself into his immobile limbs. The temperature inside the empty wagon, whilst still reducing each breath to a semi-crystalline cloud, was apparently much warmer than the howling blizzard beyond the double-boarded walls. On the spur of the moment Gram had chosen wisely. Nothing would be abroad in this weather. Not even Arctic polar bears pushed their luck when the elements took to the 'wild side'. As for humans? Superior the Nazi's might think themselves, but not against nature. She would always better them.

Gram had a rummage through his rucksack. Storms, such as now, had been known to last for days. Water wouldn't be a problem but his food stocks were lamentably low. One tin of salted beef, two of pears and a few dried biscuits wrapped up inside his spare pair of socks. Hardly a banquet! Another couple of days and he would begin to go hungry. He settled back. If he had any doubts regarding his decision to involve himself with the plight of his fellow countrymen and his beloved Norway now was far too late to allow them to linger. He should concentrate on one thing and one thing only, getting the 'plans' safely into the hands of the British. Somehow? Otherwise what the hell had it all been about? He listened. The storm was lashing the canvas fabric of the roof. There was little danger the heavily painted fabric would succumb to such a battering. He was safe for now. The shriek of the Arctic wind shredding the frozen branches of the adjoining forest apart like some crazed demented beast did nothing to add to his comfort. Every now and then there would be a thump. The wagon would protest a momentary shudder as pieces of ragged timber rattled off its frozen carcass. The wind was certainly strong enough at the moment to flatten a human body off its feet. One hundred and thirty kilometres an hour at a guess. There was still some way to go before it could rip whole trees from the ground, although it had been known to happen. Gram crouched lower in the corner of the wagon finding security in the two opposing walls. If it did happen there wouldn't just be a small thump and a staccato of muffled rattling sounds – No Sir! Nothing like that at all!

Trollhiem. Dovre Mountains.

At one point Oberleutnant Holst had seriously considered shooting his sergeant and leaving his body suspended by its genitals from any convenient telegraph pole. That was before the blizzard ceased. One minute a howling shrieking beast the next an almost serene crystal indigo panorama of twinkling stars and black jagged peaks. Quite remarkable thought Holst who had never really been one to appreciate nature's staggering abilities or her inherent beauties. Fahnenjunker Buttner had escaped 'eunuchification', as Holst called it, by the skin of his scrotum. One more hour of battling the 'white hell' could well have seen the whole operation abandoned.

The approach to the train was a text book exercise. A blast from Holst's whistle and the sides of the rock face came alive with his men belaying towards their objective machine pistols at the ready. Holst himself led the remainder in a dashing charge along the track bed. With a crash of timbers the doors to the wagons were flung asunder and each blasted with a prolonged burst of automatic fire. It was the same story the length of the train.

"Empty Oberleutnant. There's no-one here."

Holst reached the engine's footplate. A feint glow of red embers cast an eerie reflection across the glimmering metalwork.

"Bastards." spat a furious Holst grappling for the safety catch on his pistol. He had forgotten to release it in his eagerness to get his hands on his 'quarry'.

"Shit." he snarled in anger and hurled the useless weapon at one of the glass portholes in the engines front bulkhead hoping it would at least do some damnage. It didn't. The gun disappeared in a ricocheting whine somewhere across the fuel bunker where it sought refuge amongst the logs and frosted coals. Holst closed his eyes. All that was needed now was for someone to tell him they had arrived too late. Now he would most definitely shoot them – providing he could first find his pistol.

"Bastards!"

Trollhiem covered quite a large area. But at its centre barely twenty dwellings comprised what most would have considered the hub of the community. A deathly silence, bolted doors and even more heavily secured window shutters met the arrival of German staff cars and the accompanying truck filled with heavily armed paratroops. Not even a dog barked. Holst alighted from his car.

"Get the bastards out. I want the lot of them on the road here in five minutes." Buttner scurried away.

To the splintering sounds of breaking glass and timbers and the cries of children savagely torn away from their peaceful slumbers Holst stood in the centre of the road carefully cleaning the more inaccessible parts of his pistol. Every now and then he consulted his wristwatch.

It was eleven and a half minutes before the last of the village's sleeping residents were roughly manhandled into a double line before him. With a final harsh snarl from the German sergeant the assembled crowd grew quiet. Holst raised his pistol to eye level and carefully examined it.

"My name – is Oberleutnant Holst -. "he said in a loud voice. He lowered the pistol to his side. "Today – a train came to your town. It was carrying a very important cargo. Gold bullion -." There was a murmur from the crowd. "– Gold stolen from Oslo by terrorists. This gold is required by the New Order to pay for arming and protecting your country against attack by your enemies – the

British -." Holst paused and slowly scanned along the line of shivering bodies. "- We have just come from your station. The train is empty. Completely empty. To move so much gold in such a short time must have required a great many helpers. Some of you people here perhaps? Now. If you will tell me where it has gone you may return to your beds and continue with a peaceful night's sleep-." A number of heads in the crowd turned. Holst waited for a reply. None came. He felt his anger rise.

"You damnn Norwegians -." he exploded. "You have no damnn gratitude. We come to your country to protect you and this is how you repay us? Well my friends. We have another side to our generous characters. One that I can assure you knows how to repay your fucking treachery -." Holst screamed the last few words. "If I do not have the information I require in the next ten seconds three of you will be shot. If that doesn't produce the answers I need, three more will be shot, then three more and three more. This street will run with the blood of your children before your eyes – Do you understand?" Holst raised his pistol into the air and advanced two paces forward. He began to count.

"One-two-three-four-five-six- -."

"The train wasn't carrying gold. It was carrying the King and his Ministers." Holst scanned the back row for the owner of the voice. Hvaldal stepped from between two of the older women in the front row.

"The King!" growled Holst contemptuously. "The King of Norway? Travelling in a goods train? Do you take me for an idiot? Cretin. You will be the first to be shot you arsehole. Sergeant! Take this damnn fool away and shoot him." There was a shriek of despair from Hvaldal's rear and an excited chatter of angry voices. Buttner moved quickly to Holst's side.

"It might be the man is telling the truth sir. Remember Richter. You sent him to Dombas in the first place to hunt down this King of theirs. Maybe this train was carrying this King and his cronies and not the gold – sir?" Holst fixed the Fahnenjunker with a stare. "But Richter said the driver of the train - -." He stopped. Suddenly his eyes narrowed.

"Richter. Richter. Of course. Stupid. I thought something was wrong. No German officer would ever speak so arrogantly to a fellow German officer -. Huh! Clever bastards. So that was their game." A few paces brought him eyeball to eyeball with Hvaldal.

"Why do you volunteer this information?" He fixed Hvaldal with a glare.

"Because I have a wife and child. I don't wish to see them killed." Hvaldal replied.

"So how is it that of everyone here only you know about the train?"

"Because sir. I am the station master."

123

"Ah! So. You are the stationmaster. That is good. So why Mr Stationmaster does the King of Norway travel in a filthy goods train – eh?"

"Because it was the only train they could find sir." replied Hvaldal. Holst wheeled aside then sprang back and smashed the back of his closed fist across Hvaldals face. Hvaldal reeled but managed somehow to keep his balance.

"You're a liar Mr stationmaster. Show me the house this King of yours is in. Where is it?" Hvaldal pretended the blow had stunned him. He gave a moan and held his head in his hands for a moment or two. It gave him time to think.

"He – he isn't here now. He left. About an hour ago. Three cars. By the forest road. They left by the forest road I swear to you."

"The forest road? What is that? Where is it? Where does it go? Answer me you lying swine." Hvaldal moaned again and rocked his head back and forth as if in great pain.

"The mountains. It goes into the mountains. It's a tourist road. Goes nowhere. It's nothing special Oberleutnant sir." Holst pushed his face up close to Hvaldal's. He whispered, forcing the words out through twisted lips.

"The mountains you say. Nothing special you say. They had better be there Mr Stationmaster -." Holst pulled away. "Sergeant! Make a note. What is your name Mr Stationmaster?"

"Bengt – Bengt Hvaldal sir."

"Good. Well Mr Begnt Hvaldal, stationmaster of this town. If your information proves good you will be well rewarded. If not -." Holst turned to the crowd and in a loud voice. "– I will return and I will shoot you personally myself, together with anyone else I can prove is connected to you or your family -. Is that clear?" Holst waited for a second or two for his words to sink in. "Meanwhile you are all free to return to your homes. Go! Get the hell from my sight -." Holst turned on his heels. "Sergeant. Come. Let us find for ourselves this forest road and this very important Norwegian troublemaker of 'Royal' standing. A King is just as useful a find for us as is his ransom. Don't you think?" Buttner nodded his head. Quite frankly he couldn't have cared less. All the Fahnenjunker wanted was to get out of these blasted freezing conditions and into a warm bed somewhere – preferably with a good willing woman. But that would be asking far too much in this man's army!

Dovrefgell Mtns.

Borg spun about his rifle coming level with his shoulder. It was barely discernible but the feint crunch of snow underfoot reached his ageing ears.

"I'm sorry Sergeant. I didn't mean to startle you." Olsen emerged from behind one of the trees.

"You didn't sir." replied Borg looking off beyond where the Captain stood. "Is everything alright sir?" he growled suspiciously.

"Eh? Oh. Yes. Sorry. The er- camp. It lacks some of the finer facilities. The er- personal ones. If you know what I mean?" Borg grinned. He understood perfectly. Laughter and the sound of excited chatter came from the direction of the camp.

"They're getting a bit boisterous sir. Shall I go quieten them down?" Olsen kicked some of the snow away from the top of his boot.

"No. Not just yet. Give them ten more minutes then get them turned in. The local men can stand the watch. It's been a very long day."

"Yes sir. Shouldn't you also turn in sir? It's time you yourself took a rest-Sir." Olsen smiled then laughed.

"Borg. You remind me of my father. Never order the boss to do something when you can suggest it -. Well. Maybe you're right."
The blizzard had abated. The whiteness now replaced by a grey lingering hue that in the distance promised good weather for the rest of the night.

"Two hours. Wake me in two hours. You and I, Astrup and the Lieutenant can take turn and turn about. Two-hour shifts. That way we keep everything together -."Olsen turned to go. Borg cleared his throat.

"You've kept everything together very well so far sir. They should give you a medal for all this lot sir. If you don't mind me saying so." Olsen stopped in his tracks.

"A medal. Hmm. Do you think so? There's a thought." Olsen paused. A medal for young Bergstrom without a doubt. But it would be little comfort to his distraught parents. God how he hated and loved this blasted war. The excitement, the risks, the immense pleasure knowing you were fooling the enemy and running him ragged. The dangers. The loyalty of the men. The love and deep affection they had for each other, for their families, for their country. Their own personal pride. 'What did you do when the Nazi's came daddy?' 'What was that ribbon and that shiny thing for -?'

"A medal?" Olsen turned. The sergeant was shouldering his rifle and fumbling at his greatcoat pockets. "The lads certainly. And you Borg. I wasn't convinced when you offered your services back in Lillehammer. For that I apologise unreservedly. You have been all any officer could have wished for and more. I don't think we would have got this far without you." The old sergeant bristled with pride and came expertly to attention.

"That is kind of the Captain to say sir. Only doing my duty sir. Like any good loyal Norwegian sir." Olsen laughed loudly.

"No Sergeant Borg. Much, much better than your average loyal Norwegian. Believe me. Much better."

The leading car fishtailed twice before pointing its bonnet to the sky and leaving the track. If such could have been called 'a track'. Knee deep in loosely piled snow and a solid concrete banana-skin ice sheeting over its rutted surface. Two figures emerged arms flailing in an effort to keep upright in the waist high undergrowth. Holst's driver slued to a halt. Sergeant Buttner swung from the front passenger door and plunged down the small incline.

"Imbeciles. Fat heads. Can't they do anything right?" Oberleutnant Holst bounced in anger in the rear of the vehicle. Buttner returned his breath clouding out the warmed interior of the car.

"Get that damnn car back on the road." snapped Holst angrily. The German sergeant winced.

"Sorry Oberleutnant sir. The car has a flat tyre." Holst fixed him with a glare.

"Then get it fixed – idiot." Buttner snapped off a quick salute.

"Yes sir. Right away sir." The sergeant turned on some of the men who had got down from the truck and snarled off a series of commands.

The forest road proved to be no more than an upgraded logging track that to Holst's way of thinking should never have been given a vehicular access status in the first place. If the King of Norway and his entourage had passed this way the blizzard had done sterling work in obliterating any signs of it. Holst decided there was time for him to stretch his legs. Get the circulation going again. A walk to the tree line and back. Fifty metres or thereabouts.
Buttner was waiting for him when he returned.

"A few more minutes Oberleutnant sir. There doesn't appear to be any other damage." Holst nodded and turned his attention to scanning the trees and the ridge rising beyond.

"He's here. Somewhere near. I can feel it in my bones Fahnenjunker." He paused to raise a gloved hand to shield his eyes from the greyness of the night sky. "Where are you, you old privileged one? Where? Where?"
Buttner sensed his officer had acquired a more benevolent mood after his little jaunt. He chanced his luck.

"The men sir. They could do with a short rest sir. Something to eat? A warm drink?"

"A rest!" Holst turned around in astonishment. "A rest? Are you serious? Do you think this King of Norway will be taking a rest?" Buttner pressed home his advance.

"Yes sir I do. I doubt he is having any better a time of it than we are. And sir, he has been running far longer. He can't be very far ahead of us. Not on this road. If we rest our men now -." He stopped and pointed to a small hut a couple of hundred metres away on the edge of the forest. "- in that hut say for a couple of hours. We could send out a scouting party. My guess would be they would find this King's location pretty quickly sir." Holst kept his eyes on the hut. A warm drink and a good fire. The more he thought about it the more the idea appealed to him. And the sergeant was right. It was 'bloody' cold!

It was Astrup's watch and was nearing its end. Borg appeared through the trees with ten minutes more to go. The sergeant wagged a gloved finger along his moustache to remove any ice particles gathered there. Astrup smiled to himself. The old bastard had lost none of his old styled military training and was advancing at a measured pace oblivious to the deep snow barring his way.

"The locals on their toes are they -?" Borg asked. Astrup nodded.

"They look a keen bunch – if you know what I mean Sergeant." he replied. Sergeant Borg unhitched his rifle and handed it out.

"Here. Keep your eyes open. We don't want any mistakes. Look after this for me. I'm going to look for pine cones."

"Pine cones! But Sergeant you won't find any pine cones in this deep snow -!" Borg looked the young boy direct in the eyes and gave a groan.

"For heavens sake use your imagination boy." Astrup cocked his head to one side, frowned a little, then suddenly it struck him.

"Ah! Yes. OK Sergeant. Pine cones it is then -. Only – I usually say I'm going for a crap -." Borg's face showed its disapproval. He moved away grumbling to himself and shaking his head.

Hvaldal was still in hurry when he struggled the last few hundred metres into the logging camp. Olsen had to order him to stop talking so they could understand what it was he was saying.

"– And when – and when – when they found the train – it was empty – they came down to the town -."

"Ooh." gawked Larsen and mimicking a high kicking goose-step. "Der train it is empty mein fuhrer – Er? What was it we were looking for mein fuhrer?"

"Shut up Larsen." snapped Olsen irritably. "Stop pissing about." The young Norwegian just grinned in Olsen's direction. Hvaldal continued.

"The bastards – threatened to shoot us. All of us. If we didn't tell them where you were." Larsen couldn't resist.

"So what did you do?" Hvaldal eyed the boy's grinning countenance.

"Well we didn't ell them. What do you take us for?"

"So what did they do then?" asked Larsen wide-eyed.

"They shot us all dead -." replied Hvaldal seriously. The small clearing erupted with laughter that rolled away beyond the buildings and up the undulating slopes of the narrow valley to become lost in amongst the heavily ice-bound trees.

Higher up the slope and far enough away to catch only the last feint peals of laughter Fahnenjunker Buttner brought the other three men of his patrol to a halt. He motioned for them to squat. Through his binoculars he could make out the tops of wooden buildings and what appeared to be movements amongst the trees. Then from amongst the trees and somewhat closer he detected a lone figure emerging from behind a large overhang of snow. Buttner dropped closer to the ground. Behind him the three paratroopers followed suit. The figure of the man, dressed in a greatcoat and military style hat, paused for a few moments. He appeared to be listening to the sounds of laughter coming from the direction of the buildings. After a moment or two more he moved on, across the hillside but parallel to the trees. He had a strong military bearing and Buttner could now see he sported a fine bristling moustache of white hair.

"It's him. It has to be. Christ Almighty – and he's alone." Buttner felt his pulse quicken. He had been right all along. The Royal party was having just as much difficulty moving across the area, as were they. Here he was. The King of Norway and he Fahnenjunker Buttner had him bang to rights. Buttner couldn't resist a smile. He had visions of the Oberleutnant's face when he returned with his Royal prisoner. Delightful, just delightful!

Borg was adjusting his trousers when he thought he heard the swish of skis. He was about to growl his disapproval that Astrup should have been keeping an eye on him when suddenly a hand appeared before his face and hauled him bodily off his feet. He crashed with a thud into the deep snow. A face came into his line of vision then the point of an automatic pistol.

"My apologises for the rough treatment Your Majesty, but you are my prisoner -." The face spoke in Norwegian but with a harsh German accent. The man's smock and hat left no doubt. A German paratrooper.

"If Your Majesty will agree to come quietly my man will release you. Please nod your head if you understand." Borg felt the hand across his mouth ease a little. He nodded. Slowly with the German to his rear keeping his hand less than a few centimetres from Borg's mouth, he felt a pair of hands hauling him to his feet.

"Tell your man to take his hand away. I have given you my word -!" snorted Borg crossly. The hand disappeared. Borg looked around. They were four in number. A patrol. Borg was cross with himself. If he hadn't had been so engrossed in 'looking for pine-cones' he would have seen them coming. Silly old idiot. Such would never have been the case in his earlier years. For a few moments Borg contented himself with fastidiously attending to his attire. If these Germans thought him to be the King of Norway, he had better act like one.

"Well Gentlemen -." he said at length. "We appear to be outnumbered. Four to one. The odds would seem to be slightly in your favour. You have secured for yourselves a rich prize. My congratulations - -?" Borg looked from man to man.

"Fahnenjunker Buttner Your Majesty. These are some of my unit." replied Buttner.

"Fahnenjunker! Oh dear. I had hoped one of you might be an officer. At least a Major or something higher. What will people say? The King of Norway captured by a German sergeant. Well Sergeant. I warrant there is going to be a promotion in the offering for you for this day's work. Lucky man. So? What happens now?"

"I – er. My officer, Oberleutnant Holst, is nearby. Please be good enough sir to follow me."

"Follow you? I see. And where am I following you to. Where is this officer of yours?" asked Borg.

"About half a mile sir. On the other side of the hill sir. I'm afraid Your Majesty will have to walk -." Borg drew himself up to his full height.

"I see. Well if that's the only way. I suppose I could manage that distance. Surprising as it may seem to you young man, we King's do actually use our feet to get around." Buttner smiled nervously and held out his hand indicating the direction he wished his prisoner to take. Borg squared back his shoulders. He just hoped that Astrup or one of the others might have seen what was happening and had the wit to report back to the Captain instead of trying to rescue him. If not, he didn't relish the thought of what might happen once these Germans discovered their mistake. Especially this Fahnenjunker who would already have his sights set on an Iron Cross and some meteoric rise in status. Borg winced. It hardly bore thinking about.

Astrup had seen and heard everything. From nearby cover his and the sergeant's rifle against automatic machine pistols was a definite mis-match. Borg might also get hit in any crossfire. He waited until the Germans and their prisoner had disappeared over the crest of the hill before high-tailing it back to the logging camp.

East of Dovre. Gudbrandsdal Valley.

When the blizzard ceased, the sensation was similar to sitting alongside a railway line with an inter-city express train thundering by. Suddenly the ear-splitting scream was gone supplanted by a whispering residue of gently wafting breezes tumbling erratically in the beast's wake. The sky cleared to a rolling pasty mist of sleet sodden clouds. Gram sat up in amazement and walking slowly to the door gave it two almighty slams with the side of his boot. The sheet of snow and ice cracked under the onslaught and toppled to the surface of the freshly laid snow below. Gram peered out. The mountains of newly piled snow glared back. He regretted now having left his skis near Lillehammer. Progress on foot through the deep drifts was out of the question. Stupid is as stupid does. The words flashed through his brain. There was nothing for it now but to go back to the valley road and try for a vehicle or perhaps another train going west. That would mean a walk into Dovre. And possibly more Germans. 'Bollocks'!

Logging Camp. Dovrefgell Mntns.

"Borg? His Majesty? Well I suppose that figures when you think of it." Olsen's eyes narrowed. "It looks as if the swine believed every word I told him." Hvaldal nodded enthusiastically.

"If I hadn't had been standing beside you so would I. You were very convincing Captain."

"Hm. Too bloody good from the sounds of it -." Olsen scratched at something under the peak of his cap. He hadn't had a decent wash let alone a bath for what seemed ages.

"I suppose we must take it these Germans are not as totally stupid as we think. Once they get Borg back and start questioning him they will soon realise they have the wrong man. You can bet your life they'll beat the crap out of him to get to the truth. We must cut them off before they get him back."

"We outnumber them at least two to one. Let me take my people. We will surround the hut and take them out." suggested Hvaldal hopefully.

"And the Sergeant?" said Olsen. Hvaldal hadn't got that far in his thinking.

"No. There might be a better way. Astrup. Get me my fancy dress uniform." Astrup disappeared. The stationmaster frowned.

"My Gestapo uniform." said Olsen putting the confused man out of his misery. "Meanwhile. You can gather together your men. I want you to circle the hill. Keep your eye on me. I don't want any shooting until I have the Sergeant in my hands and out of danger. Whatever happens tell your men I am the one in the Gestapo uniform and not to shoot me. I want to keep all I have in one piece, at least for a little bit longer." Hvaldal grinned.

"OK Captain. Don't shoot the ugly one in the Gestapo get-up. Will do sir."
Olsen couldn't help but smile as the eager stationmaster hurried away.

From the lee of the wooden hut Major Holst scanned the opposite tree line through his binoculars. He counted five in number. One more than the total compliment of the sergeant's patrol. Then coming fast from the rear another man on skis. He squinted through the lenses. There was something familiar about the man's attire.

"Damnn. Bloody Gestapo. What the hell -?" Holst followed the man's progress as the figure swept in a large circle to bar the patrols approach.

"Gunshe!" One of the burly paratroopers detached himself from the nearby group.

"Herr Major." Gunshe saluted.

"My ski's- now if you please." rattled Holst angrily.
Gunsche drew himself up sharply and scurried away. Holst raised the binoculars again. Bloody Gestapo. What the hell did they want – interfering in Wehrmacht business? Damnn meddlers.

Olsen didn't mince words. The best form of defence was always a bold attack. On the run in from the hilltop he concentrated on his anger so that by the time he had slammed to a stop before the surprised German paratroopers his face had a look of thunder.

"Sergeant! What the fuck do you think you are doing removing my prisoner without a by-your-leave?" Not waiting for a reply Olsen turned to Borg. "Your Majesty. My profuse apologises. These idiots will be reprimanded for their stupidity." He rounded back on the stunned German sergeant. "You cretin. What do you think you are doing? Can't you see His Majesty is all but exhausted? Release him at once."

"But – but Hauptsturmfuehrer. I – I -." Buttner got no further. Olsen gabbled out a string of oaths and -.

"How dare you argue with me Fahnenjunker. How dare you question a superior officers orders? Release him at once – At once do you hear?" The stupefied Buttner looked at Olsen then at his prisoner. From the corner of his

131

eye he could see the swift approach of the Major. "My officer Hauptsturmfuehrer – my officer -."

Holst slewed to a halt his skis showering a fine spray of the freshly fallen snow over Olsen's uniform.

"Major Heinrich Holst. These are my men Hauptsturmfuehrer. Can I be of assistance to you?" Olsen stepped back and to the side so that the Germans were all before him in a group. Hvaldal and his men should be fixing their positions. Too far away to be of immediate assistance but effective enough to cause some confusion and to stop the Germans in the wooden hut from coming to the help of their patrol. The next few minutes were going to be very tricky. Olsen hitched his machine pistol across his midriff.

"Good morning Major. An unfortunate mistake has occurred. Your men. They have my prisoner. As he doesn't, fortunately, appear to have been injured, I must ask you to order them to hand him over. We can overlook their stupidity in this instance as very little harm has been done." Holst drew himself up then peered at the pathetic figure of Borg. The old Norwegian sergeant was breathing heavily. Climbing the hill had taken its toll. Borg hadn't looked up once since the patrol had stopped walking. The arrival of more Germans and the gabble of guttural conversation had been of little interest to him. He couldn't see how he was going to extract himself from this one. Today might well be the end of his soldiering – for ever? Once they arrived at their destination and they discovered he wasn't who they thought he was, the crap would hit the fan, the fan being he himself.

"Fahnenjunker! An explanation if you please?" growled Holst.

"His Majesty was wandering about alone in the trees Herr Major. There was no guard or any sign of the Hauptsturmfuehrer's men sir. We took him prisoner as per your orders Herr Major." Holst beamed and jabbed his ski sticks pointedly into the snow.

"There you are Hauptsturmfuehrer. The man was escaping. Obviously. You should be congratulating my men for re-capturing him, should you not? My orders, from General von Falkenhorst, are quite explicit. His Majesty is to be returned to Oslo forthwith. The Gestapo must have much better things to do. You will allow my men to proceed with their duties Hauptsturmfuehrer."

"Proceed? My God Major! A little joke on your part? His Majesty is a prisoner of the Gestapo. You expect the Gestapo to take orders from the Army? This is a civilian matter. You have no jurisdiction here -." Olsen got no further. The Major's brow creased and a look of recognition registered in his eyes.

"My God! The voice. You're not -." Holst dropped his sticks and made a grab for his pistol. He got no further. Olsen pressed his finger on the trigger of the machine pistol. A spray of automatic fire sent the group of Germans spinning back. At so close a range it was impossible for him to miss. Olsen moved the weapon back and forth across the tumbling bodies until the magazine was empty. One by one the writhing limbs became still. An unreal silence followed. All Olsen could hear was the sound of his own breathing. Rapid sharp intakes of breath none of which seemed to satisfy a need somewhere deep in his heaving chest.

"Dear God! This is disgraceful. Disgraceful. Germans shooting Germans? This is not a civilised Army. My God, whatever next - -? Borg had raised his head his eyes wide with horror.

"Fucking wake up you blabbering idiot. It's me – Captain Olsen." snarled Olsen angrily. Borg tried to focus his ageing eyes on the figure before him. He didn't manage it. Suddenly both eyes rolled upwards as he collapsed across the snow in a dead faint.

Olsen looked down at him. "Oh brilliant – absolutely brilliant," he muttered. " - Just what I need right now, a limp bag of old bones!"

Further along the valley came a rattle of gunfire. Hvaldal's men had taken the sound of firing as a cue to open up on the remaining Germans clustered around the wooden hut. From above more sounds and the swish of ski's. Astrup, Eric Krefting and Kristian Schwartz slid into view.

"Captain sir. Everything alright?" Schwartz crouched over the prone figure of the old sergeant. Olsen nodded and pointed to the bodies of the Germans whose lifeblood was beginning to blot the pristine snow in large configurations of the brightest crimson.

"You could say that I suppose. The Sergeant is in shock. Check out that lot. Collect anything useful then get Borg back to camp as quickly as you can. He's not to walk. He's had more than enough for one day." Olsen took one last look at the results of his handiwork then, his breathing having returned to normal; he pushed off along the slope in the direction of the ensuing battle.

Several explosions from grenades had set fire to one wall of the log cabin. Hvaldal's men were in cover amongst the trees. The Germans, it was difficult to say how many, were pouring a hail of concentrated fire from the doors and windows. Olsen watched as two of Hvaldal's men disappeared in a flaming gout of explosives from a well-aimed stick-grenade. Olsen cursed. They outnumbered the Germans by two to one but these Germans were trained paratroops and not members of a Sunday afternoon Rifle Club. Bravery was one thing, foolishness quite another. Hvaldal had seen the Captain's approach. He grinned as Olsen sliced to halt alongside and scrambled for cover in the shallow hollow.

"Everything alright? And Borg?" he asked. Olsen nodded.

The cabin stood almost fifty metres away and was set back amongst a clearing of the roadside trees.

"What's your situation here?" With the point of his rifle the stationmaster indicated his men's positions and two of the enemy lying prostrate in the front entrance to the cabin. The hut was surrounded. The Germans couldn't get out. Likewise, to Olsen, neither could Hvaldal's men get in, not without incurring a great many casualties.

"Tell everyone to pull back another fifty metres. The bastards will have to come out eventually. If that fire keeps burning it will be sooner than later. Let them make the next move. Meanwhile I think you and I should work our way around. I want to take a look in those vehicles. My guess is we were not expected. I warrant their radio equipment is stashed there. If so – we have them for sure."

Olsen was correct. The Germans radio and all their reserve ammunition were stored in the back of the lorry. Olsen made a mental note of the waveband. An urgent cry brought them to their feet. Suddenly the air erupted in a cacophony of gunfire and small arms explosions. The Germans were making a break for it. Olsen thought twenty in all, perhaps a few less. Realising the Norwegians had also positioned themselves behind the vehicles the German paratroops scattered out amongst the trees. Olsen with Hvaldal in his wake clutching their skis headed for a narrow defile that ran directly up the sloping hillside. They arrived breathless at the top of the narrow belt of trees. Below twenty metres or more half a dozen German paratroopers slogged their way towards them.

"Grenades? Have you any grenades?" asked Olsen. Hvaldal remove two from his pocket. Olsen clipped on his skis.

"They'll try to cut across then back towards the road. I'll draw their fire. Wait until I'm down to the right of them. Then give them hell." The stationmaster checked the pins on the grenades and nodded.

There was no accuracy involved as Olsen's machine-pistol emptied its magazine onto the onrushing Germans as he flashed across their front. Nevertheless, two of the paratroopers went sprawling from half a dozen ragged bullet holes. A hail of return fire slapped the branches behind him as he crashed for cover behind a dip in the undulating forest floor. More bullets blew tiny eruptions in the snow around him. From above came a movement followed by a violent flash. Two of the Germans literally flew through the air towards his position then crashed lifeless bare ten metres away. Hvaldal's first grenade found its mark. Almost immediately there came another explosion. Olsen watched horrified as Hvaldal's body flew high up into the air then crashed limply down head first amongst the branches of a nearby tree. The result of a grenade. Although where had it come from Olsen couldn't tell? The still smoking body of the stationmaster remained skewered amongst the trees lower branches where it swung grotesquely from side to side under its own momentum. Olsen let out a snarl of anger. The remaining two Germans had stopped, frozen like statues, the explosions and the sight of Hvaldal's body lying lifeless in the broken branches of the tree seemingly transfixing them to the spot. Olsen sprang to his feet and leaped forward. The paratroopers had barely time to react before Olsen was amongst them his machine- pistol punching out holes in their camouflage smocks like a swarm of demented leaf-cutter bees. Both men toppled over backwards, almost dead before they hit the snow. Olsen swung about grabbing for a tree to stem his headlong rush. He levelled his gun and pushed off again. Let one of the bastards be alive. He wanted revenge so badly he could taste it. Hvaldal's body was still swinging; the man's outstretched arms reaching lifelessly for the blood soaked snow. "Bastards. Bastards. Bastards -." Olsen spit out his curses as each of the six bodies received a further injection of steel from his shaking hands. It wasn't necessary to ensure their entrance into their Nazi Valhalla. They were going to hell anyway. Only he wanted to be sure of that and the sooner the better to his way of thinking. German bastards.

It was getting lighter as Olsen made his way back towards the hut. Untangling Hvaldal's body from the tree had been a much more difficult task than he had imagined. The grenade had shattered the frozen branches apart making sharp bayonet hooks that hadn't wanted to release their tormentor to one of its own. Olsen suspected the stationmaster's death had been occasioned by his own negligence. The pin of a grenade was still attached to the man's forefinger. Olsen had been reluctant to try and remove it. At a guess it was Hvaldal's own grenade that had exploded either prematurely or he had fumbled it in the deep snow and been unable to find it in time. Whatever, his loss was a tragedy after all the man had done for them over the past couple of days.

The wooden hut was still burning fiercely. German paratroopers lay all around in various poses of death. Hvaldal's men were collecting whatever weapons and ammunition they could find.

"Captain Olsen." Two Norwegian riflemen approached. "Aage Hanson, Captain of the Rifle Club. Been having a spot of trouble I see." Olsen stared at the man. It was amazing how his countrymen had taken up the habit of understatement. Too many English films. Mind you half the British population was of Scandinavian extraction anyway. Especially the Scots.

"Oh. Do you think so?" Olsen replied. Two could play at that game. Aage Hanson smiled sheepishly.

"Yes. Sorry Captain -." The hillside suddenly reverberated to the sounds of gunfire. Olsen looked up. "A few stragglers. Don't worry Captain, we shall get them all. Every last one of them, of that you can be sure. There will not be any survivors -." Hanson ran his eyes over the area then -. "Bengt?"

The use of the stationmaster's Christian name meant the two men must have known each other reasonably well. Olsen grimaced.

"No. I'm sorry Captain. I'm afraid he didn't make it." Hanson's face dropped, then his shoulders.

"Oh – shit -." He turned away and for a time stared off down the road.

"Damnn it all. How the hell am I going to tell - -? What a bloody mess. What the hell did we do to deserve all this; God Almighty -." Olsen allowed his chin to fall down on his chest. He had no answer for the Rifle Club Captain. After a minute or more the man turned around again. His eyes were moist, his lips set hard against each other. He was using all his inner strengths to keep control of his emotions. Olsen slung his machine pistol across his shoulder.

"How many men did we loose?"

Hanson shook his head. "Seven or eight I think. We also have some wounded. Mostly not serious. We can't take them back to town. The Germans are bound to come looking for this lot sooner or later. We can hide some of them in the outlying farms. Get them back on their feet then depending on our English and French friends look towards what to do next." Hanson rubbed at his eyes. "What about you and your cargo?"

Olsen stared off to where several of Hvaldal's men were re-grouping on the far hillside and to where his own men and the gold awaited his return.

Whatever was his next move it was wiser the fewer people knew about it the better.

"Make it disappear then join the nearest units and kick the shit out of these bastard Germans I suppose." Hanson attempted a smile.

"Very wise Captain. If you should come across any of the Nazi bigwigs in your travels take care to string one of the bastards up for me will you, and – make sure he dies slowly – please!"

Dovre.

German paratroopers were everywhere. Reinforced by numerous drops during the previous day.

Gram made his way slowly amongst them. No one paid him any attention, which he again put down to his NS armband. The centre of the town was a shambles. A major battle had taken place here. Gram turned off the central thoroughfare and found himself on a narrow road flanked both sides by tall imposing houses. There were no Germans he could see but the pavements were busy with local people coming and going about their lawful business as if the war, not the few paces he had come, was another world away. Here again none of the Norwegians paid him any attention. Perhaps the odd hard faced glance as they gained sight of the motif on his sleeve.

From the first floor window of one of the larger houses hung the flag of the National Samlung, a temporary headquarters. The halyards were fastened under the lower sash and the hated flag flapped uselessly against the lower timbers in snagged trails of dismembered jute. That to Gram's mind symbolised all that could be said of these traitorous Norwegians and their psychotic leader. A number of pairs of ski's protruded from the banks of snow heaped along the driveway. Gram helped himself to a newish looking pair, slung them across his shoulder and continued off down the street whistling to himself, not expecting angry shouts from the house's occupants who he correctly surmised would probably be sleeping off the previous week's victories. He turned the corner. Right again! He grinned widely and made towards the outskirts of the town.

Back at the railway station German paratroopers were resting under every conceivable shelter and spilling out in every other direction taking their ease wherever they could. Dovre had never seen so many people in the whole of its history. Store of rations and military supplies littered the yard and platform areas. Gram selected an upturned ammunition box and squatted alongside ration boxes that had been opened for one of the numerous German field kitchens springing up in the rear of the cantilevered platform shelter. Over the next half an hour several of the tins and cartons, embossed with the sign of the 'black eagle', found their way into Gram's haversack. For all he knew they could have contained boot polish. Truth was he wasn't going to hang around long enough to find out? Rucksack bulging and with a number of the tins scouring a path into the muscles across his back he left the goods yard and turned away from the yard in a westerly direction. This was a route that would bring him alongside the advancing German units. Unfortunately it was also the only one that would take him where he wanted to go at the fastest possible speed.

Gram travelled on through what should have been night. The going was arduous. Freshly fallen snow not yet settled or hardened by the northern Arctic winds made for exhausting work. By early morning he had covered less than half the distance to Dombas. Continuous sightings of Germans on the road below were discouraging. He had half expected to hear the sounds of fighting in the distance. Some indication he was nearing his final goal. So far there had been nothing. Not even the odd star flare over the distant mountain peaks.

It was mid-day or thereabouts when Gram had decided to leave the steep valley slopes and was crossing over the first ridge of the forested mountain. The going downhill on the leeward side giving instant relief to his aching limbs and his progress that came much more in keeping with what he had originally envisaged. So engrossed was he to make up time he hadn't spotted the German paratroopers moving down through the trees on the opposite slope. They had obviously spotted him and were taking a line to intercept. Gram counted a dozen or more. With a flick of his body Gram slammed to a stop. Judging the distance, as the crow flies, the Germans were perhaps a kilometre away. Double that for the Germans to be near enough to hail him and a good part of that on the uphill slope. Gram turned his head. The ridge above was perhaps two hundred metres away. Ahead was a dip in the hillside. One good push would take him down then up towards the ridge to within perhaps fifty metres of the top. He would have to scramble the remaining distance on foot but by then the Germans would be well within rifle range. Gram looked back. The leading Germans had changed direction and were now skiing directly downhill adjacent his position. Gram bent his knees in readiness.

In mid-winter the small stream coursing through the valley froze solid. For almost five months of the year one could ski across the narrow strip of pasture land and not realise the stream was there. The first three German paratroops did exactly that until the thin crust of snow covering the icy shallows gave way. With a string of oaths the next two paratroopers slid into a mangled heap as their ski's suddenly shot away beneath them. Their angry cries brought the advanced group to a halt. Gram stared down in disbelief. The remaining Germans were also coming to a halt and looking for a safer passage across the hidden obstacle. With a determined leap Gram took off from his crouched position and shot towards the dip his sticks gouging huge holes in the smooth whiteness of the slope. Behind he could hear howls of anger. The Germans had realised what was happening. Through the wind whistling past his ears he heard the sharp crack of rifle shots. Nothing came near. Gram pushed on almost willing his body to fly up the opposing slope. When eventually his momentum reduced to a slow run he stopped and looked back. The paratroopers had recovered their surprise and were moving rapidly down the valley floor on both sides of the hidden stream. Gram calculated he had two minutes at the most to gain the opposite side of the ridge before the leading Germans would be in range. This was going to be a climb for his life – literally.

Dovrefgell Mountains. Nr Hjerkinn.

Olsen could tell why those that lived here called these mountains the top of the world. The view across the numerous cloud-shrouded peaks was breathtaking.

The convoy of lorries moved slowly nose to tail along the zigzag of road. Larsen was driving with Hansen, who with the death of Hvaldal had elected to guide the convoy up through the treacherous wilds of the narrow mountain roads, sitting sandwiched between them.

"This will take us up to the main road between Hjerkinn and Storen. It's just on the other side of that range of hills," said the Rifle Club Captain pointing. Olsen wiped at the condensation of the window glass. He needn't have bothered; the ice layered on the outside was almost two millimetres thick.

"How long? We're sitting ducks up here for any German plane?"

"At this pace – perhaps an hour. We may be lucky. If the main road is full of 'Allied' units moving up the valley towards Dombas, our German friends will be putting all their efforts into trying to stop them. They won't have time to come looking for us." Hansen's optimism was precariously placed. If the 'allies' had landed in sufficient strength and 'if' their battle plan was to attack through the Gudbrandsval and 'if' they had sufficient by way of heavy artillery, something the Germans had been going to great pains to push northwards and westwards as fast as they could, then perhaps -?

The perimeter around Andalsnes had to remain in Norwegian hands for at least a further three to four days.

"Hm – Let's hope so." growled Olsen.

Six vehicles to the rear Ivor Astrup was feeling decidedly apprehensive. For the last two kilometres he could swear that every now and then small wisps of steam had billowed from beneath the truck's bonnet. Eriksen and the Lieutenant sat alongside heads nodding to the constant bumping and rolling of the vehicles' suspension. Sleep was impossible but both men had been making a brave effort to attain it. As Astrup looked back through the frosted windscreen his worse fears were confirmed. There was a 'pop'; the engine gave a misfire and a gaseous cloud of angry white vapour poured up over the cab.

"Bollocks!" he snarled. "Come on you blundering great cow-frau. Don't start playing stupid games with me now." It was pointless of course. Astrup knew it.

But ranting at the rattling chassis as it hopped along in the foot deep snow somehow made things easier.

"What is it?" asked Eriksen.

"She's overheating." replied Astrup.

"I didn't think all that was from heavy breathing -," quipped Eriksen,

"We had better pull over. Let the rest passed. We don't want to seize-up the engine." Astrup looked for a suitable passing place in the gouged out faces of the surrounding rock face.

Lieutenant Ringe was out and waving on the remainder of the convoy before the truck finally lurched to a stop. Astrup bashed the retaining clips to the bonnet aside and stuck his head underneath. Ringe joined him.

"Well? Have you found anything -?"

"Yep. Lots of things. God knows what they are all for?" Astrup replied.

"You're about as much use as a moulded butter-cream coffee pot." growled Eriksen trying to see passed Astrups hunched shoulders. Astrup slammed the bonnet back down.

"I volunteered to drive the bloody thing not re-build it, arsehole!" Lieutenant Ringe stepped in between them. "Alright the two of you. Let's keep a lid on it shall we?" Astrup shrugged his shoulders and grumbling moved away. Ringe removed his goggles and held them out for Eriksen.

"You had better see if you can get up ahead of them. Bring Larsen back here - ." he pointed to the slope of the valley and the convoy making its way slowly down the winding road. "Tell him to bring some tools – otherwise we might be here forever." Ringe looked at Astrup who still had his back to them.

"Nobody's perfect you know." snapped a still irritated Astrup. Ringe shook his head and motioned to Eriksen who donned his skis and with a nod took off down the mountain. Ringe watched him negotiate the first of the snow-covered ridges. For anyone with less than Eriksen's experience such an order might have been out of the question. When it came to travelling this countryside on skis these lads were the specialists. Eriksen's rapid progress showed it. Ringe turned back.

"Coffee -?" he grinned, at the still disgruntled Astrup who was beginning to circle the truck and was kicking at anything of substance with the toe of his boots. Astrup's grim countenance immediately brightened. Now coffee, there was something he knew exactly what to do with.

Larsen spotted the swiftly approaching skier long before the others.

"Company coming up on the left sir. I think it's Eriksen".

Olsen checked the magazine of his machine pistol.

"Damnn. What now? They must be in trouble. You'd better pull up."

140

"We've broken down sir." gasped a drawn expression as Eriksen doubled over with a sudden pain in his side. The manic slide across the valley had taken more out of him than he realised. "Other side of the summit. Ringe says – Ringe says, could Olaf come and take a look at it – sir."

"Is it something we can fix?" Olsen realised the question was stupid even before he asked it. Eriksen rolled his eyes.

"Not sure sir. Maybe. What shall we do if we can't?"

Olsen's first reaction was to say – 'Take yourselves off into the mountains and shoot yourselves', but knew such talk wasn't going to help matters. Instead he turned to Larsen.

"You'd better get your skis. Take some tools with you. Pick up some of the other lads, Hansen here will help you. If you can't get it going, wait there. I will send you some help the minute we make contact with Hagan's people." Larsen made for the door handle. Olsen leaned over to Eriksen. "You may need the password. Remember – it's 'Fridtjof'. Use that and ask whoever is questioning you to find someone in authority. Got it?" Eriksen nodded. "Good. Best get moving then. Be lucky." Olsen slipped across into the driving seat and looked up at the sky.

"You should be safe for a few more hours. Keep your heads down. We've come this far. Let's not fuck it up now -."

There was nothing Larsen could do. The truck needed a new fan belt, which without the correct material was impossible to fabricate. Rolf Bergstrom scratched thoughtfully at his grizzled chin and amidst trying to remember when he had last shaved hit on an idea.

"Didn't we come passed a quarry down in the valley. If we roll her back. Maybe we could get some help from there?" Larsen dropped the heavy bonnet back on its cleats and snapped shut the springs holding it in place.

"Well I'm out of any other ideas. I'll let the engine tick over; otherwise she is likely to freeze solid on us. If you want me to run her back down there you had better get everyone up here in front. With this weight inside her I could loose it. Tell everyone to keep their distance." Bergstrom took a look at the road, the thick covering of snow and the numerous twists and turns to the valley floor. If the young lad could keep to the widened ruts of the convoy's passing and if the load didn't move, perhaps then -.

"Keep the door off its latch. If anything goes wrong promise me you will get the hell out of it. Stuff the gold." Larsen thought back to all the trouble he had gone to over the past few days. He had no intention of letting go his charges now, then again nor was it time to play the hero. He smiled and hitched up into the cab of the truck. A reply might have worried Bergstrom for it was bound to have been less than truly sincere.

Dovre – Dombas.

He was lucky. To have gained the ridge with just the one hole in his body whilst all around seemed to be raining bullets was little short of a miracle. There was blood. He could feel it. Warm at first, becoming cooler as it seeped into a slushy mess inside the sleeve of his jacket. The arm still functioned. It needed to. A few more minutes and the German paratroopers would make the top of the hill. His tracks would leave them in no doubt as to the direction he was running. His only salvation, keeping the distance. In this terrain at least five hundred metres, preferably more.

Gram no longer cared if his decision to run had been the correct one. Cross-country running had never been top of his agenda. He had left all that sort of physical exertion to those of a stockier more compact build. His forte was the slalom, downhill racing. Fast and furious. The thrill of imminent catastrophe. Beating the odds. That's what really hyped his enthusiasm. Now all that training would need to pay off.

Unfortunately the bottom of the valley flattened out to a wide strip of open country almost a kilometre wide. At that point there would be Germans both behind and ahead on the winding Dombas road. It wasn't looking particularly good. Gram pushed on.

He never saw the first line of Norwegian troops dug in behind their scooped out hollows, the white of their camouflaged hoods blending almost perfectly with the drifts of crystalline snow. The Lieutenant appeared in his direct line of vision a rifle held above his head standing a hundred metres ahead inside the tree line. Gram thought the man German and had been about to flick a change in course when the figure brought the rifle down and levelled it in Gram's direction. At that distance he couldn't possibly have missed. Gram straightened his body and slammed sideways to a halt. It was then he spotted the half dozen or more figures lying prone each with a rifle trained at various parts of his anatomy. Gram let out a long gasp of air and a smile of relief as he recognised the light blue peaks of their forage caps under the hoods.

"Drop the rifle." came the sharp command in his native tongue. Gram looked down. There, not five metres away, lay another of his fellow countrymen. The boy, who from his fresh waxen features wasn't a day over sixteen, pointed a rifle nearly as tall as himself, at a point somewhere between Gram's hairline and the bridge of his nose. "Slowly – if you please." the boy added. Gram did as he was bid letting the stock gently on the surface of the snow before releasing his grip on the tip of the barrel. The Lieutenant indicated for him to come forward.

"Identify yourself." The words were hardly out of the man's mouth before a shot rang out. Instinctively Gram flung himself down. Suddenly all hell broke loose as the Norwegian riflemen opened up in the general direction of the gunfire. Gram lay in the snow pretending as best he could that he was dead. The firing went on for what seemed ages. At one point two flares popped, one green one red. It was difficult to tell from his spread eagle position who if anyone was winning. The minutes dragged by with excruciating slowness before the automatic rattle of the German machine-pistols slowly began to fade. One thing the German Alpine troops were quick to learn in Norway, spraying the trees with bullets from machine pistols was useless against the single marksman with his rifle. Only when the Germans could attack in numbers and with the added support of heavy artillery did their general advance make proper headway. In a case such as this, small skirmishes, the Germans were outclassed every time by the deadly aim of Norway's volunteer riflemen, much to Gram's relief.

"You may get up now." said a voice nearby.
Gram lifted his face from the snow. The Lieutenant was giving hand signals. Some of the Norwegian soldiers left the safety of their dugouts and moved out in pursuit of the German paratroopers. Gram looked across in the opposite direction. The young boy sat grinning back at him.

"Can I pick my rifle up now?" growled Gram. The grin on the youth's face never changed as he shook his head and gestured for Gram to move in the Lieutenants direction.

"What's wrong with your arm?" The Lieutenant pointed to where the disturbed patch of snow had blotted red on the ground. In the excitement Gram had almost forgotten his arm. He glanced down.

"They nicked me a while back. Stupid of me really." The Lieutenant frowned.

"Unusual for them to shoot at one of their own or one of their lackeys?" there was a hint of a sneer behind the question. Gram reached for the armband and worked it carefully down his sleeve.

"That's because I'm not one of theirs -." He looped the sodden NS emblem from over his wrist. "It's stood me in good stead these past few days. I – er, borrowed it – so to speak. The owner – well he didn't want it any more." Gram grinned, "He – wasn't up to it. Physically -!"

Dovrefgell Mntns. North of Dombas.

Harald Bergstrom brought the truck to a sudden stop. Olsen, who had taken the opportunity to catnap, came awake instantly and grabbed at his gun. Borg placed a hand across the Captain's chest.

"It's alright sir. They're our people sir."
Ahead the road was blocked with two farm carts joined between by a length of stout roughly hewn pine-tree. A tall figure ducked below the tree-trunk and came towards them. The figure wore the uniform of a Norwegian Army Lieutenant.

"Who are you lot then -?" he asked then seeing the total length of the convoy, "Christ what have you lot got. The Bloody Crown Jewels?"

"Fridtjof." replied Olsen winding down the window and making sure the barrel of his gun wasn't restricted in any way. "Special consignment."

"Oh Yes. Fridtjof who?" asked the Lieutenant acidly. Olsen looked at the man then back along the long line of vehicles lining the road behind. He was tired. They all were.

"Lieutenant. I will ignore your obvious lack of respect considering the lateness of the hour and the fact the cold has probably dulled your senses." Olsen smacked the barrel of his machine pistol down on the door-frame with a resounding crash. "Now fuck off and fetch your commanding officer –. There's a good chap." The Lieutenant stared up at the barrel of Olsen's gun.

"Er - -. Yes. Well. Right. Er – OK. Hmm." The Lieutenant backed away slowly and did a smart about turn. He covered the distance returning to the barrier in half the time previously.
Borg stroked the brush of his moustache lovingly and chuckled.

"Do you think you impressed him with your command of the Norwegian language sir -?"

"Norwegian? Impossible Sergeant. It's an English word isn't it?" Borg gave a shrug of his shoulders and shook his head.
"You're both wrong. It is in fact a German word," said Bergstrom nonchalantly.

"German!" Both Olsen and the sergeant turned and stared at him.
"So I believe. My brothers and I made a point of looking them all up once. Rude words. You know what kids are like? It's from 'old German', it means- -." "Fuck

off-," piped Olsen and Borg in unison. Bergstrom beamed a big smile. "Well –
Yes, something like that-."
Both men turned back to peer through the windscreen.

"Well let's hope that the Lieutenant doesn't know that." murmured Olsen
softly.

Dovrefgell Mntns. Nr Hjerkinn.

The quarry was a single face hewn out of the massive mountain in the
shape of a horseshoe. In the clearing, a short distance from the face, stood a
small planked cabin surrounded by trees on either side. It was apparent that
everything that would not be of immediate use was to be preserved. The local
men who worked the quarry careful to protect nature's seed-blown gifts. The
small cabin produced nothing in the way of assistance to the Lieutenants
problem. No fan belts and now this!
Larsen's legs protruded from beneath the cab of the truck. Rolf Bergstrom
peered knowledgeably into the engines interior, a torch in one hand a spanner
in the other.

"Well? What's the verdict now then?" Ringe moved in a little closer.

"She's had it I'm afraid – radiator's gone!" replied Larsen from somewhere off
in the depths. Ringe stepped back and turned to the others.

"Alright. Step forward the man who stole our radiator." The Lieutenant was
hoping to put a smile on the faces of the semi-circle of glum countenances
staring back at him. He needed have bothered. No one was in the mood for
joking. Night was just around the corner and the temperature was dropping
like a stone. Ringe shrugged his shoulders.

"Well I suppose we had better try to find some help then." The Lieutenant
stepped aside as Larsen grunted his way from beneath the rusting chassis.
"Larsen. You stay put with young Bergstrom. There must be some farms
hereabouts. The rest of you Hanson men had better pair off. Take different
directions. We will meet back here in two hours. We need alternative transport.
See what you can find."
As Hanson's riflemen sorted themselves out Ringe motioned for Astrup and
Eriksen to join him.

"We three had better stick together. Larsen -, If anything happens, any
trouble, fire three shots off in quick succession -." Olaf grinned and scrambled
to his feet.

"No fears on that one Mr Ringe sir. If I get into any trouble you will hear me
screaming."

With night almost on them the Lieutenant had insisted there be no fires and that Larsen and Bergstrom find a suitable position away from the cabin but near enough as to keep an eye on the truck and its precious cargo. No heroics. If the Germans came Larsen was to allow them to take the truck. He and Bergstrom were to pull back and warn those returning.

The two of them had found shelter under a part of the quarry face that overhung near the base. For all their manly inhibitions it didn't stop them from huddling together in an effort to keep out the biting cold that whipped in flurries around the floor of the quarry causing it to let out soft plaintive moans as it scurried by. Larsen ruffled his shoulders and arched his back.

"God! My bones are beginning to crack. They're like frozen twigs." Bergstrom turned his head and winced at a sudden pain in his neck. Larsen was right. Everything was starting to stiffen up. It felt like minus forty degrees, but in truth was probably only half that. He tried a smile.

"You always were ones for the home comforts you townies. How's that delightful little wife of yours?" Larsen looked askance.

"Mind your own business you cheeky young squirt. You're too young to be asking questions like that -." then grinning, "- Although from what I hear you're not doing too badly – Ingrid! Isn't that what she's called - to hear tell?" Rolf snuggled his face down inside his padded hood.

"I don't know what you are talking about -." he replied coyly. Larsen laughed. The young Bergstrom's inquisitive chatter fell silent from the boy's own embarrassment.

"God!" Larsen shivered. "I think someone has just walked over my grave." He glanced about feeling the hairs rise on the back of his neck.

"Something's not right. Don't you feel it? It's like someone is watching us." Rolf cast his eyes around the tree's perimeter.

"Trolls." he announced cheekily. "Forest trolls. If we keep very still and quiet we may just see one." He turned to meet Larsen's gaze.

"Arseholes!" retorted Larsen huffily.

"Yes. Apparently they have those as well. Our Peter said they were situated - - ." Bergstrom got no further. A rattling noise above their heads and icicles, some whole others in pieces, fell with a clatter from above the overhang. The two scrambled to their feet and paced backward faces turned up to the inky blackness. Then a howl. A long piercing blood freezing call that drifted away across the tall fir trees to the opposite side of the valley. Larsen snatched at his rifle and aimed up into the dark.

"Christ. Wolves." Rolf Bergstrom snatched at the wavering barrel and gripped it fast.

"No. No it's not. It's Harald. Wolves wouldn't come this far down into the valley." Larsen gaped at him in astonishment.

"Harald! What the hell -?"

"It is I tell you. It's Harald. It's his danger signal. He must have come back to warn us something is wrong. It's a signal the three of us agreed to use if ever we needed to warn each other."

"What?"

"You stay here. I'll go up and find out what's happening." Rolf moved away.

"You'll? – Hang on. What do you mean? Hey! Wait up." Larsen dropped his aim and made to follow. Before he had gone two paces Bergstrom had disappeared up the rock face.

"Damn it! You young idiot! Come down." he hissed angrily. There was no reply. Only the scuffle of boots and the rattle of falling debris to indicate Bergstrom's passage up the ice laden rocks.

At least ten minutes had gone. Only the odd mini-avalanche of ice and loose rock disclosed Bergstrom was still moving somewhere above. Larsen moved back from the rock face and stood impatiently stamping his boots into the loose snow. The more he stamped the more he was sure Bergstrom had got it wrong. Had something happened to the Lieutenants patrol he felt sure one of them would have managed to get off the warning shots. It didn't make sense.

At that precise thought Larsen felt his blood turn cold. A scream, not animal, echoed out from the darkness above. The mini-avalanche turned to a torrent of loose rock. He raised both arms to protect his face when something crashed past his head and hit the ground with a resounding smack beside his feet. Larsen felt the rush of air and was flung backwards hitting the hard-packed snow some metres away. Hurriedly he raised himself on both elbows. A dark form huddled nearby. It was Bergstrom. Larsen knew it even before he reached the crumpled body.

"Rolf! Rolf! Can you hear me – Rolf?" The boy's eyes were closed. Larsen couldn't see any blood but he knew almost instinctively Bergstrom was dead. He removed his gloves and felt carefully around the boy's face. There was nothing to indicate what might have happened up there. His neck had probably broken on impact as he hit the frozen ground. Hesitantly Larsen felt for a pulse. As he suspected, nothing. The boy's skin was still hot from the climb. He knelt forward and placed his cheek alongside the boy's lips. He wasn't breathing. Larsen crumpled into the snow alongside the boy's head his hands still clasping the fresh unshaven skin.

"Rolf. Oh Rolf – You stupid, stupid, stupid - - -." Larsen's head sagged forward. Tears sprang to his eyes and rolled down his face to fall as tiny diamonds of ice into his lap. "Bastards. Bastards. For God's sake - -." He opened wide his mouth. He wanted to scream. But it was some time before anything human came from within.

Lieutenant Ringe stopped in his tracks. He thought he heard something strange on the wind but then dismissed it as his imagination. It would be minutes later when he heard the three shots echo out across the desolate mountaintops to warn the others below in the next valley that all was far from well.

Norwegian Army HQ. North of Dombas.

Headquarters 'Dombas' was alive with uniforms from every quarter of the European Continent, with the exception of Germany. Allied officers in various ranks of resplendent military attire moved to and fro with purpose. Olsen stroked at his unshaven jowls and felt distinctly out of place in his bedraggled state.

"Captain!" A familiar voice came from behind. Olsen turned. It was Colonel Hagan minus head-wear and with both sleeves rolled up to below the elbows. He beckoned.

"Pedersen said you had arrived. I'm sorry I didn't come down to meet you. Things are getting sticky. Why don't you come into the office."
The Colonel's office was one of disarray. Maps, files, papers of all description littered the few flat surfaces available.

"You will be pleased to know your stray lamb is safe. We have just received a call from one of the local farmers using your codename. The cargo is safe but I'm afraid one of your men has been killed. We don't know who – there are no further details." Olsen took in the news. One man killed? What the hell had happened?

"Pedersen has a lorry standing by if you want your people to go back up there tonight – otherwise you can leave it until the morning?" Olsen unslung his machine pistol.

"German!" Hagan pointed at the gun. "Efficient is it?" Olsen removed the two remaining clips of ammunition from his pocket.

"At close range. A bit wasteful otherwise. I – er, liberated it. It was in the possession of a very inept lout. He – er, had no need of it any more." Hagan smiled. "I think sir. I would prefer to move at night. Less trouble from their planes. Have arrangements been put in hand in Andalsnes?"

"The town is still burning and the harbour is in one hell of a mess. Fourth Division are still mopping up pockets of German resistance. There's no water or power. One of the reasons I came down here to organise things. A bit closer the action." Hagan rummaged amongst the papers on the desk. "Two destroyers are coming in. Tonight and tomorrow night. We have been ordered to ship out the gold in three batches so as to spread the risk. The destroyers are waiting off the harbour at Molde. It's too risky to come in during daylight." Olsen rubbed at his eyes. He needed a bath. At the very least a shave and a change of underwear.

"Well. It will take most of the night to get back to the truck and transfer the cargo. It will have to be tomorrow night. If we leave here at dusk tomorrow you can expect us in Andalsnes within four to five hours thereafter -." Olsen paused and thought for a moment. "Wouldn't it be better if we were to come straight through to Molde itself?" Hagan grimaced.

"No. Not really. You would have to use the ferry. The Germans have been trying to take it out for days. There's something else. The King. He and his people are to be taken off in Molde. The British are bringing in a cruiser, the 'Glasgow'. It just wouldn't do to have you all bottled up in one place." Hagan rummaged again and came up with a sheaf of papers.

"Passes. For the dockyard. The Allies have no idea what your cargo is. They have orders to give 'Fridtjof' all and any assistance. Just use your codename. It should have the desired results. One more thing -." Hagan thrust the papers into Olsen's outstretched hand. "The Germans. They have paratroopers disguised as our own men all over the place. Be on your guard. Trust no-one Captain."

Dovres Mntn's. Nr Hjerkinn.

The shadows were falling back on themselves as the truck from Dombas trundled into the quarry. Harald Bergstrom and Erik Krefting approached the log cabin from opposing directions. They breathed a sigh of relief when the door to the cabin opened to reveal a beaming Eriksen.

"Bjart! Thank God. We had word you were in trouble -?" gasped Krefting. Eriksen half shrugged then lost his smile when he realised the other man was the elder Bergstrom brother. He moved aside for the two men to enter. Astrup was on his feet having been disturbed by the noise.

"Ivor. What's been happening?" asked Krefting already bothered now by Eriksen's grim countenance. Harald Bergstrom was already checking out the sleeping forms in the cabin's sleeping quarters. He spotted Larsen.

"Olaf! Olaf!" he shook Larsen by the shoulder. "Olaf. It's Harald. Wake up. I can't find Rolf. Where is he? Wake up man." Larsen shook his head, as much to rid his fatigued brain as to focus his bleary eyes. Suddenly he became wide awake.

"Harald!" Bergstrom shook him rudely by the shoulders.

"Yes Harald. Rolf. I can't see Rolf. Where is he? Is he with the Lieutenant -?" It was Astrup who plucked up the courage to provide the answer.

"He's dead Harald -." The room already silent took on a frozen hush. Harald Bergstrom turned with a look of utter disbelief. "He – fell from the quarry in the dark. There was nothing anyone could do." Bergstrom looked across the sea of faces, white and grim in the lessening gloom.

"Dead! What do you mean? Rolf dead? What -? Fell from the quarry? What the hell was he doing on the quarry? What- Why was he up there in the first place? Dead? Larsen -." Bergstrom spun about. "Olaf? You. You were supposed to be taking care of him. What the hell were you doing – Eh? What the hell happened? Answer me you bastard."

Larsen sat with his head bowed. Tears ran down his cheeks. Bergstrom grabbed him by the seam of his smock and hauled him to his feet.

"You were the eldest. You promised to look after him. What was he doing up there in the dark? Answer me you swine or I'll break your fucking useless neck -." Bergstrom hauled the distraught man off his feet. Larsen gagged, the chord and the collar of his smock snapping tight about his throat. Astrup and Krefting looked at each other. Krefting nodded. Astrup's rifle butt caught the enraged man across the back of the neck. With a grunt both men collapsed to the floor in a tangled heap. Astrup waved the end of his rifle in Berstrom's face. The intent was obvious.

"What's going on in here?" Lieutenant Ringe pushed his way to the front of the crush. "Bergstrom. What's the meaning of this?" Bergstrom scrambled to his feet and waved a clenched fist in Larsen's direction.

"That useless idiot let my brother go larking about on top of that quarry and now he's dead. Well he's not going to be on his own. I'm going to beat the crap out of him. He deserves hanging, the negligent bastard -." Astrup stepped forward.

"No he doesn't Harald. Larsen won't tell you what really happened, but I will. Your brother heard a wolf call – OK. A wolf call. He thought it was you. Your signal for danger. Remember -?" Bergstrom straightened up and pulled his head back. Astrup continued. "So he went scrambling up the quarry before Olaf could stop him. Only it wasn't you was it Harald? It really was a wolf. We've checked. There are tracks everywhere up there. It wasn't your stupid 'danger' signal. The wolf must have gone for him when he made the top of the quarry. He fell. Now do you understand?" Bergstrom turned.

"Is this true Larsen?" he asked quietly. Larsen wiped at the tears now flowing freely down his face.

"I didn't want you to know. It was no-ones fault. It was an accident. A lousy rotten accident." Bergstrom put his hands to his head and let out a cry. The men parted as he flung wide both arms and crashed headlong making for the door. Astrup made to follow. Ringe put out an arm to bar his progress.

"Leave him. Nobody's to follow him. Let him alone. Two brothers in the space of a few days. How do any of you think you can help?" Ringe waited for a minute viewing the circle of grim faces then. "OK. You. Astrup. But keep your distance. We don't want him to come to any harm in his present state of mind. For God's sake be discreet. Keep out of sight if you can."

Some distance away and somewhat further to the north a lone wolf caught yet another cry of anguish on the circling currents of the howling bone-chilling wind. He listened. Man! No friend of his kind. He turned away. Somewhere distant he had detected a scent. One he knew well. It was that time. Thrusting his powerful limbs into action he hesitated only a fraction before moving silently on.

Andalsnes. More & Romsdal Fylke. C. Norway.

From this view point the Colonel's brief description of the town and its harbour seemed excessive. It wasn't until the first of the convoy entered the small streets leading to the quayside Olsen began to appreciate the extent of the fighting that had taken place. Many of the buildings were gutted shells and the streets themselves an obstacle course of fallen masonry and burnt-out vehicles.

The gates to the docks were locked. A heavy chain fastened securely by a large padlock barred further progress. Olsen stepped down from the cab of the truck. As he did figures began to appear from behind a stack of wooden packing cases stored dockside for further transportation. Soldiers. Clad in similar smocks to his own.

"Lieutenant Jensen -." said one of the figures training his rifle in Olsen's direction. "Your papers Captain, if you please." Olsen made for his pocket.

"No Captain. Keep your hands where I can see them. I think I can manage to assist you -." The Lieutenant approached and helped himself to the sheaf of passes from Olsen's pocket. He held them up to the weak insipid yellowing moonlight that fogged the whole of the deserted dockside area.

"These have no names Captain! Where did you get them?"

"Colonel Hagan. 'Fridtjof'." Olsen replied, fusing the two names together. If the Norwegian Lieutenant was genuine he should recognise at least one or the other. The Lieutenant smiled.

"Fridtjof'? Why didn't you say so?" The Lieutenant lowered his rifle and smiled. "I'm sorry Captain. There are still too many Germans roaming about in our uniforms. We can't be too careful." He handed back the passes. "Open the gates." The Lieutenant shouted off into the gloom. Two more figures scurried from behind more cargo boxes inside the dock area and leaped on the heavy chain, which soon clattered to the frozen ice with a resounding thud. "It's straight ahead sir. If you would care to get back on board I will show you the way."

The convoy followed a single line of railway track towards the entrance of a huge freight holder. The dockside cranes, the only two on this quay, had been reduced to mangled heaps of scrap metal. Four large bomb craters showed where the German planes had scored some success in their attack upon the British Naval parties that had arrived in the port that morning, the advance guard of what would become the Allies attempt to thwart the German ambitions in their occupation of Central Norway.

The building was of prefabricated concrete and of ample capacity to give cover to all Olsen's vehicles. Olsen was impressed. The Lieutenant too felt pleased with himself.

"It's usually used for the storing of valuable cargoes. Only a direct hit will get through that lot -," he grinned pointing a finger at the heavy beamed ceiling. "The German paratroopers have no heavy explosives or at least if they have they are not using them. Small stuff. Just to keep us on our toes. I suppose they plan not to ruin it for themselves ---as and when they finally get here in the right numbers." Olsen just nodded. The Lieutenant was only voicing what most rational Norwegians were thinking. So far the Allies had landed precious little in the way of numbers of troops required. The Germans had held the whole of Southern Norway now for over a week. Any commander worth his salt would have prioritised the bringing in of mass reinforcements and war materials. It would take a miracle for the Allies to bring sufficient strength to bear against them to halt an eventual collapse. Olsen had looked but the only miracle he had come across so far was that they were managing to outrun their pursuers and at this moment in time were still a good few hours ahead. Miracles on a larger scale? That wasn't in his power. The Lieutenant turned to go.

"I will send some trolleys down to help you move your cargo to the dock. It wouldn't be wise to take the trucks onto the quayside. German reconnaissance planes come over at regular intervals. It's not worth the risk sir."

"Fine. Good man. Thank you Lieutenant. Perhaps some of my men could help you?"

"No thank you sir. Not unless you want to risk them getting shot. Your men need proper passes. My people are jumpy. Not knowing who are friends and who is the enemy. It would be best your men not move beyond the building entrance for the time being sir."

"Well we can't stay cooped up in here all the time. Can't you contact the Colonel? Tell him what we want? We've come too far to get shot by mistake now – What's your name again?"

"Jensen sir. Per Jensen." replied the Lieutenant.

"Well Per Jensen you've done a bloody good job so far. This place is perfect. Who else knows what our cargo is?"

"Just the Colonel and the Harbour Master of course." Olsen removed his hood and repositioned his hat.

"Good. That's just how it should be. Let's keep it that way shall we. Now. Come on -. About those passes – surely you can organise a few pieces of paper. If you can organise something this good -," Olsen waved his arms around, " – I refuse to believe a few bits of paper are going to screw it all up -? Hmm?"

Dombas. On the Lomshurrungen.

Grams great sense of relief at his salvation from the pursuing Germans lasted all of ten minutes. He wasn't surprised the Lieutenant's men kept their distance. The NS armband was less than popular in these parts. But the Lieutenant himself seemed somehow distant to his questioning as to his true identity? Why were the Germans trying to kill him? He also appeared to hold little knowledge of what was happening in the area or the positions on the latest Allied units. It was almost as if he and his unit had been spirited into the valley from some distant planet and told to make the best of it. Gram's' suspicions were no less appeased when one of the Lieutenants men produced a German field dressing kit with which to attend to the wound on Gram's upper arm.

"War booty?" Gram grimaced as the man applied the bandage with less than a mother's tender care. The medic just stared and nodded. Not a word passed from his lips throughout the whole procedure. He finished with a satisfied grunt and slouched moodily away.

"So. Where did you say you were making for when our German friends ran into you?" So far Gram had refrained from mentioning the file strapped around his middle. Getting the plans to the proper authorities meant first being behind friendly lines and preferably close to a 'staff' HQ of the Norwegian or Allied armies.

"I was in Oslo when the Germans came. I have a girl. She lives in Molde. I promised her I would come."
The Lieutenant seemed to brighten up with the mention of the female sex. He laughed and nodded his head vigorously.

"Ha. A woman. Now it all begins to make more sense. So. You risk life and limb to cross half of Norway to be with a woman! Yes. But of course. This – woman. You must like her very much?" Gram gave what he hoped was an embarrassed smile. The Lieutenant clapped his gloved hands together. "Love and War. Amazing. Man's passion for both. A formidable combination when brought together. You are either very brave my friend or very foolish – or then again, very clever perhaps -." The Lieutenant' eyes narrowed. Gram tried to appear innocent. "The question is – Do I believe you?"

"Why shouldn't you? It's the truth." protested Gram. The Lieutenant stared at him for a long moment of time. His face showed he wasn't convinced.

"We have orders to check out the area. Our German friends have dropped dozens of small units similar to the one you encountered. My men should return shortly. Then we must move on. So what of you my amorous friend -? Molde you say?" Gram nodded. The Lieutenant raised his rifle then much to Gram's relief, swung it across his chest where it came to rest cradled in the man's arms. He gestured.

"Humph. I suppose you had better be on your way then. Try not to run into any more of the opposition. You may be less lucky next time." The Lieutenant raised one arm and pointed. "That direction. I should keep moving if I were you. Good luck. Don't do anything foolish. I should hate to think of you not getting what it is you are after -." The man smirked, a leer of a grin spreading down one side of his face. Gram shouldered his rifle and clipped on his skis. He had already made up his mind these men were not Norwegian. At least if they were, they were not regular army or volunteers. Possibly NS in disguise? Scouting the area for the Germans? Now he better understood the signal flares. At least his theory made sense. That was why the German paratroops broke off the engagement so rapidly. These men were fifth columnists -. But all this was speculation. If he was correct and the Lieutenant suspected he knew, what would happen next? A bullet in the back? How far down the slope would he get? At that moment one of the Lieutenant's men hailed him. Someone had spotted something lower down the valley. The Lieutenant gave Gram a nod and moved away. It was now or never. Gram pushed off and made for a gap in the semi-circle of firing positions. Several of the men appeared to have their rifles trained on his passage but none made any effort to stop him. He waved as his skis took him through and into the forest beyond. Every second he expected something to knock him off his feet and hear the report of the rifle shot that would end his foolish quest. It wasn't until he had gone a good half a kilometre the noise in his ears of his heart pounding in his chest began to die away. The further he travelled the more he began to doubt. Had it all been just his imagination? After all, he had never been in the company of Norwegian regulars before. What did he really know of how they should be? Whatever the true situation he had come through unscathed yet again. How long could his luck last?

Gram slid to a halt. No more idiotic lapses of concentration. Very carefully he scanned the surrounding countryside. A full three hundred and sixty degrees. It was as he had expected. But then wasn't that the trouble. He wasn't looking for danger, other than the usual problems that Mother Nature herself threw up. He must be more careful. Luck wasn't an infinite commodity. He pushed off in the direction the Lieutenant had pointed. Towards the darkening image scooped from the distant mountain range. Around him, from here on in, the valleys ran slowly down into the Romsdal, the West Coast and the North Sea and the comparative safety of his own kind. He hoped?

Andalsnes Harbour. Andalsnes.

The German helmets came in very handy for shaving. Olsen shook the excess water off his shaving brush and viewed his reflection in the trucks wing mirror. Three days growth of beard felt considerably better swimming around inside the German helmet than on his face. He stroked the silky soft skin around his chin.

"Bergstrom Sir." Sergeant Borg's gruff voice came from behind. Borg was accompanied by Ringe, Larsen and the surviving Bergstrom brother Harald.

"Corporal Bergstrom. I've decided to let you go with Lieutenant Jensen. His men are joining up with the 5th Division as soon as they are done here and he needs a good man. This business with your brothers will make things more difficult for all of us if you stay – so I want you to go -." Bergstrom straightened his shoulders but said nothing. "You have been invaluable to me and the others. I'm just sorry things have gone the way they have. I'm putting Larsen here in your place -."

"But Sir -." Larsen interrupted. "I couldn't take Harald's place. He's a much better soldier than me -. He's -." Olsen cut him short.

"That is not your decision Larsen. The abilities of the men in my unit are for me to decide. You will take Bergstrom's place and that is an end of it." Larsen shrank back. "Borg. See that Corporal Bergstrom has everything he needs." Olsen put out his hand. "Good luck Corporal. I hope we shall meet again." Bergstrom took Olsen's hand and gripped it tightly.

"Yes Sir. I hope so too. When every last one of these damnn Germans lie dead – Sir." he replied.

It was very much later, when the shadows across the fjord had joined hands that the sleek ghostly bows of the destroyer appeared silently through the dark mirrored waters. Larsen dropped down from the wreckage of the cargo crane.

"She's here sir – Look -."

Olsen, Larsen and Schwartz had been discussing the situation. Larsen had wanted to know the Captain's intentions when the gold was safely away.

"Do? - - To tell you the truth I hadn't even thought about it. Join up with the fourth or the fifth divisions I suppose. Carry on fighting until it's over. What else is there?"

"But I mean – when the fighting is over, couldn't we stick together somehow – you know?"

"Stick together? Well I suppose it might be possible. There's bound to be a resistance. I can't see us beating these arseholes the way things are going. I suppose we could form a resistance group of our own. 'The Bullion Gang'? It has a nice ring to it." Schwartz gave a frown.

"But won't you be going with the gold sir? At least until it's safe in London?"

"Safe in London! No chance. I'm a soldier not a bloody banker. Not on your life. Once I've handed this lot over I'm off to kill myself some Germans. As many of the little swine as possible." Olsen strained his eyes to pick out the destroyer's form. He grunted. "Yes. I see her. Good. Schwartz. Go and find the Lieutenant. Tell him to start moving out the trolleys." Schwartz clipped off a salute and hurried away. "Just look at that Corporal. You've been with the gold longer than any of us. Isn't that just a sight for sore eyes?"

"Certainly is sir. The last thing I remember having lines like that had long blonde hair and wore nothing under her ski jacket but a velvet purse and masses of smooth white skin." Olsen stared down at him.

"For Christ's sake Corporal. Do you have to?" he groaned.

Romsdashorn * *(See End Notes. Maj. Frank E. Foley.)*

At about the same time as the destroyer was arriving in Andalsnes harbour Gram encountered a British Army roadblock. The soldiers were part of the 148th Brigade, elements of the BEF Independent Forces some of which landed on the West Coast near Andalsnes prior to the main force. These special squads were part of the Maurice Force sent in to reconnoitre the area west of the port.

Within two hours Gram was taken to one of the Allied temporary headquarters at the Hotel Bellevue in Andalsnes. Here he was introduced to one Major Frank Foley. This encounter with what was a British MI6 operative and the senior man in Norway had been deleted from Gram's final report. Censored by his SOE masters. The file regarding these events is still closed to this day. *(ADF. See End Notes. Just one protest.)*

Andalsnes Harbour. Andalsnes.

"Eighty tons!" The Royal Naval Captain almost sprayed a mouthful of the clear liquid back in Olsen's face. "How the hell did you manage to get all that lot here in one piece?" Olsen sniffed at his drink. Gin or whisky? Whisky wasn't his favourite tipple.

"Good question Captain. Hard work. A lot of cheek. Some damn good lads and a fair portion of simple good luck I suppose." There was a knock on the cabin door. Another Royal naval officer entered.

"Yes Lieutenant?" said the destroyer's Captain.

"Bad news I'm afraid sir. The Frenchman sir – he's gone aground. Her Captain says he will have to wait until dawn to float her off." The destroyers Captain tried hard to hold back a grin.

"Oh dear. What rotten luck. Still – they will insist on driving on the wrong side of the road. It can't help matters can it?" He turned to Olsen.

"Well there you are Captain. Sorry about that. It looks like you will have to wait a little longer."

"A Frenchmen?" Olsen removed the glass from between his lips. "A French destroyer? But where will she take my gold?" The ships Captain gave a chuckle.

"What's the matter? Don't you trust her?"

"Trust her? No – it's not that. But if she takes the gold to France it will be the same as handing it straight to the Germans on a plate. France will be occupied soon."

"Occupied?" The Royal Navy Captain gave a look of surprise. "Good heavens man. What makes you think that?" Olsen replaced the glass on the tray provided and took a step towards one of the portholes.

"With the greatest of respect to you for all you are trying to do for us here in Norway but if the Germans that enter France are only half as good as the Germans we are fighting here – then France is doomed Captain, believe me!"

"What makes you think the Germans will try to occupy France?" Olsen peered out through the glass ring in the cabin wall.

"I think Norway is what you would call a trial run. The Germans knew we had no army to speak of and fully expected the Allies would attempt a rescue operation following their invasion. They will be taking very careful note of your reaction times, the calibre of your forces, your ability to reinforce and resupply. It's all a precursor Captain. A lead in to what the Germans expect will be their hardest battle. France. Sooner than later if I have understood things correctly France will go down." The Royal Navy Captain squared back his shoulders and pondered Olsen's words before giving a nod of the head and emptying the contents of what remained in his own glass down his throat. He moved to the cabinet and the array of alcohol bottles clipped therein.

"Hmm. Well then. Let's hope we are going to be ready for them when they come. As for your gold. You needn't worry. This is a joint operation but all the gold is to go to England no matter whose flag is flying at the masthead. From here all the destroyers will go to Scotland. We should be there ourselves by the morning."

"But can't you take it all sir? Come the morning the German's may have found the Frenchman. Then what happens? We can't stay here much longer." The Royal Navy Captain nodded to his junior who taking the cue exited the cabin closing the door behind him. He turned to Olsen.

"Look Captain. We have our orders. If we should be spotted by Jerry and cop one on the way back we could loose the lot. Can't be done I'm sorry. As much as I sympathise and would like to help. Her let me refill your glass. Let's just hope for all concerned your present streak of good luck holds. Cheers." Olsen allowed the man to pour another measure of the crystal clear liquid into the glass to join that still languishing in the bottom. He raised the glass and took a gulp.

"Mother of God! he gasped, managing to expel the words before his throat constricted in a series of uncontrollable spasms. "What – what the hell was that?" The ship's Captain looked on bemused.

"What? Oh. Yes. I see. It's – er- . It's called 'potcheen'. I have this aunt of mine in Donegal. She's eighty-five years old this year. Swears by it. Why? Don't you like it?" Olsen dabbed at his eyes and tried to focus them. It took some effort.

"Like it? I don't know? I've just lost all the taste receptors and the skin from inside my mouth. Good God! Don't let that stuff anywhere near my gold. Does – does your War Department know you have this stuff aboard?"

"War Department? Probably not. But then - neither do our German friends -." He smiled and waved the bottle. "Another? – To keep out the cold? – Perhaps?"

Olsen awoke to the sounds of raised voices coming from beyond the freight door opening. Astrup was already on his feet.

"What is it?" he demanded angrily.

"Don't know sir. Some problem down on the dock I think."

The British destroyer had slipped her moorings before dawn, her Captain eager to be gone from the narrow confines of the fjords and the ever-present danger of enemy aircraft. Phase one of the gold's removal from Norwegian soil was securely under-way.

Norwegian marines drawn up in a semi-circle and brandishing bayonets on their rifles were determinedly barring the landing of a group of French sailors. The sailors, in true Gallic fashion, were noisily complaining in loud and less than friendly expletives at this treatment by their allies. Olsen with Ringe in tow were just in time to meet Colonel Hagan and his Lieutenant Per Jensen arriving on the scene. Hagan had his pistol drawn and was forcing his way into the melee of bodies.

"What's going on here?" he demanded angrily. Then seeing the blank look on some of the Frenchmen's faces switched from Norwegian to English.

"Silence -." he thundered. It had the desired effect. Instantly there was a calm. A young fresh-faced French Lieutenant stepped forward.

"You sir. You are the commander here?" he asked in broken English. Hagan nodded.

"Colonel Hagen! And you sir? What is the meaning of this disgraceful behaviour?" The Lieutenant drew himself up and saluted. Then pointed.

"Our ship Colonel. She is fast – not going. My men sir. They must be here. It is not safe on the ship sir."

The French destroyer was still aground where she had bottomed out the night before. Hagan peered off into the gloom.

"Where? I can't see her. Where is she?"

"But that is so Colonel sir. She has the camouflage. But she is there sir I give you my word." Hagan looked again. Still seeing nothing he shrugged his shoulders irritably.

"Yes. Well. Alright if you say so. I suppose -." He turned to Olsen.

"Captain. Escort the Lieutenants people to the freight building will you. See that they get something to eat -." The Colonel cast his eyes over the grumbling group of men, " – and perhaps something to drink, unless they have brought something with them." The French Lieutenants face broke into a smile as he nodded his head appreciatively. Hagan returned the look with one of disapproval. He didn't care for the French sailors' apparent lack of good discipline. Olsen drew the French Lieutenant aside.

"What's with the panic to come here. Why all the argument?" he asked, using what little French was in his vocabulary and resorting to English for the word 'argument'. The French Lieutenant consulted his wristwatch.

"07.05 hours mon Capitain. It is said the Germans come every morning at 07.15 hours with their planes. My men does not wish to be outside without the protection -." the man replied. Olsen grinned. "But this is not amusing Captain when you have nothing for safety n' est pas?" whined the Lieutenant.

"No Lieutenant. It is not amusing. However. You and your men are an hour early. Norwegian time is 06.05 hours. You must alter your watch. A natural mistake. But one that could make things difficult between us if you and your men don't correct your clocks – n'est pas?" In true French style the Lieutenant stared nonchalantly off into space as if the suggestion didn't really warrant his attention. Olsen almost laughed. It was the reaction he had half expected.

"You have no need to worry Lieutenant. The Germans are very punctual. I suggest we find you some of that 'protection' you are so keen to acquire." Olsen waved ahead. "Shall we?"

The six Ju87s of 1st /GI. now stationed at Stora (Stavanger) came in from the south spot on time. Four of the German aircraft peeled off and headed for the harbour the screaming from their wing sirens filling the inlet with a terrifying wailing noise. Inside the freight holder the loading of the gold for that days' shipment went ahead as if nothing was happening. Olsen, Ringe and the French Lieutenant followed the course of the diving aircraft from the comparative safety of the freight building entrance. Olsen had a pair of binoculars trained in the direction of the French destroyer that up until now had not fired her guns at the German aircraft. No doubt so as to remain hidden with her camouflage as long as possible.

"Do you think they will spot her sir?" asked Ringe. As he spoke the two remaining Stuka's executed a half roll and dived down in the opposite direction in a direct line to Olsen's gaze. The destroyer's Captain knowing the game was up gave the order to open fire. Small white and black puffs of anti-aircraft fire peppered the grey backdrop seconds before Olsen observed a large reddish explosion occur on the destroyer's foredeck. One of the Stuka's bombs had found a mark.

"There's your answer Lieutenant," growled Olsen lowering the binoculars and passing them to the French Lieutenant. Eagerly the man jumped to his feet to obtain a better view. Olsen grabbed him by the rear of his tunic and hauled him to the ground.

"Careful Lieutenant. It won't help matters you getting yourself killed." The French Lieutenant gabbled something Olsen couldn't catch and as a sop to Olsen's grumbling knelt forward on his knees, as high as he could stretch.

The raid lasted less than ten minutes. Suddenly the sky was clear of aircraft. Only the odd pulverised railway wagon and the crackle of burning timbers bore any witness to their destructive passing. The French Lieutenant got to his feet.

"I must go to my ship Captain. Maybe she is not too bad?" Olsen was suddenly distracted by a shout from behind. Astrup was on his feet and pointing excitedly.

"Sir. Look. The gold." Olsen turned his head. On the dockside a number of trolleys were burning furiously. Smoke beginning to billow from beneath their canvas coverings. Someone shouted "Fire!" That was the signal for a general confusion as the fire was outside the building. Olsen was on his feet and running.

"Snow -." he bellowed. "Throw the snow on it." Most of the men began by scooping great handfuls of the powdery substance in the direction of the flames. Others, seeing the progress useless used whatever came to hand. Hats being the most favoured. Ringe was using a German helmet. One of the French sailors appeared with a stirrup pump then began running around in circles looking for a water source, the water in the dock being out of reach for his hand bucket. The French Lieutenant had removed his jacket and was thrashing the flames with it like a thing possessed.

Slowly the flames were brought under control. It took the best part of a quarter of an hour before the last flickering tongues were finally extinguished. Olsen looked down despairingly at his hat. A useless mush of dripping fabric. The French Lieutenant, his face and hands blackened, surrendered the remains of his tunic to a heap on the ground. He grinned.

"What is 'snow'?" he asked. Before Olsen could reply the Lieutenant's gaze came to rest on a series of shining metal rivulets oozing cautiously from beneath the smouldering debris at his feet. His mouth dropped open as the feeble early morning rays from the sun flashed a glittering reflection back into his eyes.

"Sacre bleu. Q'EST Que Sais? I though it was ammunition. What Captain Sir is this?" Olsen looked down and rolled his eyes. The destroyer's cargo was on a need to know basis only.

"That Lieutenant? That – you haven't seen. Comprehend?" Olsen kicked some of the charred ashes over the gold spray and looked around for Larsen. The gold bars would need re-packing before loading aboard the ship.

"Which is Captain Olsen?" A voice of authority made him turn.

"My Captain monsieur-." murmured the French Lieutenant, averting his eyes as the man approached. Olsen came automatically to attention and replacing his sodden hat gave the man a salute as befitted his rank.

"Olsen? My regrets Captain. My ship she has lost its forward guns. The German plane. Without them she is practically defenceless. To attempt to take your cargo now would put it at great risk. Something I have orders not to do. I propose to return to the harbour at Molde for to make the repairs. I am most sorry monsieur." Olsen removed his hat and tried to press some of the water from the material between his fingers.

"Yes Captain sir. I do understand. It was most unlucky. Most unfortunate. I do thank you for trying sir." The French Captain gave a shrug of his gilt braided shoulders.

"Unfortunate? Yes – unfortunate indeed. But not as unfortunate as what is happening to your country at the moment. Ces terrible. Mais – Do not despair. I am sure another ship will come when the Allied command receives my signal. Have heart – n'est pas?" Olsen caught the look of sympathy in the Frenchman's eyes.

"Yes sir. Thank you sir." The French Captain gave a nod and turned away. The French Lieutenant retrieved his tunic from the ground and placed it gingerly over his shoulder.

"If my Captain had knowledge of your –er cargo? I am not so sure he would have come to that same decision monsieur." Olsen laughed and patted the young Frenchman playfully on the back.

"Cargo? What cargo is that then?" he smirked innocently.

As the French Captain and his crewmen boarded the launch for the return to their ship Per Jensen arrived with bad news.

"I'm sorry to have to report the Colonel is dead sir. Rifle fire from the woods. He died instantly sir."

"Dead? What the hell is going on? I thought all the local areas had been cleared of the bastards?"

"They had sir. But it's practically impossible to be sure of getting every last one of them sir. Sorry sir." Olsen dropped his head and turned away. They say that bad news comes in batches of three. No ship, no commanding officer. What next he wondered? The Lieutenant waited. After a few moments Olsen raised his head and looked around. The colonel had long been known to him and had gained quite a reputation within the ranks of the Norwegian army. He would be sadly missed.

"OK Lieutenant. The first thing I need will be some of your men to move this lot back under cover." Olsen kicked over the traces of charred timbers. "The Colonel. Did he give you any indication earlier of when the next ship would be in?"

"No sir. The man who could tell you that would be the harbour master. I know there's nothing due today. You could have a long wait sir."

That was all Olsen needed. But negative thinking wasn't going to get the job done. Apart from which he had a hankering to get back to his unit and obliterate some more of these bloody jackals that were killing his friends and tearing the heart from his country. God damnn them their selfish arrogance. Damnn them to hell!

The Harbour Masters office was a shambles of broken glass and scattered files. The man himself looked in less better shape. He wore a well-fingered shirt collar open at the neck covered with a mercantile marine jacket that had seen recent scorching and was full of masonry dust. His face was drawn and haggard and had obviously not seen a good night's rest for many days. Olsen took all this into account but still sensed an atmosphere of suspicion to his unheralded presence there.

163

"But we have been here now for nearly five days. There must be some news!" The harbour master pushed himself away from the desk and tossed a handful of shipping forms amongst the debris laid out before him.

"News! Oh if it's only news you want there's plenty of that. None of it good. You want news Captain?"

"Try me." snapped Olsen.

"Alright. Let's see. Molde. The harbour master there reports this morning that the Allied forces have received orders to dis-engage. Pull out. How's that?"

"Pull out!" Olsen stopped in mid-pace. "Pull out! But that's impossible. They've only just bloody-well arrived?"

"Yes Captain. I couldn't agree more. But they have new orders. They are to move north. It seems Narvik is to be the new front. Central Norway is no longer tenable, not important."

"Not important! What bullshit is that? Don't they realise that will leave the whole of Central Norway at the mercy of the Germans. That will mean almost immediate total occupation of three-quarters of the country. Are they insane?" The harbour master shook his head.

"That's what I said at first Captain. But then you have to think about it. We are finished here. Molde is under almost constant attack. There are no roads through the mountains to the North. None that an army could use. If we stay here we shall be trapped up against the coast with nowhere but the water to go. The allies, it seems, can't reinforce from the sea in sufficient numbers in time to stop a general rout. They have no choice. And what's more to the point Captain, neither do we." Olsen stared at the man. He was of course correct in his analysis. With no declaration of war the invasion had come as a complete surprise. It was ridiculous to think other foreign governments would have laid contingency plans for such an event or in the event to sacrifice tens of thousands of lives on such a tenuous campaign. Norway would have to be sacrificed. That should have been obvious.

"So why go north?"

"I don't know Captain. Maybe the British think if they hold the north it will provide a launch-ramp for future actions against the Germans here in the south. I'm no military planner. Who can say what they are thinking?"

"So -. And what the hell happens to us?"

"Us? One assumes we die Captain, if we are stupid enough to try and stop the bastards on our own -. Other than that I'm full out of answers."

The harbour masters parting words rang around Olsen's head as he crossed the bare expanse of the quayside and entered the freight building. A large group was gathered around a small figure lying on one of the raised platforms.

Olsen pushed forward. Borg was kneeling alongside the Lieutenant. Larsen was gingerly unbuttoning the man's tunic. Ringe's face was contorted with pain.

"What's going on here Sergeant?" Olsen growled.

"It was a mistake Captain sir. The Lieutenant put on the wrong cap as he was leaving for the gate. These men here thought he was a German sir." A number of Norwegian soldiers stood nervously looking on. Borg handed Olsen a German forage cap. "They took a shot at him. Fortunately, as far as I can tell, they are not particularly good shots. It's his shoulder -." Olsen looked down into Ringe's face.

"You stupid bastard man. What the hell were you thinking?" Ringe tried a smile.

"I – I wasn't sir. As – as you can see. Sorry sir." Olsen gave a sigh.

"Never mind. You had better save your breath. God Almighty –." At that moment Per Jensen arrived with a number of his men.

"Trouble sir?"

"A misunderstanding Lieutenant. My man here needs a doctor. Is there one near?"

"In the town sir. If you will allow me." Per Jensen gave instructions for his car to be brought then -. "Captain Olsen. A word with you sir. In private."
Olsen nodded to Borg and bent down.

"Hold on in there Lieutenant. You're much too valuable to me to lose. We will have this sorted out in no time." He knuckled Ringe playfully under the chin. "I will see you later."
Per Jensen waited for Olsen to join him a short distance from the group.

"We have orders sir to withdraw northwards. They want us to split up into small groups and make our way over the mountains. It's a shame about your man. Bad timing. There are no hospitals left standing in the town. If the doctor says he can be moved you should consider taking him with you, although there is an alternative. I'm sure the Germans will treat him well?" Olsen's reaction was almost instantaneous.

"Over my dead body Lieutenant." Per Jensen grinned widely.

"Somehow I thought you might say that." The Lieutenant shouldered his rifle and pushed the pistol holster on his waist belt into a more comfortable position. "Well I suppose this is farewell. I hope you make it sir." Per Jensen extended a hand. Olsen took it. "Oh yes. I almost forgot. The radio announced this morning that Germany has just declared war on us. Apparently as from 06-00 hours this morning it is legal for us to shoot any of them, if we see them. It er makes you wonder what the hell it is we have been doing for the past two-week's sir. Doesn't it?"

Andalsnes Harbour.

Loading the bullion boxes back aboard the trucks was almost complete when sometime later Olsen entered the freight building. Schwartz hurried to meet him.

"Sorry sir, but its Sergeant Borg sir. He said he wasn't feeling well. Larsen is with him, two trucks down sir." Olsen stopped and took a deep breath. He had assumed number three in the sequence of 'bad news' to be the harbour master imparting the information on the imminent withdrawal of the Allied forces. Something in the back of his mind indicated otherwise.

Borg lay on his back on a blanket between two stacks of wooden crates. Larsen had a grave look on his face.

"How are things Corporal?" asked Olsen, fully expecting the worst.

"I don't know sir. He was trying to say something just before you got here. I couldn't make it out." Olsen clambered aboard and bent down over the old man's prone figure. He felt the side of Borg's neck for a pulse. After a few moments he withdrew his hand.

"I'm sorry Olaf. He's dead I'm afraid." Larsen looked askance.

"What? But he can't be. I was -. We were talking together only a few -."

"Yes- Yes. I know -." Olsen pulled together the loose folds of the blanket and covered the whiskered face. " It was his heart. I didn't say anything before. You remember when he collapsed. At the lumber camp. When the paratroopers nabbed him. Thought he was the 'King'? All of you thought he had just fainted?" Olsen rose to his feet. "He knew then I suspected it was something other - -."

"You knew! And you didn't send him home? Away from all this?" Larsen looked accusingly in his direction.

"Send him home? What? And tell him he was no use. No longer wanted? Would you?" Olsen held the younger man's stare. Larsen though about it for only a few seconds before dropping his gaze.

"No sir. Of course not." he replied. Olsen stared down at the roughly folded blanket and thought of what else he should be saying. God. How he was beginning to hate this mess.

"So Corporal. No Lieutenant and now no sergeant. That makes you my second in command – and please, no arguments this time eh?" Larsen nodded his head. "Remove the stripes from his tunic and put them on yours. He would have liked that – Sergeant."

Olsen jumped down from the truck.

"We've all come a long way. We've licked the Germans at every turn. Sergeant Borg and the others would have wanted us to finish what we all started. Together. What do you say – Sergeant?" Larsen looked up through the veil of tears that had gathered in his eyes. He grit his teeth tightly together and with a flicker of a weak smile Olsen knew he had his answer.

Dusk and the convoy of eight trucks slowed to a stop beside a cluster of wooden huts. The road sign a kilometre back indicated this would be the entrance to Afarnes Harbour. Olsen showed his pass to the two Norwegians guarding the gates before being waved on.
The quay was deserted. Astrup and Krefting joined Olsen who was standing staring out over the black water.
"That's west isn't it sir?" said Krefting, as an excuse to open a conversation. "It's a long time since I've seen a sunset like that in winter sir." Olsen stared grimly off into the distance at the reddish reflection spreading across the inlet below the darker mountain backdrop.
"I'm very much afraid that is not a sunset. If I'm not mistaken that I think is Molde – burning!" Both the two men moved closer towards the edge of the quay and craned their necks. It was Astrup who spoke first.
"You don't suppose we are too late do you sir?" Olsen turned his head.
"Too late? Well there's only one way we are going to find out. The both of you take the next ferry. If there's the slightest sign of trouble - don't dock. Use your guns if you have to. Turn the thing about and get your tails back here. If we are too late – then it's back to the mountains. Germans permitting." Olsen looked them both over. "See the sergeant. Exchange your rifles for two of the German machine pistols. Make sure you have spare clips. Whatever happens I want you both back here alive – Understand?"

The mood inside the hut was sombre. Olsen awoke to an almost claustrophobic silence. Apart from Schwartz and Theodore Storm on guard outside, the rest of the men sat around two long wooden tables drinking coffee from an assortment of salvaged receptacles. A few of the men were smoking, layering the foetid air with swirling blankets of grey smoke which was adding to the already oppressive atmosphere.
"For gods sake cheer up the lot of you. It's like a funeral chapel in here." Olsen sat up stretched at his aching limbs and gave an over exaggerated yawn. "It probably won't be all that bad in Molde – otherwise the King and his people

wouldn't be there -." Larsen, who had been feeding the Lieutenant sips of warm soup from a bowl, looked up.

"It wasn't that sir. We have just been thinking about what to do when all this lot is over – the gold I mean." Olsen looked around the array of young unshaven faces and felt a pang of sympathy. Lads of such tender age shouldn't have been worrying about such dilemmas as this. Partying, skiing, polishing up their finals in education, fornicating – well why not, that's what he had done. Even though he had chosen the army it hadn't detracted from all the usual pursuits of youth. Instead, each and every one here was trying to decide how best to survive the next few days and if so what the future now held for them living under 'occupation'. No wonder they were feeling depressed?

"Well. There's no point in worrying about that now. One job at a time. First off – we get the gold safe. Then we - -." The door flying open interrupted Olsen. Theodore Storm entered.

"The ferry. It's back sir." Suddenly the whole atmosphere changed as the men made a rush for the open doorway. Olsen got to his feet thankful for Storm's intrusion. He hadn't quite worked out what it was he was about to say to try and lift their spirits. Larsen tried to make Ringe comfortable on the mattress beside the open stove. The Lieutenant attempted a smile as Olsen hove into view. The doctor in Andalsnes had done his best but the wound required a more expert opinion and more delicate surgery than he, the doctor with his limited knowledge, could offer. Olsen hoped the news was good. If only for his Lieutenant's sake.

Astrup stood astride the ramp as it rattled down on the stone dock. With a leap he gained the shore.

"Sorry it took so long sir. It's chaos over there. We saw the General and the King. He wanted to shake our hands sir. Can you imagine -? And he's waiting for you sir. He says the 'Glasgow' won't sail without you sir – and – and – What else did he say Erik?" Krefting already had a wide smile on his face. He couldn't help but laugh at Astrup bubbling over in his excitement.

"I'm sorry about him sir -. Major Ording was there sir. He said to tell you the destroyer made Scotland this morning and that the first shipment of the gold is now in England sir." A burst of cheering rent the air as the assembled gathering went wild with elation. Olsen waited.

"Alright – Everybody. Alright. That's good news. Anything else?"

"Yes sir. The Major's orders are, you are to cross on the next ferry. The 'Glasgow' will have to leave soon. There's apparently another ship on the way from Tromso to take the rest of the gold. But you Sir, he insists you leave immediately." Olsen glanced across at the six trucks carrying the remainder of the gold. Krefting read his mind.

"Don't worry sir. The other ferry will be on its way back by now." Olsen consulted his watch.

"OK. Krefting and myself will take this run. Eriksen and Schwartz the next." He turned to Larsen. "Do you think you and Astrup can bring the last two trucks over alright?" Larsen hitched his rifle to his chest.

"Yes Sir. No problem Sir." he replied.

For a few seconds Olsen scanned the tired but happy faces of his men. Confident, eager, yet still only boys for the most part. Inwardly he was very proud of them and sought for the right words to express, in a downbeat manner, his heartfelt emotions.

"Yes. Well thank you Sergeant and er – well that goes for all of you. You've done a fantastic job. Every man jack of you. You're er a credit to our country. They should be proud of you. I know I am. Really -." Astrup, ever the clown of the proceedings, cleared his throat.

"That's nice of the Captain to say so. I was er wondering sir. When they gave you this operation. Was there er any mention of a commission for its safe delivery, you know – the gold? Five percent say?" Olsen forced back a grin.

"Astrup. If I don't see your ugly face coming over that horizon with my last two trucks and 'all the gold intact I will personally swim back over here and stick my machine pistol up your rear orifice – Got it?" Astrup grinned even wider and rolled his eyeballs. "Aye aye Captain Sir." He chuckled.

Molde Harbour. Molde. More & Romsdal Fylke.

From the ferry Captain's bridge it was evident Molde harbour and its sprawling dockside was no place to be. The last air raid had taken place as dusk was falling. From Olsen's viewpoint the German planes must have had a 'field day'. Not a single building appeared to have escaped damnage. Fires were burning everywhere. A huge pall of angry grey smoke spread out like a huge umbrella across the narrow blacked-out headland, too high in the night sky to give any real protection from the wheeling Stukas that come the dawn would return to finish what they had started.

Olsen scanned the horizon to his rear and glanced for the twentieth time at the watch on his wrist. Dawn wasn't that far away. Certainly not far enough to give him any peace of mind. Under the cover of night the harbour still bustled with activity. Hundreds of Norwegian and Allied soldiers were encamped amongst the disarray of dockside cargo and military supplies thronging the quay. The Allied command's order for evacuation seemed to have stalled in mid-stream. Very few vessels plied the waters as the ferry Captain reversed his engines and slipped gently into the dock.

Olsen gave Krefting his instructions. Take the two trucks with the gold to the dock gates, find cover and await further orders. Olsen himself would remain at the ferry terminal for Schwartz and Eriksen's two trucks to arrive. Together they would seek out the Norwegian HQ and the 'Glasgow'.

Meanwhile in Afarnes Larsen had fared no better than his superior officer having also spent the last couple of hours staring out across the expanse of water in the hope of spotting Olsen's ferryboat returning. The two ferries should, all things being equal, have passed each other mid-way. He occupied a prime position on a wooden fire escape overlooking the harbour master's tiny office. A powerful pair of binoculars would have been a welcome addition to his military accoutrements. Instead he had to make do cupping both gloved hands around his tired eyes as he peered intently out across the grey water at the landmass with its dark cloud covering in the far distance. The first grey fingers of a new dawn were approaching. Larsen shivered and had just decided to give his eyes a rest when suddenly the far horizon lit up with a bright flash to be replaced almost instantaneously with a huge orange ball and the rumbling roar of an approaching express train. The sound of the explosion rumbled up against the backdrop of mountains and tumbled away. Astrup came pounding down the quay.

"What is it?" he shouted. No sooner were the words from his mouth when a second flash appeared, nearer but still beyond Larsen line of vision and again followed by the sounds of explosions. Larsen craned his neck and stood on tiptoe, almost overbalancing himself on the narrow landing. After a time he stepped back. Astrup held up his arms in frustration. "Well?"

"Our ticket out of here – I think." growled Larsen huskily.

"What! Fuck-! Do you think they got them 'both'?"

"How would I know -." snapped Larsen, "I can't see a bloody thing from here in this light. Although I can't see what else the Germans might be interested in out there." Astrup swung about and aimed a careless kick at the nearest mound of snow.

"Shit. So what the hell do we do now?" Larsen shifted his gaze to the remaining two trucks drawn up alongside the ferry ramp.

"We move. Get the hell out of here. Get both trucks tanked up and ready to go. We'll give it another half an hour. If either of the ferries have got through we should be able to spot them by then."

"Tanked up? Why? Where are we going?" Astrup stared at him. Larsen looked up at the mountains then ran his eyes from left to right and back again. He smiled, freezing the vacant look.

"Good question Ivor. But we're not out of options yet." The screaming wail of diving German aircraft cut across Larsen's reply. Both men looked skywards. From the sea and growing larger by the second came two evil looking black vultures. German Stukas.

"What say we get the hell out of here?" Astrup shouted loudly as both of them took to their heels.

"Take cover – air raid." screamed Larsen seeing the rest of his squad leaving the bunkhouse to observe the diving planes instead of seeking a wiser option to shelter in the buildings lower basement. Two shattering explosions came from behind as Larsen with the rest piling down on top of him sought the protection of the basement steps. The Stukas roared overhead barely thirty metres from the dock the slanted black crosses on their wing tips mocking at the absence of any retaliation from below. Larsen stuck his head above the parapet. A muffled explosion and a single flaming fuel tank sailing high across the empty dock signified the German pilots aim for the trucks had scored at least one hit. Astrup's was the only voice to break the following moments of silence.

"So - what now Sergeant?" Larsen looked down and scowled.

"Now? Well right now Astrup, you go and find me another truck. I don't really care where from as long as it's roadworthy. I want two trucks ready to roll in twenty minutes and that includes reloading the cargo which I should imagine is strewn halfway across the bloody harbour – and try to remember not to put any loose bits anywhere other than with the rest. – Understand?" Astrup sprang to his feet and saluted.

"Yes Sergeant. At the double Sergeant – Oh just as a matter of interest Sergeant. Where are we going?"

"Vestnes."

"Vestnes? But that's miles away?"

"Yes Ivor -." Larsen retaliated getting a little fed up with Astrups' constant goading. "But there's a ferry at Vestnes isn't there? Unless of course you would prefer to swim?"

Molde Harbour:

The two explosions witnessed by Astrup and Larsen sunk both ferryboats in mid channel. The raid of six German aircraft from Sola had taken advantage of the early morning dawn affording their German pilots more visibility above the expansive layer of thick rolling smoke that covered the town which kept them from view until the last moment. However the initial attack on the ferries gave warning to the hundreds of military personnel still thronging the town and the dock areas.

"This is an air raid warning - This is an air raid warning. Clear those vehicles from the area immediately. Clear all vehicles and movable equipment – -." A massive explosion blanketed out the metallic exhortations from the cars' loudspeaker. At the far end of the street one of the tall buildings' disintegrated inside a mushroom cloud of dust, debris and raging flame.

Olsen put a hand up to his eyes against the glare of the bomb flash.

"Sound your horn damnmit." he snapped angrily. "If they won't move run the idiots over." Theodore Storm glanced at him askance. Olsen turned away. Just then the door of the cab opened and a head appeared.

"Get this bloody thing out of here you stupid oafs. "a voice snarled. Olsen recognised the angry tones and leaned forward.

"Certainly Major Ording sir. I have already suggested to my driver he mow everything down in his path to clear the way."

"Johan! For pity's sake! My god am I glad to see you -." Major Ording hung to the swinging door as the truck lurched forward. "Quick. Tell your man to get under cover. Take next left. There are some garages -."

The raid lasted less than ten minutes. Once the German Stukas had expended their bombs and strafed at everything within gun-sight they departed. Ording led the small group across the debris to his car, their destination Allied Combined Headquarters. As the Major's car drew up a large group of Norwegian officers gathered. They had recognised Olsen. A cheer went up followed closely by a ripple of polite clapping. Olsen squeezed out of the car embarrassed.

"Johan! So you did it you young rascal? Never doubted it for a second." General Ruge appeared from the rear of the group, which respectfully parted forming a channel between the grinning officers. Olsen and the Major walk through.

"The King conveys his deep gratitude and appreciation. But for you, you young blighter, we may have never got him out safely. Well done my boy – damn fine show." The General grasped Olsen's hand. Olsen felt his cheeks turning red. He wasn't used to such public adulation.

"I er. Yes. Thank you General sir. But it wasn't just me sir. I had a lot of very good men to help me sir. Not all of whom made it through." Ruge nodded. He knew only too well what Olsen was feeling.

"Yes Captain. It's a dirty business. We often lose the best – Is there – anything you need?" Olsen thought for a moment.

"Yes sir. It's my Lieutenant sir. He was wounded, back in Andalsnes. He can't stay here sir. Would it be possible for him to go with the 'Glasgow' – to Tromso sir?" Ruge cracked his face with an even wider smile.

"Still as shrewd as ever Johan. Still. How can I refuse?" Ruge set his eyes on Olsen's. "You're a damn good officer Captain Olsen. A damn good man -." Ruge turned to one of his aides. "See the Captain's Lieutenant gets a pass to board the 'Glasgow'." Olsen snapped off a smart salute.

"Thank you sir."

"No need. It's a pleasure. Now -. I must go. There's still lots to do. I look forward to hearing all about your 'adventure's' from you personally, later on Captain. It's good to have you back." Without pausing Ruge turned away, his entourage of staff officers following meekly in his wake. Ording and Olsen looked at each other. Staff jobs had to be done, a necessary requisite for any army, however small. But neither man would have exchanged their present work for the duties of a safe desk or pushing a pen for the 'old school'.

"So Johan. Would you like to go and freshen up? Get something to eat? Ording hadn't failed to notice the dishevelled condition of Olsen's uniform. Olsen nodded. Together they mounted the steps to the building.

"Look Arne. I'm not going on the 'Glasgow'." Ording stopped dead in his tracks.

"Not going? But you have to. There will be nothing left here to stop the Germans. All Central Norway is due to fall in the next few hours. You can't stay here. You will be trapped." Olsen suppressed a laugh.

"Trapped?" That was exactly what the Germans had thought he had been for the past three weeks. "No. Not quite. I shall take to the mountains. My men want to continue the fight. As it happens – so do I. We still have a lot we can do here in Norway. I can't do that in England." Ording shook his head. Not that it had come as a complete surprise.

"Somehow that's just you Johan. You always loved a good scrap. Always have to be at the sharp end of things -. So. Where will you go?"

"Hmm." Olsen stared around then shrugged his shoulders. "Don't know really. I hadn't decided. Somewhere I can do the most damnage. Wherever there are Germans – or traitors." Ording continued his stride drawing level.

"Well. Let's just hope there aren't too many of either – in the long term." he grinned.

"Sir! Captain Olsen sir!" Krefting came running up the steps. "I've just heard sir. The ferries. They've both been sunk!"

"Sunk?" Olsen paled. "Are you sure? Larsen and Astrup? Did they get across?" Krefting shook his head blankly.

"No sir. They must still be in Afarnes unless - - ." Krefting left the rest of his thoughts unspoken.

Vestnes Ferry Terminal. Vestnes.

The two trucks had travelled through the brightening dawn at speeds no sane person would have considered rational. Larsen was in no mood for 'rational'. In his and the truck behind, driven by Astrup, who for the past thirty kilometres had wished he had stayed at home, was the last of his precious charges, almost eight tons of it. He had no intention of allowing the Germans even a partial success. If Norway was to fall to these thieving jackals she would do so leaving nothing but her bare bones for the invader to gnaw upon.

The coast road ran downhill to the ferry terminal. At a glance Larsen saw the ferryboat was already docked. He banged on the door of his cab and indicated for Astrup to draw up alongside.

"Drive straight on. Don't stop for anyone -." he screamed and signalled for Astrup to go on ahead. Astrup needed no second bidding. Being in the lead he was able to reduce the speed to something he considered wouldn't get them both killed. It didn't last. With Larsen sounding his horn and bumping Astrup's rear tailgate the two vehicles entered the dockyard at breakneck speed. Judging the narrow confines of the loading ramp with millimetres to spare Astrup crashed on board. It required he had to stand almost upright on the brake pedal to stop the whole thing from careening off into the sea at the bow end. Sweating and mumbling to himself, the truck eventually responded and came to a hissing halt. Two seconds later Larsen hit him from behind. It was only a nudge but sufficient to send him head first at the trucks windscreen.

"You bloody pillock!" Astrup shook the fog from his eyes and stormed down from the cab. "Bloody pillock!" he repeated as Larsen emerged from his cab. Larsen drew himself upright. Then smiled and pointed to his sleeve.

"Bloody pillock Sergeant – if you don't mind." he replied accentuating a huge grin. "Please remember my rank Ivor."

Behind there came the sound of running feet. From the direction of the quay two figures appeared through the gloom. One was the ferry's Captain the other had on a coast guard uniform.

"Hoy! You there. What the hell are you doing? You can't do that!" called the one in the coast guard uniform. Larsen looked at Astrup then back again at the man.

"That's strange. We just have. Did you not see it?"

"But – but, but -." the man began to stutter. Larsen held up his hand.

174

"No. I know what you're going to say. Do it again. Sorry. We only do it once a day. If you missed it you will have to come back again tomorrow."

The man stared back disbelievingly. "But – but -." he began again. Larsen waved him down, then tapped the door of his cab with the tip of his machine pistol and pointed it directly towards the man's flapping mouth.

"All aboard those that are going with us to Molde then -." he chirped, then to the man in the Captains' uniform. "If you are the Captain of this here vessel we are leaving for Molde immediately. By order of His Majesty the King." Larsen smiled as the men's mouths sagged open even wider. "I am assuming you have heard of the King-Yes? So. Gentlemen. Shall we. In your own time of course." Larsen made a point of looking down at his wrist. There was no wristwatch there, however -. "You have five minutes. Best get to it. Unless of course you want the Germans to flip a stick of bombs up your stern?"

That did the trick.

Harbour Masters Office. Molde.

Concerned for the rest of his men and their precious cargo Olsen refused the offer of food and a warm bath. Communications with Afarnes was best served through the offices of the coast guard but that radio mast had been destroyed in the last air raid. The mast on the harbour master's office was still standing.

"Why the hell are they not answering?" growled Olsen impatiently pacing back and forth across the wooden floor.

"Perhaps they can't! Afarnes was hit very badly last night. The harbour masters office might not be there any more -." The harbour master gave Olsen a look of sympathy. He continued trying.

After another half a dozen attempts Olsen banged his fist on the table.

"Damnn it. I'm going over there." he snapped.

"What? But you can't. How?" Olsen had thought of that.

"The Captain of the 'Drivas'. She has the rest of my cargo aboard. I'll have to ask him to risk it. We have to try for those last two trucks. We've come too far to fail now."

"For God's sake man. That's suicide. Don't you think you've done enough already?" Olsen squared back his shoulders.

"Enough? My men are over there. What do you suggest I do? Leave them to the good graces of the bastard Germans?" The harbour master thought the whole deal crazy. He wasn't prepared to leave it at that.

"No Captain. I don't. But have you thought what could happen taking a ship of that size across the fjord? You might lose her not to mention everyone on board. Then what price your bravery?"

"If I don't try I don't deserve my commission. I can't just leave them can I -? They're not just bloody good soldiers they're friends of mine -."

"Well thank you Captain sir it's good of you to say so -." Olsen spun around. Larsen with Astrup grinning over his shoulder stood in the open doorway.

"Olaf! How the -? What on earth -?" Olsen jumped forward and grabbed the younger man around the chest hauling him up off his feet. Larsen grimaced.

"I –I say Captain sir. Steady on sir -." A welcome he had expected but this was totally over the top. Olsen dropped him to the floor.

"Steady on nothing you young bastard. Where the hell did you spring from? How did you get across? Swim?" Larsen ruffled at his collar.

"Well it did cross my mind sir but the gold was too heavy. No. We crossed from Vestnes. We – er stole the ferry – sir."

"Vestnes! But that's miles from - - You stole a ferry?" Larsen grinned sheepishly.

"Well – Yes sir. We had to. We couldn't have brought the gold across without one sir." Olsen gave a whoop of joy and grabbed Larsen off his feet for a second time. Astrup looked on bemused. Then seeing the harbour master getting to his feet he stepped back.

"I hope you are not thinking of getting that familiar. I'm not sure how much more banging around I can stand after the past few hours." The harbour master burst out laughing.

"Will a handshake do instead -." he said offering out his hand.

48 hours Later:

The German Storch came in, slowly skirting the craggy slopes of the silent fjord like an ungainly albatross, its pilot fighting against the sudden updraughts given off from the glassy surface waters below. Captain Olsen watched its progress from the edge of the small forest that clung perilously to the mountainside that dropped sheer away in places. How these magnificent fir trees managed to grow in such inaccessible places was always a wonder to him.

The town of Molde and its harbour were still visible through the haze of smoke and mist that was beginning to form as the evening cold descended. Amongst the men who had elected to stay were Astrup, Schwartz, Krefting, Eriksen, Lerdal and the Storm brothers. Three new men had joined the small band believing Olsen's message of a continued fight in the North may yet provide a starting point for an ultimate victory against the Nazi invaders and anyway, what alternative was there but to stay and die or surrender?

The German plane continued panning the black landscape hoping for a sight of its quarry amongst the darkening peaks.

"Do you think he saw us sir?" Larsen stood with his back pressed into a crevice between the rocks.

"One might have hoped so Olaf. I hope he sees thousands of us in the days to come. Dear Adolf may think he's got himself another little honey-pot with Norway only he's forgotten one thing -."

"Oh. What's that sir?" puzzled Larsen. Olsen pressed his lips together in a funny kind of grin.

"It takes a hell of a lot of bees to make honey – and bees sting Olaf my friend, - bees sting -!"

From high above the mountains looked dark and dangerous. Nothing lived amongst these ice-capped gigantic cathedrals unless you could call the small outcrops of Arctic fir and the odd brush-stroke of clinging lichen a part of normal life. The German pilot shivered. Earlier he had espied a curious configuration on one of the lower slopes north of the burning harbour. Gliding down he made out the letter 'H' * with some kind of marking drawn down through the letter's crossbar. It was certainly man-made. Someone had taken the trouble to mark the whole thing out with rocks. Quite what the purpose was a mystery? Shrugging his shoulders he pushed the 'stick' left and away towards the smoking town. He had other things to do. His masters in Oslo wanted answers – so too the gilded fat-cats in Berlin. They were worried. The pilot snorted to himself. They had good reason to be. For once he was glad he wasn't going to be amongst those who would be held responsible for all this 'mess' – if and when the time came.

*('H' * See – End Notes.)*

END NOTES.

CASE WESER – EXERCISE. (Hitler's 'Fuhrer Order)

GREGERS GRAM. 'Just one protest' 18/5/44.

CAPT. JOHAN OLSEN. (+ Fridtjof + Rinnan)

VIDKUN, A.L.J. QUISLING. (+ Josef Terboven)

PERS TEUNAN alias JOSEPH BRUN. (+ 'H')

Major FRANCIS E. FOLEY.

PAUL ROSBAUD (Griffin) + HANS F. MAYER (Marty)

The Fuhrer and Supreme Commander
Of the Armed Forces.   Berlin.
1st March 1940.
9 copies.

Fuhrer Order for 'Case Weser–exercise'.

1. The development of the situation in Scandinavia makes it necessary to
prepare for the occupation of Denmark and Norway by formations of the
Armed Forces ('Case Weser-exercise'). This would anticipate English action
against Scandinavia and the Baltic, would secure our supplies of ore from
Sweden, and would provide the Navy and Air force with expanded bases for
operations against England.
The protection of the operation against action by English Naval and Air Forces
will be carried out by the Navy and the Air Force within the limits of existing
possibilities.

The forces employed on 'Case Weser-exercise will be as small as possible
having regard to our military and political strength in relation to the Northern
nations. Weakness in numbers will be made good by skilful action and surprise
in execution.

The basic aim is to lend the operation the character of a *peaceful* occupation,
designed to protect by force of arms the neutrality of the Northern countries.
Demands in this sense will be made to the governments concerned at the
beginning of the occupation and the necessary emphasis will be given, if
required, by naval and air demonstrations.
Any resistance which is nevertheless offered will be broken by all means
available.

2. I order General of Infantry von Falkenhorst, Commanding General XX1
Army Corps, to prepare and command the operation against Denmark and
Norway as Commander Group XX1.
He will be immediately subordinate to me in all respects.
His staff will comprise of officers of the three services.
Forces detailed for 'Case Weser-exercise' will receive special orders.
Naval and Air Forces employed will remain under the command of
Commander in Chief Navy and Commander in Chief Air Force, and will
operate in close liaison with Commander Group XX1. Of the Air Force, one

Reconnaissance Wing (F) and two Motorised Anti-Aircraft Regiments are not subject to this ruling, but will be under immediate command of Group XX1 until the occupation of Denmark is completed.

Forces detailed to Group XX1 will receive supplies from branches of the Armed Forces concerned, in accordance with the requirements of the Commander.

3. The crossing of the Danish frontier and the landing in Norway will take place *simultaneously*. The operations will be prepared with the utmost possible speed. Should the enemy take the initiative against Norway, we must be able to take our own counter-measures at once.

It is of the utmost importance that our operations should come as a *surprise* to the Northern countries as well as to our enemies in the west. This must be kept in mind in making all preparations, especially in the choice of dumps and embarkation points, and in the briefing and embarkation of troops. Should it become impossible to conceal preparations for embarkation, officers and men will be given false destinations. Troops will be informed of the true objective only after putting to sea.

(a)   *Occupation of Denmark* (Weser-exercise South').

Task of Group XX1: The surprise occupation of Jutland and Funen and subsequent occupation of Zeeland.

For this purpose troops will push through to Skagen and to the east coast of Funen as quickly as possible, securing the most important points. Bases in Zeeland will be occupied at the earliest moment to serve as springboards for the further occupation.

The Navy will provide forces to secure the Nyborg-Korsor route and will seize the bridges across the Little Belt with all speed. If necessary it will also assist in landing troops. It will also be responsible for coastal defence.

The *Air Force* will provide air units primarily for purposes of demonstration and dropping leaflets. Danish ground installations and air defences will be secured.

(b)   *Occupation of Norway* (Weser-exercise North').

Task of Group XX1 the surprise occupation of the important places on the coast from the sea and by landing from air.

The Navy is responsible for preparing and carrying out the sea transport of the invasion troops and of the troops to be transported to Oslo afterwards. It will ensure sea-borne supplies. Norwegian coastal defences are to be prepared with all speed.

The Air Force, after the occupation, will ensure adequate air defence, as well as the exploitation of Norway as a base for the prosecution of the war against England.

(c)   Group XX1 will keep the High Command of the Armed Forces constantly informed of the state of preparations and will submit a timetable. This must indicate the minimum lapse of time necessary between the issue of order for 'Case Weser-exercise' and their execution.

'Just one protest'. 18/5/44.

The plan to blow up the Oslo Labour Offices dropped into Gram's lap with barely a few hours to spare. The following day, the 19th May 1944, was the day upon which the Germans had decreed all the young people resident in the city must have registered for the 'draft' and the day upon which the 'archive' files of birth and residence were to be collated. (It was suspected the 'draft' under the guise of 'labour conscription' might result in the young men being inculcated into Norwegian 'Nazi' Wehrmacht units and thus be available to the Germans as front line troops).

Within two hours of being notified by one of the 'Oslo Gang' leaders, Gunner Sonsteby, Gram had prepared the necessary explosives to 'take care' of the 'problem'.

Unfortunately it was then found that due to the extra workload given the civilian workers at the Labour Office to prepare for the coming day's work, the usual time for the workers to leave had been extended. The offices would be full of Norwegian civilians until late in the evening. Nevertheless Sonsteby decided the 'job' would have to be carried out regardless. Too many young Norwegian males' futures depended on it.

The three men entered the building by means of a key Sonsteby had obtained from a 'friend'. (The third member of the group was Max Manus, another recruit to the 'Oslo Gang'). Leaving Manus to protect their rear, Sonsteby and Gram worked their way up to the buildings second floor.

Whilst Gram busied himself setting the explosives Sonsteby stepped inside the Reception Room where most of the late night work was in progress. At a signal from Gram he had lit the fuse, Sonsteby bawled out a warning at the top of his lungs to the effect that everyone had less than two minutes to evacuate the building which was about to explode. Fortunately, in the climate that was then Oslo, everyone took him seriously. The building was completely empty when the bomb went off.

Gram's device destroyed the offices and all the files therein thus making it impossible for the Germans to administer the proposed 'draft'. How successful was shown by the Germans scrapping the whole idea altogether.

Captain Johan Olsen.

After lengthy and heart-searching discussion on the night of 29th April 1940, Olsen, Krefting, Schwartz, Astrup, Larsen, Eriksen, Storm and the two Lerdal brothers, returned to Molde. The rest, who had made up Olsen's unit, continued their journey north to try to make contact with other friendly forces making their way over the mountains. Northern Norway was now the only part of the country free of total occupation and was where the Allies intended to carry on the fight.

The bombing had ceased. There were a few boats in the harbour still afloat but almost everything else of military value had been destroyed. Either by the German bombs or by the Allies themselves prior to the evacuation.

The harbour master was still doggedly at his post. He found Olsen and his men some civilian clothes and suggested they use one of the boats to make good their escape from the closing German forces. A man called Brekke offered the 'Fridtjof' group, as Olsen's men were now to be known, the use of his boat providing the group take his son, Kurt, along with them. The boat, by the name of the 'Bluebird' was loaded with sufficient supplies and whatever weapons Olsen's men could find. The stores were sufficient to last the men approximately two months, the weapons, as long as the ammunition that went with them. The harbour master provided Olsen and his men with new identity papers and the appropriate passes that would allow the 'Bluebird' to transact it's business within Norwegian waters. She was a fishing/supplies boat. Suitably equipped the 'Fridtjof' group went into action.

Olsen's first destination was the port of Bergen where certain 'actions' were carried out against the enemy until the groups presence became dangerous, not only to themselves but also to the general population. The Germans had begun taking 'hostages' as a reprisal.

The group returned to Molde and berthing the boat for a prolonged stay moved inland. Over the next few days they attack German barracks and set up ambushing German military convoys wherever they went. Arriving at Lesjaverk they de-railed a German troop train. The plan was ill conceived and but for the arrival of a group of Norwegian 'partisans' lead by a man named Henry Rinnan* it could have been 'curtains' for Olsen and his men.

By mid May 'Fridtjof' was back in Oslo. The situation in the north of the country was being influenced by news from the Continent. The Germans had attacked the Low Countries and France. The Allies were having a bad time of things and it was expected the Allied push in the north of Norway at Narvik would be jeopardised.

Olsen and the group moved to Lillehammer. Here they carried out more attacks on German troop trains and military convoys. Looking for a secure base from which to operate they set up camp in the mountains. A cave was found that suited their immediate requirements and provided for shelter from the late winter conditions that still affected parts of Central Norway. Summer was still some weeks away.

On the 7th June 1940 the King and the Crown Prince finally left Norway. Three days later General Ruge, on orders from the government in exile in London, surrendered all Norwegian Armed Forces. Olsen took his men down from the mountains and left again in the 'Bluebird' and again for the port of Bergen.

Two weeks later they attacked and destroyed the power housing belonging to the Bjolvefossen Electro-Chemical plant at Alvik that supplied all the power to the town of Bergen. Having cause a general furore in the area and with the Germans now resorting to physical violence against many of the local populace Olsen decide they would have to make plans to leave Norway or inevitably be cornered somewhere in a fight to the death.

With the collapse of the Allied armies in France a pull-out from Norway didn't come as a surprise. The British now stood alone and could ill afford to denude her scarce resources on military campaigns in the near Arctic.

All the 'Fridtjof' team reached Scotland in the 'Bluebird'. In England they were received as heroes by their fellow compatriots, the King and his Government. They soon went to work for S.O.E. (Norwegian Div.) and all returned to Norway after completing their training as 'agents' in preparation for 'Operation Jupiter', the proposed Allied landings planned for the 'liberation' of Norway in 1944. (Events proved 'Jupiter' surplus to requirements following the successful D. Day landings in Normandy June 1944.)

Of the original 'Fridtjof' team Knut Lerdal was later murdered by men belonging to Henry Rinnan's group. Bjart Eriksen also died whilst in the hands of the Gestapo. He took poison and killed himself rather than reveal all that he knew. Olsen, Larsen, Krefting and the others survived to see the Nazi's defeated.

In the grander scale of things - When we speak of ordinary men there are some less ordinary than others! From these few, great things are done. For the future of mankind on our diminutive planet - it's perhaps just as well!

a)   Henry Oliver Rinnan. Rinnan was Finnish by birth but like some who took the country of Norway as their home couldn't resist the opportunity to 'work' for those who paid the most money. In Rinnan's case the NS and the Gestapo. Most of Rinnan's men were cornered trying to escape into Sweden at the wars end. A few survived, including Rinnan, to later stand trial for their crimes. All were found guilty of crimes against the Norwegian State and its people. All were executed. Last but not least Henry Rinnan on the 2nd February 1947.

Vidkun Abraham Lauritz Jonsson Quisling.

Both Ribbentrop, the Reich Foreign Minister and State Secretary Weissacker had expressed their reservations about Hitler meeting with this Norwegian 'fop'. The Fuhrer had given the matter some thought and in the end had made up his own mind.

"Major Vidkun Quisling mein Fuhrer". Hitler turned from the fireplace. The man was somewhat smaller in stature than Hitler had envisaged. Paunchy around the neckline and jowls. Not a man used to frugal living from the look of him.

"Fuhrer." said the man providing his host with a smart facsimile of the German salute. "My friend -," said Quisling pointing to a frail figure in his rear. "One of Norway's most successful entrepreneurs, Herr Hagelin, and one of my closest advisors". Hagelin bowed stiffly from the waist and smiled. Not a smile one might trust thought the Fuhrer to himself.

The conversation was led and for the most part held by Hitler himself. He wanted to impress upon these 'Norwegians' Germany's desire for a peaceful relationship with the Scandinavian countries. His desire was and always had been that they remain neutral to the present political differences, the temporary 'unpleasantness' and to this end he required a better understanding from Norway's Storting (Parliament). Germany had no intentions of enlarging the present disagreements by forcing yet more smaller nations into the conflict. But if the 'others', meaning Germany's enemies took it upon themselves to do so, Germany would have no choice but to take any appropriate measures necessary.

" It has become necessary to counter the propaganda moves of our enemies. To this end I have already given instructions to the Reich Finance Minister to allocate a large increase in funding to the Norwegian Pan – Germanic Order -." Quisling's eyes sparkled. "My information is that you are making good progress in all matters that concern our mutual interests?" The statement was more in the form of a direct question.

"Absolutely my dear Chancellor. As I have previously stated, the bulk of the Norwegian press and our Intelligence Services are almost entirely controlled by the British. Although we are crusading with one hand tied behind our backs so to speak, the latest census carried out by my people show that we now have upward of two hundred thousand people, some in very high places, ready and willing to act to remove the present compliant capitalists in our government and to take control. All we require is the Führer's assurance that he will provide the troops to secure some of the key installations in Oslo at the same time. The rest we can take care of ourselves." Quisling gave a nervous shiver. Hitler held the man's gaze for a second or two then turned back to the fire. He rubbed his hands together before the flickering flames.

For all the glowing fire from the crackling logs the large room had less than an ambient warmth factor. Hitler was most at ease with low temperatures. Obviously so not our fat Norwegian or his attendant pencil thin man of commerce. Hitler smiled to himself. But he had grave doubts about this fawning creatures capabilities. Time would tell.

(December 1939. Berlin. Germany.)

Vidkun Quisling. 1887 – 1945. Founder and leader of the Norwegian Fascist National Union Party, the NS (Najonal Samling). Became Minister President of Norway on the 1st February 1942, but was always subordinate to Hitler's man in Norway, Gauleiter Josef Terboven *, who effectively took control of Norway, on Hitler's orders, from Quisling, only fifteen days after Quisling had first declared himself to be Norway's new President following the April 9th invasion. (It was known at the time as the shortest presidential rule in history.)

Quisling was responsible for the deportation of 767 Jews to the Nazi death camps of Poland. (1,100 Jews escaped to Sweden with the connivance and help of the Norwegian people.) He was also responsible for the introduction of forced-labour of all able-bodied Norwegians to work on the road and railways and military installations under the Nazi Todt Organisation and for the arrest and execution of dozens of dissidents and potential troublemakers.

Quisling was arrested following the German surrender in May 1945. He was tried and convicted in September 1945 and sentenced to death for crimes against humanity and the Norwegian people and State. He was executed by firing squad on the 24th October 1945 in Oslo.

Gauleiter Josef Terboven.

Gauleiter of Norway from April 24th 1940 and later the Kola Peninsula. Responsible for a 'rule of terror' throughout Norway and for the deportation of Jews, trade unionists, press editors and the like. Also for the arbitrary execution of criminals and dissidents.

Terboven was a typical Nazi Gauleiter and a particular favourite of Hitler himself. Ruthless. Unyielding, barbaric and amoral.

This Nazi committed suicide by blowing himself to pieces with dynamite in Oslo on the 11th of May 1945. Good riddance.

Pers Teunan alias Joseph Brun.

The Norwegian Gram found dead in the forest went by the name of Pers Teunan. Teunan worked for the British Intelligence Service MI6 (Sec D).
A native Norwegian he was recruited in 1936 whilst in England where his work as an engineer on floating harbour installations for Salvensen Shipping brought him to the attention of SIS.
As a neutral Teunan worked throughout the Scandinavian countries and the Baltic States and had included short spells in Germany.

In January 1940 Teunan and others received instructions to lay plans for the sabotage of the harbour installations at Oxelosund in Sweden. In the summer months before the Baltic Sea became ice-bound most of Germany's imports of iron-ore came via this port. Some days before the planned sabotage Swedish Military Intelligence received information of the proposed attempt.
Consequently orders were received from London to abort the mission. Teunan with his senior operative, a Canadian by the name of Stephensen, crossed the border into Norway only hours ahead of their pursuers, the Swedish Police.

In February Teunan was known to be in Narvik – another port, this time in Norway, for the export of iron-ore to Germany via the North Sea. In March he moved to Kristiansand in Southern Norway where he was employed in the harbour masters office.

How Teunan came to be in possession of the plans for Case Weser-exercise North isn't known to this writer. However. Following the sinking of the German troop carrier the Rio de Janeiro by the British submarine HMS Truant on the night of April 8th 1940, many of her troops including a large number of her officers were rounded up by the Norwegian authorities. This was the first tangible proof the Norwegian government had that something out of the 'ordinary' was taking place. It is probable that a copy of the invasion plans came from one of these sources. It is also likely Teunan was entrusted by the Norwegian Intelligence Service to ensure they reach the safe hands of British Intelligence whom they knew had troops ships at sea heading for Norwegian waters (part of Operation Wilfred). They would certainly have known of British Intelligence's main operative Major Frank Foley who at that time was making for Norway's West Coast ahead of the German advance.

What is certain is that British Intelligence made use of the plans in their actions of the following weeks specifically appertaining to the British landings at Narvik in Northern Norway.

In 'Intelligence' matters nothing is straightforward. The background to this operation for reasons best known to the Intelligence Service themselves has, to this writer's knowledge, never been made public.

' **H** ' Following the occupation of Central Norway many small groups of 'resistors' came into being. As with all resistance movements throughout Europe they each had their own 'special' markings intended to show their defiance to their occupiers and to give heart to their fellow countrymen. In France and the Low Countries the 'V' for victory sign became popular as well the Cross of Lorraine in France in particular. In Norway the letter 'H' crossed in its centre with the number 7 – which signified unstinting loyalty to the country's exiled King Haakon the Seventh began to appear everywhere. It was to remain in use long after Norway rid herself of the tyrant's yoke and still stands today for a show of loyalty to the country, its democratic government and its staunchly loyal Royal family.

Major Francis Edward Foley

Born Highbridge in Somerset England. Educated at St John's College, Highbridge, Stonehurst College, Lancs and St Joseph's College, Poitiers, France. 1914 – Studied philosophy. Joined up in the Herefordshire Regiment 1915. Seconded into North Hant's Regiment 1917 and sent to the Western Front in France. Promoted to Captain and billeted near the village of Mory, Nr Cambrai. Wounded 1918. Returned home to England and transferred into Army Intelligence Corps. Sent to Cologne following the Armistice in 1918 then to Berlin.
Worked for Military Intelligence in Passport Control Office, British Embassy, Berlin.
Married at Dartmouth 1921. Daughter born 1922 given the name Ursula.
Worked in Berlin from 1924 – 1938. During which time he was responsible for the 'illegal' granting of hundreds of visa's to enable German Jews and their families to emigrate to England and other countries.
Arrive Oslo August 26th 1939. A bare few days before Case White, the invasion by the Germans of hapless Poland. Instrumental in obtaining the 'Oslo Report' in early November 1939 (see The Griffin & Hans Ferdinand Mayer).
April 8th 1940. Foley was one of the first to receive intelligence of a proposed invasion of Norway and activated British Intelligence's 'Emergency' plan which ordered him to expedite plans for the removal of Norway's 'heavy water' produce, the retrieval of the Norwegian Royal family and assistance to ensure the removal of the country's gold reserves.
April 9th 1940. Foley leaves Oslo for Hamar. Arrives Hosbjor on Lake Mjoso. Leaves same night for Otta, then Lillehammer.
April 10th. Makes Dombas then Andalsnes. Sets up temp HQ Military Intelligence, Hotel Bellevue, Andalsnes.
April 12th. London sends in new W/T operatives and new ciphers. British Intelligence has learned the Germans are reading many of the British cipher messages. Leaves for Lillehammer for meeting with Gen Ruge, Commander of Norwegian Armed Forces at Oyer. Ruge asks for a Liaison Group to be established - know hence as the 'Foley Mission' – to which a number of Norwegian Officers are to be attached. Foley adopts new code-name, 'Wuff'.
April 13th. First special units of British Special Forces attached to 'Maurice Force & Sickle Force' land in Central Norway. Clandestine force for 'special ops'. Contact made with 'Foley Mission' near Dombas same day.

April 16th. Foley Mission is constantly on the move between Dombas and the West Coast of Norway. Mobile units make W/T triangulation impossible for German monitoring.

April 18th. Foley received copies of German Invasion plans. Sends information ref. German Objectives to London.

April 21st. British and Norwegian positions at Lillehammer flanked by German advance. Allied troops begin withdrawal towards Trettin.

With the constant heavy build-up of German reserves and knowledge of 'Case Yellow' the British government gives the order for evacuation of Central Norway. Foley's team leave Norway with 'heavy water' consignments.

May 1st. Foley ordered back to London.

On May 3rd Foley was sent to France with orders to remove 'secret' installations to Britain. The unit was evacuated from Bordeaux in what became known as 'Dynamo 2'.

For the rest of the war years Foley was appointed head of MI6 (A1) Germany and Norway. He was responsible for the dissemination of intelligence and the security of MI6 operatives in those countries. He was also advisor to MI6 (SIS)(Sec V), and the 'XX Committee'.

British Intelligence, as is their practice, never acknowledge the role Frank Foley played in his unstinting efforts to help the oppressed of the occupied countries. The government of Israel however had no such inhibitions. Francis Edward Foley was honoured on the roles of the 'List of the Righteous' in Jerusalem in the 1960s (Dept for the Righteous. Yad Vashem. P.O.Box 3477 Jerusalem. Role No. 91034.) A grove of trees have been planted in his memory at the Harel Kibbutz.

Frank Edward Foley. A remarkable man by any standards. A great credit to his country and to all others who fight against those who would attempt to deny freedom and peace to the peoples of the world.

The 'Griffin' & 'Marty'.

Paul Rosbaud, 'The Griffin', born 1897, Gratz, Austria. Reared by his mother, his father having 'left' the family home at the time of his birth.
Rosbaud fought for the Austrian Army on the Italian Front in World War One and was taken prisoner by the British in 1917 at the age of twenty.
During his spell of incarceration he came to like his English guards and learned to speak the language reasonably well.
In 1918 following his release he went to study Chemistry at Darmstadt University and then went on to study X-Ray cinematography at the Kaiser Wilhelm Institute in Berlin where he qualified as a Dr of Radiography and Nuclear Physics. In 1933 he was well known throughout the scientific fraternity for his regular publications in a number of 'Science' periodicals of the day. He met Frank Foley in 1937 when organising for his wife to take an 'extended holiday' in England. His wife was Jewish. She remained in England for the duration of the war.
In 1939 when Foley moved to Norway Rosbaud arranged for exchange visit students to study in Oslo and began to accept Norwegian students in Berlin. Foley made an 'arrangement' with a number of these students to act as couriers for Rosbaud who's detestation of the Nazi's had prompted him to 'work' for the Allied cause.
In November 1939 in collaboration with one Hans Ferdinand Mayer, code-named 'Marty', Rosbaud compiled a list of all his knowledge regarding the German Nazi's research on military hardware for transit to Norway.
The story of the package containing what would become to be known as the 'Oslo Report' is well documented. This story is of course well outside the true facts of how British Intelligence came into the 'Oslo Reports' possession. To protect the 'Griffin' and 'Marty's' identity Foley concocted how the package was left on a wall at the British Embassy in Oslo late one November night and was 'found' by one of the Embassy staff.
The 'Oslo Report' contained details of numerous German 'secret' weapons under research or production. Not least of which were the magnetic and acoustic mine and the rocket developments then well advanced at a small Baltic port called Peenemunde – the V1 and V2.
Throughout the war both the 'Griffin' and 'Marty' were able to supply British Intelligence with massive amounts of data on the ongoing research taking place in Nazi Germany. i.e. Attempts at production of the 'fission bomb'. Heavy

Water production. The 'rocket' glider. Wasserfall, an anti aircraft missile. Close proximity fused shells. The Me 262 jet aircraft and last but by no means least the U-boat 'snorkel'.

BIBLIOGRAPHY.

Operation Jupiter.   D.Baden Powell.   Robert Hale 1982.

Norway Invaded.   T. Horsley.   Withy Bush Press 1940

Dokumente des OKW.   W. Hubatsch.   B.G.Verlag Fron Main.

Black Eagle, White Gold.   Adf.   Unpublished.

MI6 1909-1945.   Nigel West.   Westintel Ltd. 1983.

S.O.E.   M.R.D. Foot.   BBC 1984.

Ashington. John.   Personal conversations. Perrinporth.
                         Cornwall. England. 1977.

END.

'Scripts on Black'.

Chance! Being in the right place at the right time!
For most of us we would consider such to be a rare occurrence. Something that
only happens 'once in a blue moon'. But we would be wrong.
Being in the right place at the right time happens far more often than the
majority of us realise and is simply a question of 'awareness' and 'intuition.
It is true to say that there are some who are born with an acute awareness of
their surroundings and are therefore 'tuned in' to react positively to the 'main'
chance when it arises, whilst others appear to struggle when afforded the same
tantalising opportunities. I suppose it could be said we all have such a 'gift' to a
greater or lesser degree. It was therefore unsurprising to this writer to find
himself in the summer of 1965 to be the recipient of one such 'opportunity',
being, in my youth, eager to taste the fruits of life and always more than
willing, sometimes recklessly so, to seek out their mysterious source. This
opportunity came in the guise of a fellow well met.

I knew him as 'Chas'. Charles E. Broadstairs or so his British and United
Kingdom Passport said. But 'Chas' had at least three passports. I know. I had
sight of them all over a period of months. We were introduced by an elderly
Jewish impresario, otherwise known in those days as a 'theatrical agent', who
like myself at the time had a small provincial office on the outskirts of the city
from where we plied our individual trade in the world of 'show business'. (I
soon came to realise my elderly Jewish friend also plied other 'trades', but those
I must leave for another time). I was due to meet a man by the name of John
Knowles, the sole owner of 'Intermac International' and one of Manchester's
most successful entrepreneurs of the time. 'Chas', to whom I was introduced,
after we had concluded our business, was in 'Security', so he said, which I took
to mean the well being of his employer and his employers' premises. I was
wrong again. It meant nothing of the sort. I remember being impressed by his
striking good looks. He had a very likeable manner and although he was a good
fifteen to twenty years older than me I found no difficulty in enjoying his
presence that same evening at 'Mr Smith's Night Club' where we were often to
be found in the early dawn-lit hours. That was to be the beginning of a very
long enjoyable and surprisingly informative friendship. We had quite a number
of things in common, most of which I will make no mention, as they are not
pertinent to this story. What is and what was to lead me many years later to

write 'Scripts on Black', was the period of years preceding my birth in 1944 and the dire consequences to which they led. In essence, the Second World War, something in which 'Chas' participated and to such a degree I have only in the past few years slowly come to realise. (No wonder he frowned when I kept various badly scrawled notes on the subject – a number of which went 'missing'). If my memory serves me correctly my time with 'Chas' covered a period of about four years. Not that I saw him often in the later years. But now and again he would contact me and then just as suddenly disappear from the scene like a thief in the night. He had a habit of being able to blend with the shadows. Something I suspect he acquired from his 'real' masters – whomsoever they might have been.

'Chas' had a number of acquaintances in the city. I came to know most of them as time went by. All, without exception, came from what was then known as the 'Eastern bloc' countries. But that was before the war, or as I now know, at the war's end. Some came from the Ukraine others Poland and some; I am convinced, from Germany itself. All without exception fought for the Nazi's. Once I had been accepted into their 'circle', they wasted no time in explaining, in stark detail, how their own personal 'tragedies' had come to pass and how they came to be residing in this cold northern English city with its post-war grime and cosmopolitan inhabitants. (I suspect that the reason was to provide them anonymity – the same, as one who would wish to hide a tree would naturally pick a forest). They went by a variety of names.

There was Stefan. (See – Black Despair). A good looking well - built figure of a man. His name was of Ukrainian origins, but as I was soon to discover he was in fact a Bavarian born on the outskirts of Munich in the mid nineteen twenties. His was a very personal story and one which no one could but fail to commit to memory for its human tragedy and absolute obscenity. Peter was another. Peter came from Silesia but had a Polish surname. He was a friend of a man by the name of Claus Fuhrmann. (See - Black Dawn). Another went by the name of Martin. I was never convinced this was his real name or the fact he claimed to be of Russian descent. His stories of the 'Russian front' and of the 'Nazi's' retreat through his homelands held me enraptured for endless hours, but what mostly took my interest was the story he told of a Franz Werner (a name Martin used) who it transpired was SS General Hans Kammler's adjutant throughout the last four years of the war. (For those not familiar with Kammler see – Black Dust).
There were others. Some I only met in passing. Some for a week or two. Then they would disappear. Move on. Always moving on. That was the problem. It

was this constant moving from place to place that first aroused my curiosity which slowly turned to suspicion as the months passed by. Why it was these people didn't feel safe. The war had been over many years. Almost twenty years in fact. But yet these 'lost souls' still didn't feel secure. Even when in a country like mine?

The answer only came many years later when researching behind the stories and the information I was given.

Finally there was 'Chas' himself. Reputedly English, (as English as one Commander Ashe-Lincoln whom I met in 1974 far from the shores of this, my native country. It was the commander who put me on the trail of 'Ausscheiden', Goering's concept for the subjection of the British Isles. See – Black Shark). 'Chas' was born in Germany, schooled in Germany and fluent in at least four languages. He had returned to the shattered city of Berlin in 1946 and become embroiled in the 'black market', the shadowy world of 'Nazi' hunting and the politics of the embryonic 'Cold War' that was about to unfurl behind the Soviets inhuman 'Iron Curtain'. (See – Black Veng'ence'), 'Chas' Etienne Richter, his German identity. 'Andre' Macon, his Belgian identity, and who knows how many more? As I have said it was 'Chas' who was instrumental in my writing 'Scripts on Black'. But not until nearly forty years later and at a time chosen in the safe knowledge the 'establishment' would no longer care about these far-flung events. Also at a time when many of those whose stories some of you may care to read are now no longer with 'us' – - - - - if indeed they ever were?

Atlas D'four 2005.

Other Books by Atlas D'four.

Published by UkUnpublished in 2010.

UKBookland gives you the opportunity to purchase all of the books published by UKUnpublished.

Do you want to find out a bit more about your favourite UKUnpublished Author?

Find other books they have written?

PLUS – UKBookland offers all the books at Excellent Discounts to the Recommended Retail Price!

You can find UKBookland at www.ukbookland.co.uk

Find out more about **Atlas D'four** and his books.

Are you an Author?

Do you want to see your book in print?

Please look at the UKUnpublished website:
www.ukunpublished.co.uk

Let the World Share Your Imagination